D1105102

Talking Gender

The University of

North Carolina Press

Chapel Hill & London

Public Images,

Personal Journeys,

and

Political Critiques

Edited by

Nancy Hewitt,

Jean O'Barr,

and

Nancy Rosebaugh

Talking **Gender**

© 1996 The University of
North Carolina Press

Manufactured in the
United States of America

The paper in this book meets the
guidelines for permanence and
durability of the Committee on
Production Guidelines for Book
Longevity of the Council on
Library Resources.

Library of Congress
Cataloging-in-Publication Data
Talking gender: public images,
personal journeys, and political critiques /
edited by Nancy Hewitt, Jean O'Barr,
and Nancy Rosebaugh.
p. cm.
Includes bibliographical references and index.
ISBN 0-8078-2288-4 (cloth: alk. paper). —
ISBN 0-8078-4597-3 (pbk.: alk. paper)
1. Women's studies. I. Hewitt, Nancy A., 1951– .
II. O'Barr, Jean F. III. Rosebaugh, Nancy.
HQ1180.T35   1996
305.4'07—dc20   95-51645
CIP

00 99 98 97 96   5 4 3 2 1

Kristine Stiles's essay was previously published as
"Shaved Heads: Towards a Theory of the Cultures
of Trauma," *Stratégie II: Peuples Méditerranéens* 64–65
(July–December 1993). It is reprinted here with
the permission of the publishers.

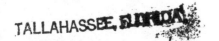

To the students,

faculty, alumnae/i,

and administrators

of Duke University,

whose enthusiasm

and commitment

have enabled all

of us to journey

together.

Contents

Acknowledgments

Women's Studies at Duke University is a collaborative effort, and this anthology, celebrating the tenth anniversary of the program, exemplifies that collaboration.

A lecture series, culminating in a weekend symposium, was conceptualized by the staff—Jean O'Barr, Nancy Rosebaugh, Vivian Robinson, and Sarah Hill—as a means to bring together the feminist community on campus and to highlight for others recent developments in the study of women, gender, and feminist theories.

That plan was made possible by various energies and resources. The energies came from Nancy Hewitt of the History Department, who organized the lecture series, and from the faculty and graduate student colleagues who suggested speakers. Graduate students Alexandra Fitts and Lily Phillips took on the tasks of researching the speakers' works, preparing publicity, and making arrangements. Tolly Boatwright, William Chafe, Kim Curtis, Jean Hamilton, Sucheta Mazumdar, Carol Meyers, Jan Radway, James Rolleston, and Anne Firor Scott all helped by introducing the speakers as dates unfolded. Our work-study students, Ashley Barfield, Rebecca Musil, and Nakeisha Neal, were invaluable in making all of these events happen.

The resources to put these energies into action came from speakers' endowments given over the last decade by alumnae/i and friends. The Charlotte Bunch Fund, the Wilhelmina D. Harland Fund, the Dora Anne Little Fund, the Women Speakers Fund, and the Florence N. Shortlidge Fund all enabled us to offer honoraria, pay for accommodations, and entertain guests in our community. The generosity and vision of alumnae/i in fostering feminist scholarship at Duke is unique.

Comments and critiques of the introductory essay were solicited in our monthly faculty seminar, where Michèle Longino and many others improved our presentation.

To Brenda Denzler fell the critical final steps of editing the manuscripts and preparing the materials for the press. We thank her, as we thank all of our colleagues, for their multiple contributions to what will, we hope, be a continuing conversation, here and elsewhere.

Talking **Gender**

Nancy Hewitt

Jean O'Barr

Nancy Rosebaugh

Introduction

Women's studies emerges in this volume as a rich, if some-times dissonant, chorus of voices. Asked to speak to the process of recon-structing women's lives, the contributors reflect, and reflect on, debates over representation, experience, and social policy. Examining diverse commu-nities, chronologies, and conceptual frameworks, they demonstrate the ways in which gender, race, class, and sexuality have modified and multiplied academic agendas in the past decade. The authors reveal as well the discor-dant notes that now mark nearly all attempts to apply feminist findings to everyday life, whether the concern is pornography, pedagogy, performance art, AIDS policy, or global politics. And they reveal how analyses of race and class and studies of men, masculinity, and gender have rearranged the score of women's studies.

Roots and Routes

For a field with a relatively short history, women's studies has sunk deep roots and traveled diverse routes. The contributors to this volume, like others who are on a long journey, look backward as well as forward as they carve out new analytical and interpretive paths. The first generation of feminist scholars showed that earlier research, in a range of disciplines, excluded women and that such exclusion mattered. In the 1970s, these scholars invented women's studies as they ranged across the disciplines, uncovering the victimization of women and recovering the active agency of those who sought to emancipate their sex. Emerging from a social movement that recognized and publicized the political implications of personal experiences, feminist academics sustained a sisterly vision that sought to embrace women inside and outside the academy. They tested popular images against practical knowledge, illuminating inconsistencies and stereotypes that shaped (or more often misshaped) laws and policies affecting women. Much early work in the field highlighted the commonalities among women across time and place, illuminating sex-based discriminations and sex-conscious protests against them.

The second generation of feminist scholars focused on women's experiences and self-presentations, emphasizing how they differed both from men's experiences and from each other. Indeed, the watchword for the 1980s was difference — racial, ethnic, national, sexual, economic, and epistemological. Although the emphasis was on women as women, attention to conflict came to outweigh the search for sisterhood as researchers and teachers sought to capture the complexity of women's lives and histories. Scholars of color in particular questioned the power relations that inhered in a sisterhood that allowed white Western feminists to set the political and intellectual agenda for women around the world. At the same time, a new concern with women's efforts to effect change led feminist scholars to downplay victimization and highlight the individual achievements and collective contributions of women across time and place.

Pursuing these analyses into the 1990s, we have come to recognize and acknowledge the fragile nature of the common ground on which women's studies was established. The fragmentation of the feminist movement and the redefinition of "women's" issues based on multiple identities occurred alongside the emergence of the New Right, all of which reinforced claims that women's different locations in the world created conflicting, even contradictory, perspectives on womanhood, women's roles and responsibilities, and the public policies that would best meet women's needs and desires. Among feminist academics these intellectual and political challenges spurred theoretical innovation, with practitioners of gender studies, queer studies, and women's studies and advocates of postmodernist, multicultural, and materialist approaches interrogating earlier interpretations and the scholars who produced them.

Conversations continued, although arguments, debates, and diatribes also characterized exchanges among those who believed deeply in the political implications and applications of scholarly analyses. Many women's studies scholars felt ambivalent about the increasingly adversarial nature of feminist discourse and particularly about the ways in which such controversies were represented in the media. Indeed, having long balanced political and intellectual agendas, commitments to professional careers and community outreach, and the power as well as the limits of sisterhood, many were more comfortable with ambivalence and conflict within the world of women's studies than with the categorical dichotomies into which our work was forced by popularizers of political correctness.

Feminist scholars cannot recreate consensus, however. Advocates of difference and partisans of postmodernism already fear that the institutionalization of women's studies has blunted its political and theoretical edge. Others worry that the category "woman" has been or will be shattered by attention to the seemingly infinite variety within the sex, that men will recapture center stage via gender analysis, and that literary theory will distance feminist academics from the larger feminist community. Only the willingness to confront these competing claims to the redefinition of women's studies scholarship and pedagogy can sustain our interdisciplinary roots and our social commitments while marking out new routes of analysis and application.

Scholars have taken up the challenge of exploring ever more diverse communities of women, and many now take as a starting point these women's own stories as the vantage point from which to reexamine male-dominated institutions. We are still asking about exclusion, resistance, and difference as they illuminate the lives of women. But we are also exploring more fully the construction of manhood and masculinities, the production and perpetuation of gender differences, and the insidious effects of gender stereotypes on social institutions and public policy.

If women's studies has been fragmented in the past decade, it has also been revitalized by scholars grappling with fundamental questions about power, pedagogy, and politics. We have returned increasingly to the personal and engaged style of early feminist writing in which the subjectivity of the author openly informs analysis. This recommitment to accessibility and to politics promises to open specialized, sophisticated, esoteric, advanced theoretical debates to a wider audience and to revitalize conversations between feminists inside and outside the academy.

As scholars of women's lives and as individuals who have been part of the women's liberation movement since the 1960s and 1970s, we sought to further that revitalization as we celebrated the tenth anniversary of the Women's Studies Program at Duke University.

Women's studies programs provide both intellectual and institutional space for growth, for reflection, and for change. Individual scholars, whether faculty, students, or alumnae/i, encounter in women's studies questions that have long concerned and plagued them but have only recently been articulated for them. In collaboration—through common reading, classroom discussion, organized seminars, and casual conversations—ideas are put forward, alternatives suggested, perspectives tried out. The process of intellectual growth is constantly challenged by the process of reflection here. A new idea is examined in the context of the new ideas of others, and each of us reconceptualizes ourselves as learners and knowers in the process. This community, like every such communal endeavor, is by no means flawless. It allows failures while encompassing us as we keep doing our feminist work.

The feminist work we are doing at Duke is exemplified in this volume. The ideas evolved in the scholarly community, where diverse perspectives not always welcomed by everyone were encouraged and where we were able to shape the printed product by multiple readings in many settings. We have attempted to use the intellectual and institutional space we have created for ourselves while not being contained by it. This to us is the challenge of the late 1990s and was articulated for us by Professor Michèle Longino, who led a discussion of our introductory essay at a faculty seminar as we were preparing the manuscripts for publication. She observed:

> Although 1990s feminism in the academy may look messier and even less vigorous than in the past, it is to my mind performing a necessary task, that of breaking out and away precisely from the "safe haven" that has been accorded it by the institution—a space that has been invaluable but also a form of containment, and is now claiming, demanding, making its own space wherever it happens to light. That "safe haven," in this case

Duke's Women's Studies Program, has triumphed over the institution that enables it by challenging the parameters of its own niche and embracing the explosion throughout the university and beyond.

Embracing the Explosion

We recognize that readers do not necessarily approach an anthology by reading straight through from beginning to end. A more eclectic journey through the chapters offered here is encouraged by the seemingly disparate character of the topics covered. For this reason, we have not attempted to review the literature relevant to the collection as a whole but have, rather, asked each contributor to provide the appropriate intellectual context for her or his own work. Here we will underscore what we see as the outstanding insights in each paper and some of the intricate interconnections among them. We hope that our reading stimulates yours and that you will make additional linkages as these authors' investigations intersect with your own. In addition, we hope that by explicitly envisioning the relationships between how women lead their lives, how gender is culturally represented by and to them, and how our public practices often rely more fully on the representations than the realities of women and gender systems, we can create the basis for future conversations. Three decades into feminist scholarship it is obvious that the issues are complex, deeply rooted in our social institutions and cultural ideologies, and open to alteration only when we articulate the processes by which they are continuously recreated.

Amy Richlin's careful account of the Roman *scholae* is a strikingly appropriate place to begin the conversation, both as the first essay in the collection and the primary introduction to one of the central themes. In her essay, Richlin recovers a neglected Roman institution, the school where boys were taught the skills of public discourse, and examines the process of learning *how* to speak that also instructed boys in *what* to speak. Working with the maxim that "content is never arbitrary," Richlin shows us that even though women were physically excluded from the *scholae*, male representations of women dominated the discourses developed there. It is this creation process, illustrating how representations of women came into being almost unconsciously, that is the central fact for us to grasp.

Richlin's essay is sobering. The rhetorical skills taught to the Roman male elite in the *scholae* survive in many of the elements of the contemporary model for speaking and debating in public places — in courts, legislatures, community meetings, even classrooms. Do the skills, developed in antiquity and employed today, continue to carry some of the same ideas about gender? Richlin suggests that they do, giving us a case study of the production of gender that takes us away from North American presentism and causes as to ask more carefully about the ways in which historically created and male-dominated practices continue to echo in our ears and resonate in our institutions.

Kristine Stiles takes another route through the processes of gender production in modern times and in a variety of settings. An art historian concerned with how political cultures of trauma visualize sexualized images, she examines the experiences of French women punished as collaborators during World War II and contemporary Romanian performance artists resisting repression. Beginning with the public humiliations orchestrated by German and then French authorities in the 1940s, she presents a rich, detailed analysis of the near universality of shaving women's heads to stigmatize them and to imprint a message of domination on a culture's visual memory. She then links this practice with a form of artistic performance, artists who mark their bodies to create a visual language, signing how the power of the state silences its citizens. She thus locates both the destruction and the reclamation of identity in the reverberating silence of shaved heads and marked bodies.

The Stiles essay contains a thoughtful afterword in which the author records responses she has received to the presentation of her work in a variety of public settings. Again and again, she hears women claiming that they shave their heads and mark their bodies of their own volition. Stiles responds with an elaboration of how representations are embedded in male-constructed cultural systems and how women share that representational space with historic symbols despite their aspirations to the contrary. She argues that change cannot occur without understanding the embeddedness of overlapping and interconnected cultural signs in historical experience. This age-old debate about the ability of the oppressed to emancipate themselves using the tools of the oppressor resonates with Richlin's analysis. Both look back to the dynamics of the production of gender asymmetry and the creation of symbol systems as the ground from which to move forward, excavating the historic bases for many contemporary practices and thereby undercutting assertions that such practices are natural or universal.

In the third essay of the volume, Mandy Merck examines the complex question of the connections between men's representations and treatment of women, and feminists' representations of, and redress against, men's mistreatment. Merck grounds her discussion in the now familiar debate on pornography, particularly as it has been articulated by Catharine MacKinnon. A cultural studies scholar, Merck takes as her central problem the model of behavioral conditioning developed by Pavlov that is overtly refuted by, but nonetheless intermingled in, the work of MacKinnon and her followers. Without taking sides in a debate that has come to divide feminist scholars and activists, Merck offers grounds for a sharper dissection of the issues surrounding pornography. She demonstrates the contradictions inherent in the idea that masculine sexuality is imbricated with bestiality. Rather than emphasizing the differences among the factions, Merck shows how much ground they share and how both sides are caught "in the old tourniquet of agency and determination." Merck argues that antipornography activists are confused about men and that this confusion stems from their indecision about whether men are dangerous by nature or nurture. Thus, she claims, they fail to address women and women's relationship to sexuality.

In taking up this most contemporary of debates as it has been framed by our ideas about men, male cultural practices, and male social institutions, Merck contributes significantly to our understanding of both the production and performance of gender in the domain of sexuality. She uncovers the processes by which we think about the issues as well as the ways in which those processes are reinscribed as we engage in our daily routines. Her subject resonates with those of Richlin and Stiles and again calls for the question: what are the narratives women and men live by, and how can we expand the repertoire? All these authors urge us to disentangle convoluted histories and contradictory ideas as the basis for action.

One action useful for creating new representational models is writing — of a newly emergent kind. The next three authors in this volume — Kathy Ferguson, Deborah Gray White, and Karla Holloway — record experiences and then reflect on those experiences in light of the ways in which they are represented in broader cultural frameworks. The writing they are investigating, whether their own or that of those they are researching, is grounded in the understanding that each woman or set of women has a particular analysis of the world they inhabit. Focusing on the testimony of individual women, these scholars move us toward a fuller engagement with differences among women and among men even as they continue to explore differences between women and men.

Ferguson's powerful essay is divided into two parts. In the first, she reflects on her evolution as a political theorist. An important part of that evolution, she believes, involved learning how to write *through* theory rather than *about* theory. Participating in a project that engages scholars from many disciplines, Ferguson explores ways of bringing the abstract and the concrete into conversation with one another. Women's studies has long provided an intellectual space where bidirectional analyses — in which theory simultaneously informs and is informed by case studies — can take place. Writing *through* theory to Ferguson suggests thinking beyond as well as by means of prevailing understandings. In the second part of her essay, she uses her kibbutz journal writings — undertaken as a political theorist and as the mother of two sons whose father is an Israeli citizen — to make meaning of everyday events as they are mediated by the power of the state. Here the continual interplay between the abstract and the concrete illuminates Ferguson's central concern: how what we see (the representation) meshes with the complexities of what is (the realities) and the possibilities and restrictions this suggests for personal practices and state policies.

Ferguson, like Richlin, asks us to think about the way institutions shape options, looking in some detail at the military state as the dominant institution in Israeli society. Ferguson also asks a version of the question posed by Stiles: is it possible to connect to something, in this case Israel, but not always or only in terms of the symbols that the thing offers? Like Merck, Ferguson demonstrates that moves against the power of the dominant narrative can become reincorporated into the power of that narrative, but she holds out hope for creating new identities *against*, even *outside of*, those prevailing narratives.

White, a social historian, explores the life stories created by African American clubwomen as they sought to present and preserve themselves in a culture that refused to portray them accurately or protect them fully. Working with the private papers of a number of African American women who led organizations devoted to racial uplift at the turn of the century, White shows how rarely these women examined the contradictions between their personal and public lives and how this dissemblance increased the difficulties both of leading private lives and being public figures.

White's extensive quotations from diaries, letters, and reports provide vivid illustrations of how African American women negotiated a cultural terrain in which representations of what women should be were coded by the sexual realities of a deeply racist society. As these women of talent traveled across America urging their sisters to undertake personal behaviors that were designed to "raise the race," they struggled with their own distaste for domesticity and their inability to confront openly the conflicts they experienced in a racially and sexually oppressive culture. Whereas Ferguson, writing some one hundred years later, can use the tools of feminist theory to locate her identities through writing, White's women could not. Rather, they adopted another stance, that of silence and dissemblance, and rode out the conflicts of their particular journey.

Holloway, like White, uses the experiences of African American women to reflect on the relationships among experiences, images, and public practices. Like Ferguson, she is writing *through* literary theory, not *about* it. She seeks thereby to identify the strategies African American women use to make meaning of their experiences. Holloway, a literary scholar, identifies one strategy as the ability to talk *with* each other rather than *about, to, for*, or *at* one another. In her words, "Our voices do our work for us."

Using literature as well as contemporary narratives about race, Holloway makes an impassioned argument that black women's voices are not heard because they do not match the circumscribed narratives imposed on them in our culture. These culturally imposed narratives continually erase the very voices Holloway is recording. Holloway, like Richlin, locates her critique in educational institutions. Her central concern is the conventional classrooms where conversations that are the source of voice are closely regulated. Her evaluation of schools as social institutions differs from Richlin's in the sense that women are present in Holloway's classrooms while missing in Richlin's *scholae*. But Holloway and Richlin are both arguing that what happens in those educational spaces silences women. For Richlin, it was the narratives created about women in their absence that was key. For Holloway, it is the insistence, even when women are present, on silence and writing rather than the encouragement of the noise that accompanies conversation. The silences captured in Holloway's tale are echoed as well in the acts of political resistance recounted by Stiles.

Holloway, Stiles, and Ferguson all resist the idea that one set of symbols, derived from elite men's control of the state, serves the multiple experiences of women and men. All are indignant with the ways in which women come to participate in a system that does not include them. White's descriptions of the tensions that women experience and learn to deny in order to survive capture concerns embedded in these more modern tales. All of the authors support Holloway in her demand that we listen to women, contrasting what we hear with what we are told and drawing energy for change from the inconsistencies and contradictions we identify. For each author, the challenge is to take apart the gender and racial dynamics that make things the way they are and set the stage, particularly through writing and talking, for the imaginative contemplation of alternate realities.

The last three papers in this collection focus directly on those alternate realities, on what might be done with the insights of contemporary feminist scholarship as we analyze their implications and applications to public policy and practice. Like the earlier contributors, Barbara Ogur, Michael Kimmel, and Cynthia Enloe have done a lot of listening. But their emphasis is on action and their proposals are provocative. Ogur, a practicing physician, has begun an oral history project with the HIV-positive women she serves in a Cambridge, Massachusetts, clinic. Frustrated by the barriers that the Centers for Disease Control's typologies impose on understanding the spread and effects of AIDS among women, Ogur began to listen. In her essay, she records the stories of the women she is treating as they reflect on how they made critical life choices, how they make meaning of their HIV infection, and how they are understood by their families, communities, and the health services. Like Holloway, Ogur speaks *with* the women she treats; like Ferguson, she embraces subjectivity to think by means of, but also beyond, prevailing understandings. Ogur argues for making women's experiences the basis for epidemiological investigations rather than fabricating partial truths about those experiences by forcing them into categories created from cases of men.

Kimmel brings us back to the case of men, but his subjects are far removed from the *scholae*, the state, and the Pavlovian conditioning analyzed earlier in this volume. Kimmel, a sociologist who pioneered the study of masculinities, takes up the question of what men can learn from feminist scholarship. Drawing both on his research into the history of pro-feminist men and on his personal experiences as a male academic who advocates studying men as men, Kimmel directly confronts the question of how the interconnections of gender and power work to keep men invisible to themselves, to the social institutions they construct, and to the cultural theories they promulgate. In many ways, Kimmel's ruminations parallel Ferguson's, for he is writing against the dominant discourse rather than from inside it. Kimmel also points out that while men as a group have power, individual men usually feel powerless and are angry and confused by the blame for the world's ills that comes their way. This raises a caution for scholars and activists who may treat the category "man" in monolithic fashion.

The perspectives of Ferguson are also echoed in the final essay of the anthology in which Enloe goes global. Ferguson and Stiles have explored the experiences of contemporary women outside the United States, while others (White, Holloway, and Ogur in particular) have focused their attention on the diversity of women's lives within the United States. Enloe challenges us by asking how women at various places on the globe and in every economic situation are related to one another through the production and consumption of material and symbolic goods. Honed by training in political science and feminist theory, Enloe's grasp of global economics, technical innovations, labor organizing, and commercial advertising—all as they relate to the shoes on our feet—provides us with a comprehensive picture of the fundamental themes of the anthology: what do women do? how is it represented? and what policies grow out of the connections and contradictions created thereby?

Journeys

The authors and editors of this volume have pursued these questions in order to imagine alternate realities that might improve the lives of us all. This common project is obscured at times by the diversity of the cases presented, but one question emerges as central to each: how do women, who as a group are subordinated to men, respond to, resist, and even wield power? Colonialism, in various forms, offers a model implicit in many of these essays. The term was first used to denote the process by which a powerful nation gained control over a dependent area or people. But the capacity of those with economic, political, and cultural resources to penetrate less powerful communities and shape them to their own needs is by no means restricted to discussions of the Third World. Now viewed by feminist scholars as a way to suggest the control men wield over women, colonialist models are also applied to illuminate situations in which one community of women—often in collaboration with or at the behest of men—dominates another community of women. These models have been applied to relations between nations, among ethnic, racial, and religious groups, or within families, factories, and classrooms; they reveal not only impositions of colonial power, but, equally important, the diverse ways that women resist such impositions.

The efforts of the authors gathered here to resist colonizing their subjects or being colonized by dominant theories, histories, and categories suggest some of the elements that foster unity among women's studies scholars traveling increasingly divergent paths. Three of these elements stand out. The first is the commitment to giving voice to those who are the subjects of research; the second is a concern with giving voice to the researcher's own subjectivity; and the third is articulating the political implications and applications to which these voices speak. All of these elements echo past practices in women's studies, and yet all transpose those practices to a new key. Recognizing silences, recovering voices, reflecting self-critically on one's own perspective, and reconnecting the personal to the political have characterized feminist scholarship within and across disciplines since the 1970s. Now, however, in the context of critiques by women of color and by practitioners of materialist feminism, postmodernism, cultural studies, queer studies, and feminist legal theory, questions of voice and perspective, definitions of representation and experience, and applications to policy and politics have been recast. Multiplicity, fluidity, and ambiguity now characterize our work.

Milestones, as moments to contemplate well-traveled paths and anticipate new approaches, are now even more valuable. For as we recognize the processual character of our work, it is important that we provide ourselves with "rest stops" where we can consolidate our efforts and evaluate our progress. In this sense the Women's Studies Program at Duke offers a case study of the changes that have occurred in the field in the past decade.

The Women's Studies Program at Duke, established at least a decade after programs at peer institutions, has enjoyed strong administrative support, wide student and faculty recognition, and important relationships with alumnae/i and donors. Women began attending classes at Duke in the 1890s, and a coordinate Woman's College educated women students from 1930 to 1972. In 1972, Duke became fully coeducational, merging administrative ranks as well as residential space, including women as regular students or through the Continuing Education Program. The latter was guided during the 1970s by its director, Jean O'Barr. In the 1980s, she built upon the institution's experience of women as students, faculty, administrators, and alumnae by claiming the Women's Studies Program as a continuation of Duke's historical commitment to women's education: with women's studies, women could be the subject, not merely the object, of inquiry. That continuity was made manifest in the program's establishment in 1983 with a desk in a corner of a large parlor room, once the scene of Woman's College lectures and socials.

In the first semester, 231 students enrolled in eleven classes; by the end of the first decade, between 1,100 and 1,200 graduates and undergraduates enrolled in forty to fifty courses each semester. The largest interdisciplinary program at Duke, Women's Studies now awards some fifty certificates to each graduating class, and in the past decade some 130 graduate students have concentrated in women's studies. As the program's second decade begins, undergraduates can major in women's studies. Nearly 20 percent of the undergraduate faculty have affiliated with Women's Studies, claiming women or gender as an area of research or teaching interest. An alumnae Council on Women's Studies led a successful $1.4 million endowment campaign, ended in 1992, and continues to advise and support the program.

With these visible markers of success, a tenth anniversary was something to celebrate, providing an opportunity to explore the state of feminist theory and practice within the safe haven of a widely recognized and well-supported program. Endowment funds were available to support a lecture series and symposium. A steering committee composed of students, faculty, and staff began to generate ideas for a theme as well as recommend scholars who could address key concerns through their current research. One of the earliest ideas—to examine feminism's effect on public life—deepened and broadened over the course of discussion. The committee sent out a call for recommendations to students and faculty campuswide, noting that

> The series should feature speakers who examine the interactions among the material realities of women's lives, the symbolic representations of those lives in mass culture, and the social policies that condition women's options and actions. Recognizing debates among academics over the very definitions of "representations" and "realities," we seek to identify speakers whose work addresses the heterogeneity of women's experiences. Finally, we envision speakers who cut across academic and activist agendas.

Drawn from the arts, humanities, social sciences, and medicine and drawing on legal, literary, liberal, ethnographic, and anticolonialist feminist frameworks, the participants in the lecture series and symposium demonstrated the multiplicity as well as the unity of women's studies scholarship today. The written record of their labors is reproduced in this volume.

Case studies are an important means of both recognizing the circumscribed nature of any individual's perspective and capturing the complexities that help move us from the contingent to the qualified. The authors in this volume each work with a specific case, drawing on their distinctive disciplinary training as well as the interdisciplinary frameworks offered by women's studies. Each author grounds an analysis of the ways gender is represented by larger social and cultural systems in the experiences of women and men living in a particular time and place. Each author, in relying on a single case, is urging us away from grand theory and the search for universals and toward a perspective that is self-consciously partial, yet generalizable. The fine detail offered by case studies allows readers to connect with the material at many levels, to imagine how things could be different, to reconsider how the public rules and private interactions surrounding their subjects could be altered, and thus to construct their own generalizations as they move from case to case. The final product is always in the making, the journey as important as the destination, the conversation more productive without closure.

Amy Richlin

How Putting the Man

in Roman Put the Roman

in Romance

A lthough women's studies began, in the 1970s, with strong roots in history, the trend of the past few years has run toward a sort of presentism, in which history before the modern disappears. As an ancient historian, I am naturally fond of taking a long view, and have argued that such a perspective enables us to see continuities in women's condition over long spans of time.[1] I hope that we have reached a new turning point, a "re-revision," in which we can drag our attention away from the fascinating glare of the present century and look again down the long cool corridors of the past.

Such a claim for the value of ancient history may seem brash, coming from the student of a culture (Rome) that has left us with almost exclusively male-authored texts. What can be done with these texts other than the kind of "images of women" work that literary theorists left behind ten years ago? Faced with a body of evidence skewed toward the elite male, Roman historians of gender have from the outset tried to see Roman sexualities as part of a system, a cultural whole, in which, for example, sexual institutions bear a recognizable relation to institutions like the army, the empire, the law.[2] Our texts give us ample material to talk about the production of male gender; and since the feminine played a part in the Roman idea of the masculine, we can at least talk about the meaning of the female for males. The meaning of the male for females, even of the female for females, can often be extrapolated. In this essay, I will be looking at a major site of male gender production in Rome of the early Empire: the *scholae*, where young men were trained in legal oratory — an institution that I will argue bears a significant resemblance to its modern descendant.

It seemed particularly appropriate to be thinking about the *scholae* in 1993–1994, a good year for trials and unusual crimes. For a while, the *Los Angeles Times* was full of nothing but the Menendez brothers, Nancy Kerrigan, and Lorena Bobbitt; as I write, the pages have been taken over by the ongoing story of O. J. and Nicole Simpson. As a feminist and a student of Roman law, I was struck by one particular feature about the way these trials worked: the lawyers' arguments are like stories — stories that take familiar patterns. The Menendez trial was in the paper day after day, and every time it appeared, the reporters noted that the prosecution was arguing that the brothers killed out of hatred and greed, the defense that they killed after years of abuse. As for Lorena Bobbitt, the *Times* subhead on January 11, 1994, read: "Defense will argue that abuse drove her to mutilate husband. His lawyer says it was jealousy." These arguments tell stories about what happened; they take the bare "facts" about the case — what's given — and fill them in. And they can work only if the stories are recognizable to the audience — the jury (and, increasingly in these days of Court TV and tabloid frenzy, the general public).

What does Lorena Bobbitt have to do with Roman history? The answer becomes more apparent with a little background information. That background has to do with a Roman institution so obscure that most people today have never heard of it. And yet it was perhaps the most important ideological state apparatus of the early Roman Empire. It was the system in which young men learned to do the work of Roman upper-class males, the system in which they learned to make speeches. The power of this system is evidenced in many ways, not least of which is that it determined the format of the speech on which this essay is based; the layout of the room in which it was given; the rank and roles (though not the sex) of the people who spoke and attended; the form, physical and otherwise, of Duke University and of universities in general; and the nature of the system that trained the lawyers who tried Lorena Bobbitt's case as well as the process by which she was tried. But for now I will pass over those aspects of the power of that system. Instead I wish to make you better acquainted with the Roman phenomenon known as the *scholae* (or "schools").

At the age of fourteen, sons of Roman citizens exchanged the child's toga for the man's toga — the *toga virilis*. This act took place in a public ceremony at a yearly religious festival, the Liberalia. The boy's father would accompany the boy to the forum, and the forum would from then on be the center of the boy's world. Here he would be handed over by his father to an apprenticeship; in the Republic, he would attend on a great orator (which meant, in Rome, a great lawyer and a great politician); by the time of the early Empire (around the 30s B.C.), he would attend the rhetorical schools. This apprenticeship of the young man was known as the *tirocinium fori*, the "apprenticeship to the forum" — or maybe a better translation would be "forum boot camp." Entering the forum, the young man entered a world wholly male as well as a public space devoted to activities marked as male in Roman culture: litigation, legislation, politics, gladiatorial combat. This space was decorated with monuments to the victories of Roman generals and framed by buildings dedicated by Roman men to the memory of their family name. Recent work in feminist architectural theory has spelled out for us how spaces can be gendered; the Roman forum is a preeminent example.[3]

Though cases were heard in the open air of the forum, the *scholae* came to be held indoors, often in the house of the teacher. At the *scholae*, the young men and their teachers practiced speaking in preparation for the "real world" of the forum. They called their practice speeches "declaiming" to distinguish them from the "real" speaking in the forum. And in order to practice, they used practice cases, called *controversiae*. Fortunately for us, a great many of these cases have been preserved in a number of ancient sources — most notably, in the work of the elder Seneca. He was an upper-class Roman, originally from Spain, who came to Rome to study as a young man just as the Empire began; and he had (thanks to his training) a spectacular memory. And so, in the reign of the emperor Caligula (around A.D. 40), he wrote a little book for his three sons, preserving for them — and us — all the best things he remembered hearing back in the *scholae* of his youth.[4]

What were these practice cases like? They were remarkable. First a "law" would be stated; then there would be a "given," the bare bones of a case. These givens are wildly improbable, fantastic, melodramatic, and very short — only a few sentences. The task of the speakers was then to devise the most elegant speeches they could on the basis of the given. In the course of doing this, they, in effect, made up stories. And these stories were highly gendered, which I think is in keeping with the function of the schools in turning boys into men. It is an axiom of mine that content is never arbitrary. So these young men, in learning *how* to speak, learned also *what* to speak. (Of course, another of their lessons was a silent one, expressed by the absence of women from the *scholae*.)[5] But another interesting thing is that these stories bear an odd resemblance to a genre of literature that seems also to have sprung up around this time: the novel, or romance. It is my contention that the content of these stories has a significant relation to the content of the ancient novel.

And so the title of this essay: "How Putting the Man in Roman Put the Roman in Romance." It sums up two ideas: that the *scholae* taught gender to Roman citizen males; and that they did so, oddly, by teaching these young men to create romance novels through oral improvisation. Of course, this title is much too cute, and so compressed that this whole long explanation is necessary in order for the reader to know what it means. But this kind of overly clever compression was a beloved technique of the *scholae*, though embarrassment was sometimes expressed; as Seneca said, some stylists are not unaware of their vices — they love them. To explain why a scholar like me makes a title like that, it might be argued that the same kind of exhaustive training, with rewards for showing off, produces the practitioners of critical theory as produced the speakers of the *scholae*, and I would again point out that the similarity is not a coincidence. Writing this article, casting the argument, ordering the sentences in artful structure and pleasing rhythm, I am following rules devised by the rhetoricians and using some of the masters' oldest tools.

This concludes what the orators in the *schola* would call my *narratio* — the presentation of the basic facts. Now I'll do a little *divisio* — like a good declaimer, I'll divide up what I'm going to talk about.

First to deal more closely with this process of putting the man in Roman. Gender, it turns out, pretty much permeated the world of the *scholae*. Gender itself was an element in rhetorical style, and it was very important to learn to speak like a man. Judith Butler has argued that gender is something performed; and David Gilmore and other anthropologists have argued that manhood throughout the Mediterranean, ancient and modern, is contested ground.[6] Certainly we see both these hypotheses confirmed within the *scholae*, where orators are always attacking each other's manhood and where students ran the risk of turning virility into effeminacy through overtraining. The great rhetorician Quintilian says that orators need "firmness of the body, lest our voice be attenuated to the thinness of eunuchs and women and sick people; this is achieved by walking, applying body lotion [*unctio*], abstinence from sex, and the easy digestion of food — that is, *frugalitas*."[7] A voice that was too songlike or too highly inflected was said to be "broken" (*fracta*) or "soft" (*mollis*), adjectives that were also used of men considered effeminate. Body movements were important, but they could not look too much like the movements of a dancer, because dancers were also considered effeminate.

Conversely, according to the elder Seneca, you had to be a real man in order to become a good speaker. He lectures to his sons about this at the very beginning of his book:

> Look, the intellects of our lazy youth are asleep, nor do they wake up for the exercise of a single respectable occupation; slumber and languor and, what is more disgusting than slumber and languor, the pursuit of wicked things has invaded their spirits: the obscene pursuit of singing and dancing keeps them effeminate [*effeminatos*]; and curling the hair and shrilling the voice into womanish cajoleries, competing with women in the softness of the body and cultivating themselves with the foulest elegances — that is the pattern of our young men. Who of your agemates is what I might call intellectual enough, diligent enough — rather, who is enough of a man? Softened up and emasculate [*enerves*] as they were born they remain all their lives, laying siege to other people's chastity, careless of their own. The gods are not so wicked as to bestow eloquence on people like *them*. . . . Go on, look for orators among those depilated and powdered men — men nowhere but in their lust.[8]

Clearly, an orator has to be not only a man but a manly man; and sexual behavior is a determinant of rhetorical ability.

Another thing that marked the *scholae* as a manly kind of place was the large element of contest that shaped what went on there. This was not really a friendly audience; the schoolmen were quick to criticize each other (often interrupting), and the performances were decidedly competitive. Seneca thinks of the speakers in terms of ranking them, and at one point he comes out and gives us his list of the top four declaimers.[9] Criticisms could be very harsh — the speakers often resorted to personal insults and sometimes attacked each other's manhood. My favorite example of one of these insults gives a real feel for the somewhat grade-school level of humor involved. This joke is a lot funnier in Latin than it is in English, though, and in order to get it across I have had to juggle the translation. Also I have to give away the punch line and explain something, which is that the main sewer line for the city of Rome was called the Cloaca Maxima, which just means "the Great Sewer." So at one point Seneca is reporting a sort of interview with the great declaimer Cassius Severus, and Cassius Severus tells this story about another declaimer called Cestius Pius, whom he strongly dislikes. He says that he went over to Cestius's *schola*, where "Cestius was talking about how great he was, as usual. He was saying, 'If I were a boxer, I'd be Muhammad Ali. If I were a dancer, I'd be Nureyev. If I were a racehorse, I'd be Man o' War.' So I couldn't contain myself and I shouted out, 'If you were a sewer, you'd be the Great Sewer.'" Cassius goes on to say that everybody burst out laughing.[10]

Much in this account is typical of the *scholae*: Cestius is extremely boastful — not unusual; Cassius Severus responds with public ridicule — also not unusual; and the rest of the men present respond by laughing — also not unusual, according to Seneca's account. This kind of thing often escalated into an exchange of insults, and this practice is reminiscent of a general Roman practice of verbal dueling, a practice Rome shares with other cultures as well.[11] We might also note that Cestius here compares himself with two figures defined by competition — in the Latin, a gladiator and a racehorse. Yet all three figures bear some stigma: actors and gladiators were *infames*, and horses are, after all, animals. The comparisons suggest the danger underlying the performance of oratory — the risk of manhood slippage.

A third and final point about manhood in the *scholae* has to do with who was there. As I said before, these texts are very little known today. I have to work hard to convince others that the *scholae* were in fact an important part of Roman culture. But some of the people who frequented the *scholae* were famous. The emperor Augustus liked to go, and he and Tiberius, his successor, were fans of various declaimers. Augustus's sidekick Maecenas, the famous patron of Vergil and Horace, liked to go, and he plays a somewhat sinister role in Seneca's stories.[12] Another great patron of the arts, Messalla, liked to go, and so did his most famous protégé, the poet Ovid. In fact, Ovid figures in numerous amusing stories about the *scholae*; not only did he like to declaim, but his poetry served as a model for younger declaimers' oratorical style.[13] Conversely, the style of the *scholae* left its mark all over Ovid's poetry — in not only style but content — and the influence of the *scholae* on all subsequent literature could thus be said to be double-barreled. Writers continued to be trained in the *scholae*; and Ovid is arguably the most influential Roman poet in terms of style and content. Finally, the elder Seneca is called the elder Seneca to distinguish him from the younger Seneca — the famous one who wrote philosophical essays and tragedies and who played such a dramatic role himself at the court of Nero. The three sons to whom Seneca dedicated his book included not only the younger Seneca, but the father of another great Roman poet, Lucan.[14]

The point is that the men who attended the *scholae* included some of the most conspicuous role models in early imperial Rome. They were at the center of government and the arts and would shape the face of Roman culture. The *scholae* included young men, of course — even primarily; they included these young men's teachers, most known to us today only through Seneca; they even included Greeks and, occasionally, a freed slave. But, to Seneca, the glory of the *scholae* were men like his friend Porcius Latro, a manly man from Seneca's native Spain; he was an outdoorsman, a hiker, with a "bold, rustic, and Spanish style" about him.[15] These are the men that Seneca is holding up as models for his sons; and he defines the orator by quoting a famous line from the quintessential Roman man, the elder Cato: "An orator is, Marcus, my son, a good man, skilled at speaking."[16] The terse simplicity of the definition is meant to enhance — and be enhanced by — Cato's perfection as a manly man, which in turn is enhanced by the fact that this definition is addressed to his son, whom he is coaching in how to be a man.

So much for putting the man in Roman. How did this put the Roman in romance?

I first started thinking about this at the prompting of a passing remark by S. F. Bonner in his wonderful book about the *scholae*. Talking about a sort of proto-*controversia*, he remarked that it has "quite an 'Arabian Nights' setting" to it.[17] Nobody can read Seneca's *Controversiae* without being struck by the wild and wonderful plotlines; when I thought about the relation between the *controversiae* and the romances of the first two centuries A.D., I could only think of a joke an old friend of mine once told me — that Cheerios are bagel seeds.[18] In much the same way, the *controversiae* are like novel seeds; their topics and their plotlines have a lot in common with ancient romances. But what is even more interesting about them — and this shows up clearly in the way Seneca presents them — is how they were performed. The theme was given, and then each speaker played a riff on it, as it were; the plotline was developed as a group project, as in some forms of hypertext. *Controversiae* were fluid, within certain (disputed) boundaries; they were never finished;

they could be performed, or created, any number of times by any number of players. Great riffs were remembered, copied, and praised; some riffs were critiqued, despised, rejected. And what is most interesting about them, to me, is that the content of the *controversiae* — the air the declaimers breathed, the water they drank, the bagels they ate — was not just any content. Themes recur, and the declaimers observe certain limits in dealing with them. As Petronius remarked about the *scholae*, it is not possible to live in a kitchen without stinking.[19] I would argue, in other words, not only that the *scholae* engaged young men in the romantic but that this engagement must in turn have had a profound impact on their culture. And not only on the young men but, in turn, on women.

Seneca's *Controversiae* are divided into ten books, each containing between six and nine items, so a total of seventy-four remain in full or in excerpt. The topics may be divided, for our purposes, into those that deal mostly with women and those that do not. Of those that deal with women, popular topics and characters include adultery, wicked stepmothers, rape, and the seduction of priestesses; of those that do not deal with women, popular topics and characters include disinheritance, tyrants, heroes and generals, rich men and poor men, abusive fathers, parricide, and pirates.

Counting up these motifs is hard, since there are many overlaps. But just to give a rough idea, the topic of disinheritance forms one of the most numerous groups, with twenty-five of the seventy-four *controversiae* dealing with it in some way. The disinheritance *controversiae* basically revolve around conflicts between father and son — a preoccupation of the *controversiae* generally, and a resonant one, considering that the *scholae* were populated largely by fathers and sons. In contrast, forty-two of the cases, well over half, involve female characters, often in a way that defines them in terms of their sexual bodies. Good women are decidedly in the minority in these cases, the outstanding example of one being a daughter who hangs herself before the house-door of her cruel father — and she is dead already when the case begins; it is her brother and father who dispute the case.[20]

A couple of representative givens show the level of melodrama typical of the cases. The titles are Seneca's own:

1.2, "The Prostitute Priestess"
Law: A priestess must be chaste from chaste parents, pure from pure parents.

A certain virgin was captured by pirates and sold, bought by a pimp and prostituted. She begged those coming to her for donations [only]. When she could not beg off a soldier who had come to her, she killed him as he struggled with her and tried to force her. Accused and acquitted, she was sent back to her family. She now seeks to be a priestess.

1.7, "The Tyrant-Killer Let Go by Pirates"

Law: Children must support their parents or be put in chains.

A certain man killed one of his brothers, a tyrant, and killed the other brother caught in adultery, though his father was begging him not to. Captured by pirates, he wrote to his father for ransom. The father wrote a letter to the pirates: if they would cut off his hands, he would pay them double. The pirates let him go. The father has become poor; the son is refusing to support him.

An obvious feature of the givens is the number of plot twists packed into them. The problems are not simple; moreover, much scope is allowed the speaker for filling in the gaps in the chain of events. A less obvious feature is the persistence of the gender stereotypes that appear in the givens overall. The tension between fathers and sons, which appears here in the most melo-dramatic terms, pervades the *controversiae* and is of course interesting in itself. But here I want to focus on what the *controversiae* do with women.

First of all, it should be emphasized that what we have here is what Seneca remembered and chose to write down. The preponderance of misogynistic remarks is sometimes staggering; a cautious analyst might be willing to de-duce only that this was Seneca's personal bias. Nonetheless, he does give us some clues that suggest he was not alone.

One of the chief skills of a declaimer was known as *descriptio* — description. Here are some examples from the case of the prostituted priestess:

(1) [Latro said,] "As for the rest, I don't know. Why do you call me to your cubicle and your obscene cot?" . . . (2) [Fulvius Sparsus] said, "What you did once you were shut in we can neither ask nor know." . . . (3) [Publius Vinicius said,] "She stood naked on the shore for the buyer's approval; all parts of her body were both inspected and handled." . . . (4) [Mento said,] "I apologize to your ears and dignity that it is necessary in this case to mention the words 'brothel,' 'pimp,' 'prostitute's earnings,' 'murder.'" . . . (5) [Arellius Fuscus said,] ". . . You were called a prostitute, you stood in a public place, the placard was put up over your cubicle, you welcomed each customer; as for the rest, even if I were in that public place, I would rather be silent."

We have some good examples here of the figure known as *praeteritio*, "pre-tending not to talk about." And it is clear that the speakers are taking a good deal of pleasure precisely in describing and thus exposing the imagined woman's prostituted body.

In a similar way, some *controversiae* expose a body that has been physically abused — often, though not always, the body of a woman. An example comes from a *controversia* in which a woman has poisoned her daughter to keep her from marrying her own lover. The (unnamed) speaker describes the scene: "The rotting corpse is brought forth, swollen with poison. . . . We have seen the disintegrating corpse, and we take the cadaver as proof of the mother's confession."[21] The production of this rotting corpse is not called for by the given; but such descriptions are typical of the *scholae* and would continue to be popular in the literature of the next century. Indeed, post-Augustan literature might be said to be characterized by gratuitous rotting corpses, perhaps due to the prevalence of political purges and forced suicides in the lives of the literary classes in those years. The gendering of such corpses as female then doubles their significance: not only the currently perforated citizen body but the always perforable female body.[22]

Another standard technique of ancient rhetoric was the use of what were called *loci communes*, literally "commonplaces." These were set pieces that the speaker could bring out and rattle off almost without thinking. The most important one in Latin literature is the *locus de saeculo*, the commonplace on the degeneracy of modern times (Seneca's tirade on modern young men, above, is a variation on it), but there were many others. And there was a commonplace on the corrupt nature of women, as evidenced, for example, by its painful insertion into one speaker's argument. This comes from a case about a woman who is tortured by a tyrant but does not reveal her husband's plot to kill the tyrant. Her husband then divorces her when she fails to bear children, and she sues him for unfair treatment. Fabianus, a speaker who loves commonplaces, is speaking against the husband: "Why did you divorce your wife? Did she burden your income with expenses? And, as is the way in these modern times, womanish ambition, running over with extravagance, goes crazy as they compete with each other, extending private losses to the very state. Did she desire gems, pearls sought from foreign shores, gold, clothing that would cover nothing of her wifely body? If she were like this, the tyrant would have corrupted her easily. . . ."[23] You can hear the creaking as Fabianus squeezes the commonplace into an argument that really does not call for it; and you can also see what the commonplace about women was like.

Akin to the commonplaces were the assumptions that were made about gender; one fragmentary *controversia* tells a great deal about rules for men as well as for women (the attributions to individual speakers are lost here):

Let an unchaste man be barred from speaking at a public assembly.

A good-looking young man made a bet that he would go out in public dressed in woman's clothing. He went out; he was raped by ten young men. He accused them of rape and won his case. Barred from speaking at an assembly by a magistrate, he sues the magistrate for slander.

He put on woman's clothing, he arranged his hair in a woman's style, he put on eyeliner in girlish primping, he colored his cheeks. . . . Give him girl's dress, give him the night: he'll be raped. . . . I pass over the deeds of his adolescence in general, I rest my case with a single night: he imitated a girl so well that he found a rapist.[24]

I would note the assumptions here about who has the right to speak — for one thing, someone who has been penetrated cannot speak — and about the direct connection between being female and being raped. The young man's assumption of female dress is described in terms very similar to those commonly used in Roman texts to describe effeminate men; thus we might extrapolate the nature of *their* experience of life.

It is important to realize, in connection with this idea about who has the right to speak, that the topics of the *controversiae* are marked by an almost complete absence of a female subject. For male characters, the declaimers had the option either of impersonating the characters themselves, or of pretending to act as the character's advocate (*patronus*). But for female characters, it was the convention only to pretend to be their advocate. There are occasions when this advocate is apparently repeating the words of his client's account; but they are very rare. The disjunction between women and the world of the *controversiae* shows up starkly in one declaimer's remark: "She was found innocent because the little woman seemed not to know anything about the law."[25]

So much for the topics of the *controversiae*; now I want to look at how the declaimers manipulated them by telling stories. The technical term for a "story" in the *scholae* was *color*, and Seneca devotes a section of each *controversia* to a discussion of the *colores* that different speakers used. He also includes among his recollections a great many fascinating anecdotes about what the declaimers thought about what they were doing as well as his own opinions about it. And here is a little reflection on what *colores* meant to the declaimers.[26] Seneca is remarking that the declaimers could not resist the temptation to attack one character in the *controversia*: "The sweetness of making an epigram [*sententiae dulcedo*] overcame some — they couldn't resist it. The dry [*aridi*] declaimers keep the *colores* they have proposed more faithfully; for nothing disturbs them — no ornament, no epigram. In the same way, women who have ugly faces are more often chaste; it's not the willingness they lack, but a seducer." Remarkably, Seneca here portrays the declaimers as seduced into story by language—the declaimer is in the place of the woman, his personal style is like a woman's beauty, and the seductive *sententia* is like the seducer of the woman, carrying her/him off into narrative. This odd gender switch here is much in keeping with the tendency of Roman critical language to call story "sweet"; as Seneca says elsewhere, "The sweetness of stories has led me off the subject" (*longius me fabellarum dulcedo produxit*).[27]

How could the declaimers use *colores* to tinker with *controversiae*? First of all, I should note that the whole structure of *controversiae* encourages invention: not only were the givens fictional—and sometimes quite unrealistic—but many of the laws were as well. Both givens and laws were passed down the generations in a sort of oral tradition as well as in handbooks.[28] Second, the givens themselves allowed for much elaboration by the speakers—elaboration that sometimes amounted to changing the given altogether. Seneca often reports indignation on the part of other declaimers when someone does this; but sometimes everyone does it, and he says not a word.

Here is one of my favorite sets of *colores* from one of my favorite cases.[29] The rule is "Let an unchaste woman be thrown off the rock"—a reference to the Tarpeian Rock, a crag in Rome from which certain kinds of criminals were thrown as punishment. Now, the law itself is quite unrealistic; as Seneca's editor drily notes, a *man* was thrown off the Tarpeian Rock, for committing incest with his daughter, in A.D. 33;[30] the punishment for an unchaste priestess was not being thrown off the rock but being buried alive. The declaimers have doctored the law and the circumstances, apparently to suit their preferences.[31]

The given is that the woman is to be thrown off the rock, prays to the goddess to save her because she is innocent, is nevertheless thrown off the rock, and lives; now they want to throw her off again. The hostility of some speeches made against her is quite astonishing. But my favorite *colores* are ingenious ones: "Aietius Pastor spoke this *controversia* before Cestius when he was already a senator, and he thought this *color* the best: she had hardened her body by means of drugs to such a degree that she bounced off the rocks, unharmed. . . . [Cestius laughs at this.] . . . Julius Bassus . . . had said, 'a virgin good at jumping.' I remember that Junius Otho Senior used a stupid *color*, which was the less bearable because he published a book of *colores*. 'Perhaps,' he said, 'she prepared herself for the punishment, and from the time when she began to sin she took lessons in falling.'"[32]

Other *colores* take greater liberties with the given. As we might expect, in light of Roman attitudes on rape,[33] declaimers in the numerous *controversiae* that deal with rape often express suspicion as to whether a rape has in fact taken place. Some excursions into plot production are more surprising.

The most complete speech among the *controversiae* is one by Porcius Latro in the case of the "Foreign Merchant."[34] The given here is that a man goes away on business; while he is gone, a foreign merchant tries to seduce his wife, fails, dies, and leaves her all his money. When the husband returns home, he divorces his wife on suspicion of adultery. Latro's speech, an extravaganza of misogyny, includes the following complete fabrication.[35] Speaking as the husband, he describes ". . . how a young man, handsome, rich, unknown in the neighborhood, moved in next to a beautiful woman who was too much at liberty in the absence of her husband; and how he perished, his strength exhausted by the continuous satiation of his daily lust, by day and by night. . . ." The given does not tell the cause of the merchant's death; Latro, in the role of the husband, has simply decided that it was due to too much sex and has made this element part of his story.

Most telling of all is the case of the "Stepmother's Wound." The given involves a case of murder in which a man is found stabbed in his bed, with his second wife (the proverbial wicked stepmother) lying next to him, wounded. It becomes an accepted ploy for the declaimers to say that she was *lightly* wounded; Seneca accepts this without comment and indeed sets aside a whole section for descriptions of the wound — for indeed the wound is produced, like the rotting corpse, as an object of scrutiny: "About the stepmother's wound some said elegant things, some foolish — no, many said foolish things. [Among the elegant ones, Hispo Romanius said,] 'Show, stepmother, show where your lover pinched you.' [Among the foolish ones, Licinius Nepos said,] 'That's not a wound, but an adulterer's love-bite.'"[36] It is notably difficult here for us to tell the difference between elegant and foolish. Meanwhile, without comment, a stab wound in a woman is turned into the mark made by a lover. Not only is the woman's status as chaste wife under attack; for her, the line is blurred between battery and the erotic.

The point here, then, is that the declaimers made up stories; and not just any stories, but stories that offered a particular version of gender, stories that took pleasure in exposing the female body, stories that express deep hostility toward women. The reinforcement of beliefs produced by this process would have been enhanced by several special features. First, imitation was considered an important means of learning and of expressing a declaimer's art. A neatly put *sententia* would normally be widely repeated, or imitated with slight variations. Second, in his discussion of *colores*, Seneca often notes that "everybody took the line that . . . [whatever]." More often than not, the declaimers seem to have moved en masse in the same direction. As in mountain climbing, there seems to have been a feeling that certain approaches were workable; occasionally someone would test out a new route, and Seneca remarks on this. Finally, the declaimers, quite consciously, were playing to the crowd. As Cestius Pius remarks, "There is much that I say not because *I* like it but because the audience will like it."[37] Thus the stories the declaimers wrote were, in a way, already written for them.

A proper *declamatio* ends with a *conclusio*, in which the speaker explains what it all means. And so I must do the same.

When I say that the *controversiae* bear a strong resemblance to the ancient romances, what does that mean? These novels themselves seem to begin in the first two centuries A.D., though they have precursors in other genres, like the story of the *Odyssey* or the tales of history. They are really novels — some of them quite long — and, as Jack Winkler points out, they tend to have a "marriage plot": two lovers meet, are separated, have a long series of fantastic adventures, are finally reunited, and marry.[38] The *controversiae* lack the main ingredients of the star-crossed lovers and the marriage, but other plot elements are shared: odd twists of fate, kidnappings by pirates, exposed children, poison, wicked stepmothers, tyrants, mysteries. In addition, many of the novels are highly rhetorical: Shadi Bartsch spends a whole book just on *descriptio* in the novels.[39]

Of course, what we would expect is that the ancient novels had a female readership. Holly Montague, building on the work of Janice Radway and other scholars of the modern romance novel, has pointed to the strong similarities between ancient novels and modern Harlequin romances and bodice-rippers.[40] We might like to imagine Cleopatra, for example, dipping into some early version of the *Aithiopika* as she floated down the Nile on her barge. However, there is no evidence to suggest that this was the case, and if it were the case, a female audience might not have found these novels all that empowering. It is true that some ancient women could read, and did read, as well as write; this would have been much affected by social class, but it is fair to say that the "daughters of educated men" (possibly 15 percent of the population) could read, though they were less well educated than their brothers. They did not, for example, go with their brothers into the *scholae*. So ancient women *could* have read novels.[41]

There is more to suggest, though, that ancient novels were read by men — in fact, the same men who attended the *scholae*.[42] Petronius's *Satyricon*, as we have it now, begins with an ironic tirade against the *scholae*, and this book is also a takeoff on the standard Greek romance. I would argue that we have to look elsewhere for ancient tales with a markedly female subjectivity and that we can find them, oddly enough, in the same place that spawned the *scholae*. Declamation seems to have come to Rome from the Near East — from Rhodes and Asia Minor as well as from Athens. Although the institution of the *tirocinium fori* was surely indigenous, the idea of having *scholae* was not; but it certainly caught on.[43] Many of the teachers came to Rome from the Greek East — farther east than Greece itself. Cestius Pius, for instance, despite his Roman name, came from Smyrna, in what is now Turkey. Hybreas came from Mylasa, just south of there. Meanwhile, the novels seem to have been especially popular in Syria, around Antioch. So we might posit a common source for the narratives of the *scholae* and the novel and also for another, more woman-centered kind of text.

This other kind of narrative was extremely popular around Syria in the second century A.D.: the Apocryphal Acts, including tales such as the *Acts of Thecla*. Thecla, a bold heroine, decides to follow St. Paul and take up a life as a preacher of the Gospel. She renounces her fiancé, dresses as a man, travels, talks back to powerful men, and has many harrowing adventures, including several narrow escapes in the arena, in one of which she is saved by direct divine intervention from being eaten by seals. I have no trouble believing that the *Acts of Thecla*, along with stories like the *Life of St. Mary the Harlot*, were widely read by women.[44] Thus even in antiquity the plotline of the novel was not intrinsically sexist, and the content could vary according to the needs of the author. While the narratives of the *scholae* were made by men and were directly involved in the production of male gender, they were not the only game in town.

So much for connections between the *controversiae* and the novel. Now, how about connections between the *controversiae* and the law? And how do these boil down to the same thing? How does knowing that Seneca's practice cases work like little novels help us to understand what happened when Lorena Bobbitt's case went to court?

This is not a question alien to legal theory. Critical legal theory has devoted much attention to narrative; feminists in particular have pursued two approaches.[45] First of all, as in other disciplines, feminists here have argued that legal doctrine and procedure are shaped by gendered narratives. As Clare Dalton points out, "The stories told by contract doctrine are human stories of power and knowledge. . . . It is only through [the] restriction of content that any story has a meaning."[46] She demonstrates how judicial decisions operate — think through — a set of stereotypes (or stories) that accord a limited range of possibilities to women. Moreover, the stories told in the court-room are told by lawyers.[47] Lucie White recounts how her client, Mrs. G., suddenly takes control of a narrative that White had carefully prepared ahead of time; if White, a feminist lawyer filled with empathy for the voiceless Mrs. G., is surprised when Mrs. G. comes up with a story of her own, we can gauge how far our declaimers might be from any Mrs. G. they might run into.

Of course, the past few years have provided us with some spectacular examples of narrative at work in the shaping of the state. In Toni Morrison's collection of essays on Anita Hill's testimony at the Clarence Thomas hearings, Wahneema Lubiano reflects on how some "narratives are so naturalized . . . that they seem to be reality . . . [and] . . . reproduce the world in particular ways."[48] Similarly, and more specifically, Kimberlé Crenshaw demonstrates how the inadequacy of existing narrative produces doctrinal exclusion, in which "the specific forms of domination to which black females are subject sometimes fall between the existing legal categories for recognizing injury."[49] Crenshaw illustrates, among other things, how prevailing narratives about rape act to discredit the woman's character; and how credibility is a function of one's place in the narrative.[50]

But the more spectacular move in feminist legal theory has been a call *for* narrative, in a bravura application of the techniques of *écriture féminine*. The idea has been to bring into legal discourse both a kind of narrative that is vivid and immediate rather than dry and abstract and a kind of content that gives voice to experiences normally excluded from law journals: being raped, being battered, giving birth, being locked out of Benneton because you are black. The last account belongs to one of the most noted writers in this area, Patricia J. Williams; her essays bear the subtitle "Diary of a Law Professor," and she illustrates her theoretical arguments with stories of her own life.[51]

Interestingly, one incident Williams recounts involves "K., a first-year student," reduced to tears by an argument over a racist problem set by another professor on an exam: "The problem was an updated version of Shakespeare's *Othello*, in which Othello is described as a 'black militaristic African leader' who marries the 'young white Desdemona' whom he then kills in a fit of sexual rage. Othello is put on trial. The students were to identify the elements of murder. The model answer gives points for ability to 'individualize the test' of provocation by recognizing that 'a rough untutored Moor might understandably be deceived by the wiles of a more sophisticated European.'"[52] Williams then meditates on anecdotal questions like this one and on the kind of in-class exercises known as "hypotheticals," of which she gathers a collection. For, as it turns out, the method of instruction favored by the *scholae* is alive and well in law schools today (and note here the casual connection to canonical literature). Williams comments, "While styled as hypotheticals, these collected exams set themselves up as instructional mirrors of real life. . . . We, as law teachers, create miniworlds of reality."[53]

This, in turn, led me to think back to my own training in Roman law, which, come to think of it, was full of hypotheticals. In my own experience — and, from Williams's list, law school hypotheticals are similar — hypotheticals are written to be melodramatic, even funny. The Roman characters in hypotheticals are always crashing their chariots, having chamber pots emptied on their togas, and marrying multiple spouses. These funny Romans also routinely beat, kill, sell, maim, and do business or have sex with slaves, for Rome, of course, was a slave society, and slavery plays a large part in Roman law. I looked in Curzon's *Roman Law*, a textbook that includes hypotheticals among the exercises for each chapter, to see how gender figures there, but found no characters identifiable as women, except for a single question in the chapter on marriage.[54] But then Curzon likes to call his characters by letters of the alphabet, as in "Advise A in the following cases. (a) A buys a slave from B" or "A, who resides in Rome, appoints his slave, B, as manager of his fruit farm in Sicily."[55] So I looked at the hypotheticals I wrote myself when I taught Roman law at Dartmouth in the spring of 1982 and found no shortage of female characters: "the widow Candelabra, a doting mother" and her daughter "Lolita, a precocious child" (more literature); Mania, the wife of Marcus Viscus; and the actress Malaria, who breaks her collarbone falling off a horse. In one case, involving the murder of "the fatcat governor of Bithynia and Pontus," the suspects include his "beautiful Bithynian slave Barbara," "his wife Impedimenta" (found in bed by her father with her husband's freed slave), "the widow Impecunia" (evicted from her apartment), and, incidentally, his "old slave, Fido." In another case, "Crismus Bonus came home from the Forum early, one day, and found his beloved wife Vanilla in bed with his trusted freedman, Manlius the actor." It seems that I cannot claim, myself, to have been immune from my training.

The Roman evidence reminds us that law has always been saturated with narrative; it is not a question of adding narrative to law but of increasing the repertoire and questioning the old narratives. Moreover, we have to deal with the weight of a history in which the old narratives were imposed on women's lives. Even the brief glimpse presented here of the kinds of narrative produced in the *scholae* suggests their probable effect on Roman women as legal persons. I have elsewhere argued that the rhetorical strategies of the Hill-

Thomas confrontation had much in common with the strategies whereby women were silenced or sexualized in the Roman forum—whereby Cicero, for example, attacked Clodia.[56] So what do we do with the idea that such narratives have been operating to silence women for over two thousand years? I always tell my students that you have to know what you're facing before you can fix it. And I would say that women's studies has given us the tools to do both. I think it is important to keep faith with history—and then to keep on working.

Notes

Translations throughout are my own unless otherwise indicated. Abbreviations used throughout work as follows (for example):

C. 10.pr.13 = Seneca, *Controversiae*, book 10, preface, sec. 13

C. 10.1.13 = Seneca, *Controversiae*, book 10, *controversia* 1, sec. 13

S. 2.7 = Seneca, *Suasoriae*, *suasoria* 2, sec. 7 (the *Suasoriae* are not divided into books)

1. Amy Richlin, "The Ethnographer's Dilemma and the Dream of a Lost Golden Age," *Feminist Theory and the Classics*, ed. Nancy Sorkin Rabinowitz and Amy Richlin (New York: Routledge, 1993), 272–303.

2. This tendency appears already in Marilyn Skinner's early literary studies of Catullus, notably "Parasites and Strange Bedfellows: A Study in Catullus' Political Imagery," *Ramus* 8 (1979): 137–52; and "Pretty Lesbius," *Transactions of the American Philological Association* 112 (1982): 197–208; in Judith Hallett's work on Latin love elegy, "The Role of Women in Roman Elegy: Counter-cultural Feminism," *Arethusa* 6 (1973): 103–24; and in my own work on Roman satire, *The Garden of Priapus: Sexuality and Aggression in Roman Humor* (New Haven: Yale University Press, 1983; rev. ed., New York: Oxford University Press, 1992); and has continued throughout the 1980s. Indeed, the question of the value of literary studies for feminist work in classics was explicitly problematized at an APA panel in 1985; statement and responses were published in *Helios* 17, no. 2 (1990). Important work since 1990 includes Carlin A. Barton, *The Sorrows of the Ancient Romans* (Princeton: Princeton University Press, 1993); Catharine Edwards, *The Politics of Immorality in Ancient Rome* (Cambridge: Cambridge University Press, 1993); and two forthcoming collections, *The Roman Cultural Revolution*, ed. Thomas Habinek and Alessandro Schiesaro, and *Roman Sexualities*, ed. Judith P. Hallett and Marilyn B. Skinner. Even critics who have kept a primarily literary focus, like Maria Wyke and Micaela Janan, factor history and material culture into their work, and Wyke has moved into popular-culture and film-theory approaches. Similarly, historians of slavery and of the family, like Suzanne Dixon and Sandra Joshel, have made gender an important part of their work. Younger

critics such as Anthony Corbeill, David Fredrick, and Jonathan Walters have adapted approaches from architectural theory, body history, and the comparative history of sexuality. Studies of Greek gender systems are perhaps better known to the general public; for a full discussion, see Richlin, "Ethnographer's Dilemma"; and Amy Richlin, "Not before Homosexuality: The Materiality of the *Cinaedus* and the Roman Law against Love between Men," *Journal of the History of Sexuality* 3, no. 4 (1993): 523–73.

3. On the Roman education system, see in general Stanley F. Bonner, *Education in Ancient Rome* (Berkeley: University of California Press, 1977); on the *tirocinium fori* and the Liberalia, see Richlin, "Homosexuality," 545–48, with sources. On the activities associated with the Roman forum, see John E. Stambaugh, *The Ancient Roman City* (Baltimore: The Johns Hopkins University Press, 1988), 104–22, and Edwards, *Politics of Immorality*, 19–20, 167–69, with bibliography; on the rhetorical use of the forum by speakers, see Ann Vasaly, *Representations: Images of the World in Ciceronian Oratory* (Berkeley: University of California Press, 1993), esp. 36–39. On feminist theory in architecture, see Shirley Ardener, ed., *Women and Space: Ground Rules and Social Maps* (Oxford: Berg, 1993); Gillian Rose, *Feminism and Geography* (Minneapolis: University of Minnesota Press, 1993); and Daphne Spain, *Gendered Spaces* (Chapel Hill: University of North Carolina Press, 1992); especially pertinent here is Silvia Rodgers, "Women's Space in a Men's House: The British House of Commons," in *Women and Space*, ed. Ardener, 46–69, the subject of which might well be compared with the Roman forum and senate house.

4. References to Seneca are to *The Elder Seneca*, 2 vols., ed. and trans. Michael Winterbottom (Cambridge: Harvard University Press, 1974).

5. On the place of Roman women in the court system, see Amy Richlin, "Roman Oratory, Pornography, and the Silencing of Anita Hill," *Southern California Law Review* 65 (1992): 1321–32. For a similar — and related — exclusion of the female from privileged discourse, see Rita Copeland, "Why Women Can't Read: Medieval Hermeneutics, Statutory Law, and the Lollard Heresy Trials," in *Representing Women: Law, Literature, and Feminism*, ed. Susan Sage Heinzelman and Zipporah Batshaw Wiseman (Durham: Duke University Press, 1994), 253–86.

6. Judith Butler, *Gender Trouble* (New York: Routledge, 1990), 24–25, 134–41; David D. Gilmore, *Manhood in the Making* (New Haven: Yale University Press, 1990); John J. Winkler, *The Constraints of Desire* (New York: Routledge, 1990), 9–11, 45–70; on gender and rhetoric, see esp. Maud W. Gleason, *Making Men: Sophists and Self-Presentation in Ancient Rome* (Princeton: Princeton University Press, 1995).

7. Quintilian, *Institutio Oratoria* 11.3.19. On Roman attitudes toward actors and performers generally, see Edwards, *Politics of Immorality*, 98–136.

8. *C.* 1.pr.8–9, 10.

9. *C.* 10.pr.13.

10. *C.* 3.pr.16. Literally, Cestius says: "If I were a Thracian [a kind of gladiator], I'd be Fusius; if I were a pantomime actor, I'd be Bathyllus; if I were a horse, I'd be

Melissio." Pantomime was like ballet. Bathyllus is still somewhat famous as the sex-object for, among others, Maecenas; the others are obscure.

11. On Roman verbal dueling, see Richlin, *Garden*, 65, 74–76, 86–87, 103, 147–48; and work in progress. An outstanding study of verbal dueling in a modern culture (Chiapas, Mexico) is Gary H. Gossen, "Verbal Dueling in Chamula," in *Speech Play*, ed. Barbara Kirshenblatt-Gimblett (Philadelphia: University of Pennsylvania Press, 1976), 121–46.

12. *C.* 2.4.13.

13. See, for example, *C.* 2.2.8–12; *S.* 3.7.

14. On Lucan and rhetoric, see M. P. O. Morford, *The Poet Lucan* (Oxford: Blackwell, 1967).

15. *C.* 1.pr.14, 16.

16. *C.* 1.pr.9.

17. Stanley F. Bonner, *Roman Declamation* (Berkeley: University of California Press, 1949), 19.

18. Thanks to Eddy Taylor of New Milford, New Jersey.

19. *Satyricon* 2.1.

20. *C.* 10.3.

21. *C.* 6.6.

22. For which see Sandra R. Joshel, "The Body Female and the Body Politic: Livy's Lucretia and Verginia," in *Pornography and Representation in Greece and Rome*, ed. Amy Richlin (New York: Oxford University Press, 1992), 112–30.

23. *C.* 2.5.7.

24. *C.* 5.6.

25. *C.* 6.2.

26. *C.* 2.1.24.

27. *S.* 1.7.

28. See Bonner, *Roman Declamation*.

29. *C.* 1.3.

30. Tacitus, *Annals* 6.19.

31. See Winterbottom ad loc.

32. *C.* 1.3.11.

33. Richlin, "Homosexuality," 561–66.

34. *C.* 2.7.

35. *C.* 2.7.2.

36. *C.* 7.5.8–10.

37. *C.* 9.6.12, Winterbottom's translation.

38. John J. Winkler, "The Invention of Romance," in *The Search for the Ancient Novel*, ed. James Tatum (Baltimore: The Johns Hopkins University Press, 1994), 23–38. The collection in which Winkler's article appears provides the most current introduction to the history of the novel in antiquity and the problems surrounding it. For a

comprehensive collection of ancient novels in translation, see B. P. Reardon, *Collected Ancient Greek Novels* (Berkeley: University of California Press, 1989). On gender roles in the ancient novel, see David Konstan, *Sexual Symmetry: Love in the Ancient Novel and Related Genres* (Princeton: Princeton University Press, 1994).

39. Shadi Bartsch, *Decoding the Ancient Novel* (Princeton: Princeton University Press, 1989). The idea that the novels and the rhetorical schools are connected goes back to the nineteenth century; see Elizabeth A. Clark, *The Life of Melania the Younger* (New York: Edwin Mellen Press, 1984), 158–59.

40. Holly Montague, "Sweet and Pleasant Passion: Female and Male Fantasy in Ancient Romance Novels," in *Pornography and Representation in Greece and Rome*, ed. Amy Richlin (New York: Oxford University Press, 1992), 231–49.

41. On the readership of the ancient novels, see Ewen Bowie, "The Readership of Greek Novels in the Ancient World," in *The Search for the Ancient Novel*, ed. Tatum, 435–59; and Susan A. Stephens, "Who Read Ancient Novels?" in *The Search for the Ancient Novel*, ed. Tatum, 405–18. The figure of 15 percent, derived from William Harris's studies of ancient literacy, is discussed in Stephens, "Who Read Ancient Novels?," 407; for female readership, see Bowie, "Readership of Greek Novels," 436–40, and the bibliography in his note 12. On the education of girls, see Bonner, *Education*, 135–36.

42. See Bowie, "Readership of Greek Novels."

43. Bonner, *Education*, 65–75.

44. For a bibliography on the *Acts of Thecla* and a brief discussion of its authorship, see Ross S. Kraemer, ed., *Maenads, Martyrs, Matrons, Monastics* (Philadelphia: Fortress Press, 1988), 407. The connection between the Apocryphal Acts and the ancient novel was first examined in 1902. See Clark, *Life of Melania*, 160 and 153–70; also see Richard I. Pervo, *Profit with Delight: The Literary Genre of the Acts of the Apostles* (Philadelphia: Fortress Press, 1987). On the popularity of Thecla and on women as readers of such literature, see Clark, *Life of Melania*, 167–69; for later saints' lives, see Claudia Rapp, "Figures of Female Sanctity: Byzantine Edifying Manuscripts and Their Audience," *Dumbarton Oaks Papers* (forthcoming). On the specularization of female characters in saints' lives, see Elizabeth A. Castelli, "Visions and Voyeurism: Holy Women and the Politics of Sight in Early Christianity," *Protocol of the Colloquy of the Center for Hermeneutical Studies* (forthcoming).

45. Easily available are several essays in Katharine T. Bartlett and Rosanne Kennedy, eds., *Feminist Legal Theory: Readings in Law and Gender* (Boulder: Westview Press, 1991), including Clare Dalton, "Deconstructing Contract Doctrine," 287–304, and Lucie E. White, "Subordination, Rhetorical Survival Skills, and Sunday Shoes: Notes on the Hearing of Mrs. G.," 404–28. Additional bibliography is provided by the editors. See also Anne C. Dailey, "Feminism's Return to Liberalism," *Yale Law Journal* 102 (1993): 1265–86, a review essay on Bartlett and Kennedy that provides an overview of the call-for-narrative school (esp. 1273–78); Kathryn Abrams, "Hearing

the Call of Stories," *California Law Review* 79 (1991): 971–1052, which examines in detail several prominent exponents of this school and meets objections commonly made to their work; Lynne Henderson, "Legality and Empathy," *Michigan Law Review* 85 (1987): 1574–1653, on audience reaction to narrative in law; and the symposium on legal storytelling in *Michigan Law Review* 87 (1989). The collection *Representing Women*, ed. Heinzelman and Wiseman, is less pertinent to this essay than its title indicates, but see Copeland, "Why Women Can't Read"; Margaret Anne Doody, "Voices of Record: Women as Witnesses and Defendants in the *Old Bailey Sessions Papers*," 287–308, on the "courtroom drama . . . [as] prefabricated scenario"; and Susan Sage Heinzelman, "Guilty in Law, Implausible in Fiction: Jurisprudential and Literary Narratives in the Case of Mary Blandy, Parricide, 1752," 309–36. Both Doody and Heinzelman link legal narratives to the genre of the novel.

Many thanks to my colleague Nomi Stolzenberg for her expert advice on feminist legal theory.

46. Dalton, "Deconstructing Contract Doctrine," 297.

47. See White, "Subordination"; cf. Kimberlé Crenshaw, "Whose Story Is It, Anyway? Feminist and Antiracist Appropriation of Anita Hill," in *Race-ing Justice, Engendering Power*, ed. Toni Morrison (New York: Pantheon, 1992), 402–40, at 422.

48. Wahneema Lubiano, "Black Ladies, Welfare Queens, and State Minstrels: Ideological War by Narrative Means," in *Race-ing Justice, En-gendering Power*, ed. Morrison, 329–30.

49. Crenshaw, "Whose Story Is It, Anyway?," 404.

50. For thoughts on race and narrative point of view in the case of Lani Guinier, see Patricia J. Williams, "Lani, We Hardly Knew Ye," *Village Voice*, June 15, 1993, 25–28.

51. Patricia J. Williams, *The Alchemy of Race and Rights* (Cambridge: Harvard University Press, 1991).

52. Williams, *Alchemy*, 80.

53. Ibid., 87, 88.

54. L. B. Curzon, *Roman Law* (Plymouth, England: Macdonald and Evans, 1966), 48, no. 5.

55. Ibid., 208, 210.

56. Richlin, "Roman Oratory."

Kristine Stiles

Shaved Heads and

Marked Bodies

Representations from

Cultures of Trauma

A multitude of representations and cultural productions emanate from social and political events located in, and imprinted with, trauma, the ancient Greek word for wound.[1] These images and attendant behaviors constitute the aggregate visual evidence of the "cultures of trauma," a phrase I want to introduce to denote traumatic circumstance that is manifest in culture, discernible at the intersection of aesthetic, political, and social experience.[2] While research in traumatogenesis has proliferated during the past two decades, few have examined the cultural formations that result from, and bear illustrative witness to, the impact on world societies of the ubiquitous wounds of trauma. Meditating on the history of trauma, British psychiatrist

Michael R. Trimble observed that its "etiology and pathogenesis . . . remains *invisible*" (my emphasis).[3] Yet, however invisible its origin and development, I maintain that the cultural signs of trauma are *highly visible* in images and actions that occur both within the conventional boundaries of visual art and in the practices and images of everyday life. This essay explores two of these sites: shaved heads and marked bodies.

Trauma may be defined concisely as "an emotional state of discomfort and stress resulting from (unconscious and conscious) memories of an extraordinary, catastrophic experience" that shatter "the survivor's sense of invulnerability to harm."[4] War, with its institutions and practices, is a ubiquitous source of trauma. But the genesis of trauma is not limited to the effects of war since the abuse of bodies destroys identity and leaves results parallel to war and its consequences. For several centuries trauma was diagnosed as neurosis.[5] But the term "post-traumatic neurosis," used to describe the symptoms of shell-shocked World War I veterans, was changed to "post-traumatic stress disorder" (PTSD) in the 1970s when the symptoms of Korean and Vietnam war veterans began to be diagnosed as stress.[6] This diagnosis refers to a heterogeneous group of causes with a homogeneous set of behaviors: disassociation, loss of memory coupled with repetitive, intrusive, and often disguised memories of the original trauma, rage, addictive disorders, somatic complaints, vulnerability, guilt, isolation, alienation, detachment, reduced responsiveness, inability to feel safe or to trust, and numbing.[7] Causes include war, shock, concentration camp experiences, rape, incest, sexual abuse, racism, shocks related to natural disasters or accidents, prolonged periods of domination as in hostage and prisoner-of-war situations, and the brutal psychological conditions perpetrated by some religious cults. I do not want to suggest that the omnipresence of trauma means that all traumatic experiences are the same. But if one considers the genocide of Cambodians, Indians and Pakistanis, Bosnians, the Kurds, or blacks in the United States, or the cultural influence of the "disappeared" among Argentinians, Chileans, and El Salvadorans, or the Boat People of Vietnam and Haiti, or the effects of the Chinese Cultural Revolution, then the occurrence and advance of trauma is staggering and global. Indeed, the world's some 40 million refugees, most of whom are women and children, offer a material image of trauma. If I were to identify the capitals of the cultures of trauma, they would be such places as the second-largest city in Pakistan or the third-largest city in Malawi, both of which are refugee camps![8]

At the nexus of the cultures of trauma is the highly celebrated new world order, which, I think, did not begin with the fall of the Berlin Wall in 1989, but with the ethos of the Holocaust and nuclear age. The epoch of the Cold War and its aftermath might be understood as an age of trauma whose threats increase exponentially, especially with the grim reality of the thriving global business in weapon-grade plutonium and enriched uranium contraband and such nuclear-industry disasters as Three Mile Island (1975) and Chernobyl (1986).[9] In this regard, the U.S. response to the so-called rape of Kuwait was, perhaps, as much an excuse to dismantle Iraq's nuclear-weapons capacity as it was to restore Kuwait's sovereignty. Where such continuous peril exists, trauma is constant. The task is to undermine its invisibility. For its concealed conditions, its silences, are the spaces in which the destructions of trauma multiply.

My past research attended to the impact of destruction in the formation of works of art that grew out of violent experience.[10] In particular, I studied the use artists made of their bodies as the primary signifying material of visual art performances, actions removed from the context and history of theater. While certain antecedents in futurism, dada, the Bauhaus, and surrealism exist for this historically specific phenomenon, it developed as a viable independent visual art medium in Japan, Europe, and the United States in the 1950s and, I think, must be correlated directly to the corporeal threat experienced by populations living in the geographical spaces most terrorized with destruction.[11] The actualization of destruction in performative works of art was a cultural sign, I suggested, a *techne* for making one's life into an aesthetic coefficient of survival. Such art not only bore witness to various survival strategies by converting invisible trauma into a representation, but, more immediately, into a presentation. Simultaneously representational and presentational, this art offered an alternative paradigm for cultural practices, one that appended the traditional metaphorical mode of communication, based on a viewing subject and an inanimate object, to a paradigm of exchange, based in the connectedness implied by metonymy. In this model, the human body held the potential for an exchange between individual subjectivities.

While I concentrated on the unprecedented physical and material violence and destruction that artists used, paradoxically, as the creative means for making art, that research was confined generally to the topic of war. Typically, although not exclusively, questions related to the interconnection between sexuality, identity, and violence I filter through that lens. Now my work examines the shared symptoms that result from the interrelated causes of trauma in war and sexual violence. This work poses such questions as what are the visual codes of trauma? and how does an understanding of these representations facilitate knowledge of the cultural effects of trauma? Such questions are not, however, concerned with the history, methodology, or therapeutic aims associated with either the research or practice of art therapy, practice that involves the treatment of individual cases. Nor does it engage in a psychoanalytic analysis of individual works of art. Rather, I seek to map the behavioral symptoms identified with trauma onto cultural representations and actions produced in conditions where trauma occurs. For I reason that the heterogeneity of traumatic causes that results in a homogeneity of symptoms may equally produce a heterogeneous body of images and actions that can function as homogeneous representations of trauma.

This study explores how visual responses to trauma may assist peoples of diverse individual, social, and political experiences in arriving at a shared language from which to construct different cultural, social, and political institutions and practices. In seeking to identify a shared body of visual representations of trauma, I have no lingering desire for holistic humanism or any need to attempt the constitution of false homogeneous communities. Rather, the goal is to acknowledge the growth and development of global networks of information-sharing systems and shared ecological concerns, and to reclaim for visual art the powerful role it is capable of playing in the development of a global humanitarian discourse of humane concern — a role threatened by the disempowering conditions of the economies and markets of art and usurped by the cynical denials of art's contemporary efficacy by many theorists of postmodernism. Identifying the visual results of cultures of trauma may hasten development of shared cultural terms through which to address disparate cultural events. Transforming visual representations into textual analysis may increase insight into, and compassion for, suffering, which is the first and necessary stage for reform.

This essay considers two sites within the cultures of trauma. Shaved heads is a representation that refers both to an image and a style resulting from a wide variety of social and political experiences outside of the context of the visual arts. Marked bodies is a representation that pertains to the performative paradigm that developed within the visual arts, an aesthetic practice that I believe is rooted deeply in cultures of trauma in accordance with larger political frames of destruction and violence.

Image 1: The community gathered in French towns and villages to shear her head with animal clippers and then smear the sign of the swastika in soot on her bald forehead. The citizens judged her a "horizontal collaborator" for having sex with German soldiers during World War II. Denigrated and denounced as a whore, she was even stripped naked sometimes before being paraded through town, a token of the emblematic territories, defamations, and controls of war. She remained solitary amidst the molesting, persecuting assembly, exiled in a particularly sordid historical moment in a throng of her countrymen and women.

Horizontal collaborators served as metonymic signifiers for the "vertical collaborators" who, under the Vichy government, maintained an upright appearance while they capitulated to the Germans, raised their hands in the Nazi salute, and welcomed "the New Europe" into their beds. These women with shaved heads were used as communal purgatives, scapegoats for the French who themselves had whored for jobs in Germany, for extra food, and for peacetime amenities, especially during the years 1940 to 1943. In 1944 and 1945, photographers Robert Capa and Carl Mydan documented the terrible brutality to women accused of sexual collaborations with the Germans; and Marcel Ophuls included documents of one such incident in the town of Clermont-Ferrand in his 1969 film *The Sorrow and the Pity*.[12] Female collaborators whose crimes were not sexual were not treated with the same kind of corporeal violations as the horizontal collaborators, whose primary sedition was to have slept with the enemy. The ritual scrutiny by French communities of the intimate affairs and bodies of "their" women suggests that these women's crime was vulvic, the vaginal betrayal of the patrimonial body of the State. The assault on, and psychological domination of, the female body and the photographic and filmic records "taken," or "shot," of her display on communal viewing stands all typify physical and scopic aggression linked to sexuality, especially sanctioned in the "theater of war."[13] War condones and ritualizes the destruction and occupation of territories and bodies. Marked as properly owned by the community, the shaved head confirms feminist's observations that wars are fought for, among other things, privilege to the bodies of women.[14]

The visual discourse of the phallocratic order may be seen in the shaved female head, the site where rule by the phallus joins power to sexuality.[15] Phallic rule is fundamental in cultures of trauma and forms the nexus between war and sexual abuse, a site where assaults on the body and identity produce similar traumatic symptoms. In his important new book *Shattered Selves: Multiple Personality in a Postmodern World*, political theorist James M. Glass argues that the justification for taking women issues from the same "perversion of power and the arrogance of patriarchal assumptions over the possession of women" that results in incest and other kinds of sexual abuse. He concludes that "to the extent that power moves beyond its ordered field and beyond its respect for the lives and bodies of others, it is not much different from political forms of power which define sovereignty as the infliction of harm, the punishment of bodies, and the depletion of life."[16]

Nowhere is this conjunction more agonizing than in the testimony of Bok Dong Kim, a Korean military "comfort woman" (*jugun ianfu*), one of the many Asian women abducted for sexual service during World War II by the Imperial Army under the name of the Japanese emperor. Kim testified about war crimes against women on June 15, 1993, at the Center for Women's Global Leadership during the International Conference on Human Rights in Vienna. She explained that after her body was unable to continue to provide sexual services for as many as fifty soldiers a day, her blood was used in transfusions for the wounded. The comfort woman provided the furniture of sex, and her body, when broken, became a mere blood bag from whose veins the life of one woman was drained into the health of many men. The ferocity of her experience is unbearable and related to the pornography now being made of the rapes of Bosnian women conquered as territory, possessed, and displayed.[17]

Hélène Cixous and Catherine Clement, French feminist theorists, identify the "intrinsic connection . . . between the philosophical, the literary . . . and the phallocentric" — which, they argue, is a bond "constructed on the premise of woman's abasement [and] subordination of the feminine to the masculine order."[18] Shaved heads signify humiliation, a visual manifestation of a supralineal condition of domination and power that joins war and violence to the abuses of rule by the phallus. The doctrine of male hegemony is global and founded in the texts of organized world religions. In the Judeo-Christian tradition, this instrument is the Bible:

> I want you to know that the head of every man is Christ; the head of a woman is her husband; and the head of Christ is the Father. Any man who prays or prophesies with his head covered brings shame upon his head. Similarly, any woman who prays or prophesies with her head uncovered brings shame upon her head. It is as if she had had her head shaved. Indeed, if a woman will not wear a veil, she ought to cut off her hair. If it is shameful for a woman to have her hair cut off or her *head shaved*, it is clear that she ought to wear a veil. A man, on the other hand, ought not to cover his head, because he is the image of God and the reflection of his glory. Woman, in turn, is the reflection of man's glory. Man was not made from woman but woman from man. Neither was man created for woman but woman for man. For this reason a woman ought to have a sign of

submission on her head, because of the angels. (1 Corinthians 11:1–16; emphasis added)

The above citation from the New Testament is anticipated in the Old Testament:

> The Lord said: Because the daughters of Zion are haughty, and walk with necks outstretched ogling and mincing as they go, their anklets tinkling with every step, *the Lord shall cover the scalps of Zion's daughters with scabs, and the Lord shall bare their heads.* On that day the Lord will do away with the finery of the anklets, sunbursts, and crescents; the pendants, bracelets, and veils; the headdresses, bangles, cinctures, perfume boxes, and amulets; the signet rings, and the nose rings; the court dresses, wraps, cloaks, and purses; the mirrors, linen tunics, turbans, and shawls. Instead of perfume there will be stench, instead of the girdle, a rope, and for the coiffure, *baldness*; for the rich gown, a sackcloth skirt. Then, instead of beauty: Your men will fall by the sword, and your champions, in war; her gates will lament and mourn, as the city sits desolate on the ground. (Isaiah 3:16–26; emphasis added)

This passage recasts the theme of women's culpability in the original fall from grace. Here the vanity and narcissism, with which she is charged, is cited as the source for the demise of men by the sword in war. He shall check her haughty and seductive ways, the Lord God, who shall mete punishment upon her body in the form of scabs, stench, and baldness.

The French were not alone in shaving the heads of women who slept with the enemy. Similar proprietary national interests, rights, and rites regarding the sexuality of German women were recorded by Bertolt Brecht in his poem entitled "Ballade von der 'Judenhure' Marie Sanders" (Ballad of Marie Sanders, the Jew's Whore, 1934–36). Brecht wrote that Marie Sanders, a woman from Nuremburg, was "driven through the town in her slip, round her neck a sign, her hair all shaven. . . ."[19] Her crime was to have slept with a Jew.

In yet another context, African American novelist Ishmael Reed summons the specter of a shaved head in his book *Reckless Eyeballing*. This time, however, the image refers to the war between the races. Advocating shaving the heads of black feminist writers whom he accuses of collaborating with white feminists, Reed growls, "They deserve what they get. Cut off their hair. . . ."[20] Reed charges black feminists with acting on behalf of white men in whose name white feminists serve to emasculate black men: "To turn the afro man into an international scapegoat . . . showing black dudes as animalistic sexual brutes." Reed's rage lives in the "colonialist program" identified by Frantz

Fanon in which "the woman [is given] the historic mission of shaking up the man," a strategy described by Gayatri Spivak as "brown women saved by white men from brown men."[21] Reed detested any association with the architects of colonization, white men, whom he labeled "the biggest cannibals [who] have cannibalized whole civilizations, they've cannibalized nature, they'd even cannibalize their own mothers."

Reed's diatribe, coupled with his misogynistic advice to shave black women's heads, offers a multifarious view of the convoluted manifestations of rule by the phallus. Kinship, race, or national identity, for Reed, resolves the question of sexual access to female bodies, and entry into them is determined by war, colonization, enslavement, incest, and rape. Here the Bible offers instruction, complete with shaved heads:

> *Marriage with a Female Captive.* When you go out to war against your enemies and the Lord, your God, delivers them into your hand, so that you take captives, if you see a comely woman among the captives and become so enamored of her that you wish to have her as wife, you may take her home to your house. But before she may live there, she must shave her head and pare her nails and lay aside her captive's garb. After she has mourned her father and mother for a full month, you may have relations with her, and you shall be her husband and she shall be your wife. However, if later on you lose your liking for her, you shall give her her freedom, if she wishes it; but you shall not sell her or enslave her, since she was married to you under compulsion. (Deuteronomy 21:10–14)

The doctrine of privileged right to women, especially "comely" women, mandated in Deuteronomy, has chilling social reverberations in Reed's text. But it also has demoralizing parallels in cultural practices. For example, the 1973 film *Soylent Green*, directed by Richard Fleischer, depicts a ravaged and famine-ridden chaotic New York in the year 2022, a warlike environment where every luxury from strawberry jam to "comely" women is guarded jealously.[22] Beautiful women are assigned to apartments as "furniture" and provided for only as long as the incoming male tenant agrees to continue to rent them or, in the language of Deuteronomy: if you later on lose your liking for her, you shall give her her freedom. Moreover, Thorn West (Charlton Heston) refers to Shirl (Leigh Taylor-Young) as a "hell of a piece of furniture" and "like a grapefruit," both metaphors interchangeable with the ways in which the actual bodies of the comfort women, mentioned earlier, were used as furniture and nutrient. But while women are without question the majority of those who suffer the rule of the phallus, this fact does not abrogate the reality that men, too, may be, and are, abased in phallocracy. Few more striking and unpredictable examples of such men exist in this constellation than the skinhead.

Skinheads derived their look, in part, from an identification with "West Indian immigrants and the white working class," James Ridgeway explains in his horrifying history of the rise of a new white racist culture.[23] Dick Hebdige adds that it was "those values conventionally associated with white working-class culture which had been eroded by time that were rediscovered embedded in [the black musical culture of] ska, reggae, and rocksteady."[24] Prevented from participating in white male power and privilege because of their class and lack of education, skins adapted an appearance of marginality with respect to Western systems of power. They also condensed a stunning array of differing cultural and political sites and meanings into an image. The result was a representation of absolute brute force signified by the shaved head but also by such articles of clothing as black army-surplus combat boots and camouflage gear. Skins visualized interconnected networks of brutality ordinarily categorized as different in culture. These include the hardened countenance of the military man, under whose sign society contracts death; the veneer of the outlaw, or prisoner of ball, chain, and spiked collar, whose transgressions bar him from the privilege to kill; the demented, dangerous, unpredictable mental patient, shaved and lobotomized; an image of ravaged diseased bodies, radiated and suffering; and, finally, the debased aspect of the concentration camp Jew, the ultimate picture of oppression.[25] The image of the skinhead contains the powerful and the abject, the oppressor and the oppressed, the killer and the killed.[26] Skins would seem to differ from the women with shaved heads cited above because they appear to be the agents in the reconstruction of their own identity. To a certain degree they are. But agency depends upon a more complex set of relations that involve not only personal will but social forces. Thus, the constitution of an image — like that of the skins — that is aimed at vitiating the threat of helplessness and powerlessness succeeds better in betraying and reinforcing the locus of its identity in the trauma of that threat.

Toni Morrison addresses this seeming paradox when she points out how the United States is simultaneously a "nation of people who decided that their world view would combine agendas for individual freedom" and the "mechanism for devastating racial oppression."[27] Morrison thus demonstrates how such apparent paradoxes are better understood as the reciprocal ways in which different languages, cultural representations, social and political institutions, and races and sexualities comprise identity. Morrison's deconstruction of this intertextuality offers further access to the links shared by black Ishmael Reed and white skinheads. "The Africanist character," she writes, becomes a "surrogate" who "enables . . . whites to think about themselves . . . to know themselves as not enslaved, but free; not repulsive, but desirable; not helpless, but licensed and powerful; not history-less, but historical; not damned, but innocent; not a blind accident of evolution, but a progressive fulfillment of destiny."[28]

Skinheads live contradiction. Their social experience is to be enslaved, repulsive, helpless, damned, and to belong to the very group who has a history and a promise of fulfillment in which they cannot share. This paradox is also the foundation for the anger that incited the dispossessed French in World War II, for Reed's rage, and for the skins' lethal frustration, a fury that takes its revenge upon the bodies of the women proclaimed their own. This delusion of possession helps to explain why the image of a happy coupling between a white woman and a black man is described in a 1981 Aryan Nation flyer as "the ultimate abomination." For if nothing else belongs to the British or American (French/German/Japanese/African/Serbian/Iraqui, etc.) skinhead, if he is socially fucked by other men, he alone will fuck her white (black/brown/yellow/red) body.[29] The vicious retaliation of the skinhead unfolds within the epistemological spaces ensured by white male hegemony, a phallic rule in which his virility becomes merely a caricature unmasking the reality of his impotence, a lack derived from the fact that he actually cohabitates the same disempowered spaces of women and all other dominated peoples. His inadequacy sustains his obsession with white supremacy where, fortified by emblematic images of superiority and power, he attempts to exercise his deprived authority.

All of these shaved heads inhabit the visual memory of culture, a memory of the history of war, domination, and colonization across whose pages bodies reach back to the Old and New Testaments and forward to the white power of skinheads, the youth paramilitary arm of ultraconservative groups whose theology is based on Scripture and who act out of a belief in their divine *right to be on top*, where power and sexual abuse fire the cultures of trauma. "Organization by hierarchy makes all conceptual organization subject to man," Cixous and Clement write, and that organization "is located in the logocentric orders that guarantee the masculine order a rationale equal to history itself."[30]

Image 2: In the performance "Test of Sleep," Amalia (Lia) Perjovschi, a Romanian artist, covers her body with white paint over which she inscribes a complex sequence of symbols resembling hieroglyphic marks, untranslatable signs, a visual language that she then animates with gestures deployed in silence — hand, arm, leg, and full-body signals enacted in her home before her husband, the only witness. Perjovschi's principal means of communication, beyond the direct but silent, intimate liaison with her husband, artist Dan Perjovschi, is through photographs, documents that he — as husband, collaborator, and beholder — recorded. Her action took place in 1988, one of the darkest years of Romanian captivity under the autocratic totalitarianism of Nicolae and Elena Ceausescu, who were assassinated December 25, 1989. In 1993, in Timisoara, site of the revolution, Eastern European artists gathered for the performance festival, Europe Zone East. Dan Perjovschi's action was to sit silently while the word "Romania" was tattooed on his upper left forearm.[31]

While shaved heads provided visual access and insight into the linkage between power and sexuality that contributes to the construction of cultures of trauma, Lia and Dan Perjovschi's marked bodies enunciate the silence that is a rudiment of trauma and a source of the destruction of identity. Silence was maintained efficiently by the Romanian secret police, the Securitate, which enforced Ceausescu's crushing control. In large measure, that organization was successful through the sheer force of rumor, hearsay that numbered the Securitate, with its system of informers, at one in six Romanian citizens.[32] No one remained above suspicion. Fear and secrecy resulted in the effective supervision of all aspects of Romanian life. Stealth was augmented by reports of reprisals against challenges to authority, threats that were invigorated by actual punishments. Extreme even among nations of the former Soviet bloc, Romanians endured their conditions in isolation. Preventing its citizens from travel, the government retained Romanian passports and politically sequestered the nation from exchange with most of the world. Romania resembled a concentration camp, especially in the 1980s when Lia and Dan Perjovschi (both born in 1961) were in their twenties.[33]

While such coercion was the most obvious process by which Romanians were traumatized into obedience, a double bind, comprised of intense nationalism coupled with economic shortage, incapacitated the people into perceiving themselves as absolutely dependent upon a government that they could not criticize without being labeled unpatriotic.[34] This paradoxical predicament reinforced what Katherine Verdery, a U.S. anthropologist specializing in Romanian culture, calls the "symbolic-ideological" discourse in Romania, a discourse that utilizes "the Nation . . . as a master *symbol*."[35] Romanian debates over national identity rose to a fever pitch in the 1980s, especially with the programmatic decimation of Romanian traditional life, the destruction of villages, and the relocation of peasants and workers into the bleak city-block houses, all of which were part of Ceausescu's massive relocation and urbanization project that followed his 1971 visit to North Korea, China, and North Vietnam when he inaugurated "a 'mini-cultural revolution,' with renewed emphasis on socialist realism."[36] The ambitious reconstruction of Romanian cities included the erection of high-rise apartment complexes in an idiosyncratic and hybrid Korean-Chinese style imitative of the International style. In the redevelopment of Bucharest, especially between 1984 and 1989, some 50,000 people lost their Beaux Arts and Victorian homes to the unrivaled, infamous, architectural complex leading to the vulgar Casa Poporlului, House of the People, funded by Romanian taxes at the expense of all other civic, social, industrial, and agricultural projects. Like its historical antecedents, Ceausescu's building campaign was aimed at a monolithic representation of power through which to arouse awe and complete compliance. An effective means of social control, its sterility mirrored the repression of interior life.

But questions related to Romanian national identity did not originate in Ceausescu's regime. They reside deep in Romanian history and consciousness, both of which have been split for centuries between the philosophical and teleological worldviews of the Occident and the Orient, as well as along the geographical political exigencies of North-South and East-West. Romanians trace their bipolarity to the occupation in A.D. 106–107 of the Roman emperor Trajan, who invaded the ancient lands of the Carpatho-Danubian people, the Geto-Dacians. Since Neolithic times the Gateo of the lower Danube and the Dacians of the Carpathian Mountains had inhabited what is now modern Romania. Such divisions make Romanians especially vulnerable to psychological fragmentation and contribute to the renowned "distrust of all the cherished notions . . . of progress and history" that is "characteristic" of Balkan peoples, according to Andrei Codrescu, a Romanian expatriate poet living in the United States.[37] The historic rupture of Romanian national identity was reinforced in, and is echoed by, the shattering of personal identity under Ceausescu. In this regard, Verdery has recognized a "social schizophrenia" among Romanians that she has described as an ability to experience a "real meaningful and coherent self only in relation to the enemy party."[38]

Artist Ion Bitzan, an admired professor of art at Nicolae Grigorescu Academia de Arta in Bucharest, provides a special example of this schism. Bitzan, born in 1924, lived through Stalin, Gheorghiu-Dej, and Ceausescu. Under Stalin, Bitzan learned as a student that transgression was impossible. He remembered the painful "unmaskings" (his term) during which students denounced each other and their professors, denunciations accompanied by obligatory applause, the same obligatory applause required at the very mention of Stalin's name.[39] His terror was so deep, he remembered, that he felt "guilty for being human" and was afraid of "being an enemy of the party, an enemy of the State, an enemy of the Soviet Union."

In 1964, one of Bitzan's paintings was selected for inclusion in the Venice Biennale. A social realist work of "a lorrie filled with wheat, a field worker, and a red flag in the corner," the socialist subject and style, like the applause, was mandated. But Bitzan felt his work was "perfect" because he had composed it precisely according to the rules for the Golden Section. When he traveled to Venice to attend the Biennale, however, he saw the assemblages and collages of Robert Rauschenberg, the American artist who received first prize at that Biennale. Bitzan returned to Romania confused, disturbed, and embarrassed by his art. He felt himself to be a provincial outsider and was humiliated by the very painting of which he had been so proud. Three years later, Bitzan also began to make collages and constructions, and to fabricate exquisite handmade papers on which he wrote in a flowing and elegant but secret, unreadable personal language. He created these works, however, only in the privacy of his studio. In public, Bitzan continued to paint in a socialist realist style. Like many Romanian artists, he capitulated to Ceausescu's frequent requests to paint "Him" or "Her" — the terms Romanians used for Nicolae and Elena. For his compliance, Bitzan earned money, prestige in the Art Academy, and the right to travel. He "sold" himself, he insisted, "but only for an hour or so a day when I worked on their pictures." After that he turned the canvases of Him or Her — emblems of his repression — to the wall and began his secret life. In telling this story for the first time, in his own words Bitzan became "ashamed" and left the room. I too felt shame. My interview had perpetrated the familiar form of an interrogation. Before contributing to and witnessing Bitzan's shame, I had been sheltered from understanding the interview form of discourse as a persecuting interrogative.

Bitzan's private collages, hand-made papers, artist's books, and indecipherable texts are all a microcosm of the conflict that characterized Romanian artists' conduct, their need to invent alternative languages and to make hidden private works. Verdery's observation about Romanians' "social schizophrenia" is related to Bitzan's experience. Comments by a number of Romanians confirm her view. Alexandra Cornilescu, a linguist from Bucharest

University, noted that survival in Romania depends upon "hedging."[40] Hedging means that one cultivates the ability to live multiple lives. Romanians learned to say one thing and mean something else, to speak in layered codes impenetrable to informers, often even confusing to friends, to use their eyes and gestures as if they were words. Or, as Andrei Codrescu confessed, "I lie in order to hide the truth from morons."[41] "Repressive discourse," Cornilescu continued, "gradually developed towards a rigid inventory of permissible topics; religion, non-dogmatic philosophy or political theories, poverty, prisons, concentration camps, political dissidents, unemployment, sex, etc., were, as many taboo topics, unmentionable and, largely, unmentioned in repressive discourse."

Nothing is more pernicious in the "discourse of fear" than the problem identified by Cornilescu when she writes that in Romania, "If an object/person/phenomenon is not named, then it does not exist." With the word "Romania" emblazoned on the surface of his body, Dan Perjovschi staked the authenticity of his existence on a name. His tattoo divulges the dependence of his identity upon his country, a territory marked by centuries of uncertainty and the challenged, manipulated, and traumatized conditions in which he and his fellow Romanians lived. But his tattoo is also an indeterminate sign signifying the synchronicity of a visible wound and a mark of honor. A symbol of resistance and icon of marginality, it is a signature of capture, a mask that both designates and disguises identity. As a signifier for the charged complexity of Romanian national identity, the tattoo brands Dan Perjovschi's body with the arbitrary geographical identity agreed upon by governments, and it displays the ambiguous psychological allegiances such boundaries inevitably commit to the mind. His action-inscription also conveys some of the content of the accreted spaces of Romanian suffering and guilt, guilt that Perjovschi addressed when he explained that in Romania, where both prisoners and citizens alike habitually were transformed into perpetrators, guilt and innocence intermingle inseparably. And he asked, "Who may point a finger?" Similarly, psychiatrist Judith Lewis Herman describes the process by which incest victims are silenced and made to become complicit in their own abuse: "Terror, intermittent reward, isolation, and enforced dependency may succeed in creating a submissive and compliant prisoner. But the final step in the psychological control of the victim is not completed until she[/he] has been forced to violate her[/his] own moral principles and to betray her[/his] basic human attachments. Psychologically, this is the most destructive of all coercive techniques, for the victim who has succumbed loathes herself[/himself]. It is at this point, when the victim under duress participates in the sacrifice of others, that she[/he] is truly 'broken.'"[42]

Only recently have such experiences begun to be verbalized in Romanian discourse. Cornilescu explains that in the media terms such as "survival," "nightmares," and "shock therapy" appear increasingly as metaphors describing the past and referring to the current transitional period. Such words comprise the languages of trauma and provide new textual evidence of the stress that punctuates the Romanian imagination.

But Romanian silences must be understood in the context of silences that result from terror threatened by the situation and its perpetrator(s), from the repressed silences shielding victims from the pain of memory, and from the *robotization* that results from chronic captivity.[43] These silences represent only some of a host of traumatic silences. All these conditions lead to what many researchers describe as the "conspiracy of silence," a complex environment that culminates in the silence remembered by Holocaust, incest, and rape survivors.[44] Herman proposes that the shame, fear, and horror that traumatized victims experience, leading to silence, is augmented by public denial of trauma and even by the behavior of mental health professionals, who sometimes treat those who "listen too long and too carefully to traumatized patients" as "*contaminated*" (my emphasis).[45]

Romanians feel contaminated. This emotion is embedded in journalistic metaphors that refer to Romania as a "dead" or "diseased body," an "organism . . . undergoing some form of therapy . . . severe pain . . . nightmares," and in need of "shock therapy." Such "therapy" is administered in a collage created by Romanian artist Ion Grigorescu, born in 1946. In a 1986 black and white photomontage, overpainted and decorated with collage elements in gold foil, Grigorescu depicted himself as St. George slaying a dragon. Entitling the work *Bine si Rau* (Good and Evil), Grigorescu montaged two photographs of himself together to create a composite image of a conqueror and a vanquished. In the image, Grigorescu appears to leap over a figure who bends over a large boulder. The vaulting Grigorescu plunges a huge wooden stake through the bent figure's back, killing the "dragon" that turns out to be simply another image of himself. Driving the stake into his own back, Grigorescu spills his own blood; it gushes from his self-inflicted wound, the life fluid of a body that spurts out and pours over the rock that breaks his fall. Set against the backdrop of a landscape image and around this striking scene, the murder takes place in what appears to be a room, an architectural space created when the artist drew faint lines of ink that traced the perspectival space of a box. In gold ink on one of the room's transparent walls, he painted a half-figure who, reclined on a pillow, wails from the pain inflicted by a foot and leg that is clad in Roman centurion sandals and that stomps on his stomach. At the top of the picture and outside of the architectural space, Grigorescu collaged a small scale that he cut out of gold metallic paper, a symbol of judgment that suspends from the sky.

In the image, Grigorescu collapsed self-sacrifice into the martyrdom of Romania. Visually comparing his suffering to that of the sacrificed Christian, he also summoned the forces of Christianity necessary to vanquish the predator, a tyrant that he slayed in the same manner required to rid the world of the mythic Romanian terror, Dracula, by plunging a stake through the heart. But Grigorescu drives the stake through his own heart, dashing its evil and shedding his blood on the rock that suggests St. Peter's church. The recollection of Roman dress and Roman Catholic faith draws the Occident into this dramatic scene of violence. Internal repression and external invasion commingle across the territories of power, faith, self-sacrifice, violence, guilt, and martyrdom. These complex threads weave through Grigorescu's image of pain as visual witness to a conflict in which all are implicated. Inside individual subjectivity, and outside that being in the social and political world of competing ideologies and teleologies, Grigorescu confesses his own culpability. Such a representation gains even more force as an authentic image of Romanian social and psychological experience when considered in light of the observation that Romanians "resist anything that resembles the construction of state power [yet] simultaneously . . . live with internalized expectations of a state that is paternalistic, that frees them of the necessity to take initiative or worry about their pay checks, hospital bills, pensions, and the like. They simultaneously blame the state for everything and expect the state to resolve everything [in an] . . . amalgam of accusation and expectation."[46]

Grigorescu's collage is made even more compelling by the fact that these photographs are self-portraits of a performative action the artist undertook in private to prepare this work. His private ritual suggests an exorcism of self undertaken in secret, stealth demanded by the political exigencies of 1986, the year of the work's making. Such hidden performances recall other actions Grigorescu did before the gaze only of his own camera. A self-portrait of 1975, for example, features another striking image of the martyred artist, this time with a crown of thorns encircling his neck. Another self-portrait shows the artist with an elongated neck over which is superimposed the image of the Egyptian King Tut's renowned coffin. In another series of auto-portraits, Grigorescu created body actions in his own living quarters. One series entitled *The Tongue* (ca. 1973–75) pictures only the anatomical feature of a mouth, teeth, and tongue that is gaping wide in a clear invocation of a scream.

The choking, silently screaming, entombed self-image offers other representations of Romanian self-recrimination, guilt, anger, futility, and suffering. "Sufferance" was a term Cornilescu also used in her discussion of textual practices in the contemporary Romanian press. Suffering cohabits the silences that, as literary theorist Elaine Scarry argues, "actively destroy" language, a process that brings about "an immediate reversion to a state anterior to language."[47]

In "Test of Sleep," Lia Perjovschi conjures that anterior state. As the apparatus of the dream condenses and displaces meaning, so Romanian silence registered existence as somnambulant. "Everyone in Romania silently calls out loudly," Lia said. "I wanted to draw attention to that inner life, to make it possible for people to understand it without words." Even the title of her action — "Test of Sleep" — offers textual access to the blocked layers of the performative unconscious available in sleep. Sanda Agalidi, a Romanian artist and expatriate living in the United States, has also summoned the idea of sleep in relation to Romanian social reality. She writes about the "determined will" necessary to maintain aspects of the estranged self, to create an "alternative language" — for "as the words awaken," the "bad world falls asleep."[48] In both artists' metaphors, the silence of sleep parallels repression but also approximates a space within which a different language may be formed, a language that Lia described as the "discrete communication" she enacted in "Test of Sleep." Mikhail Bakhtin, a victim of Stalin's despotism, might have compared her corporeal narrative to the heteroglossia of the oppressed who long to speak for themselves. For he observed that all social life is an ongoing struggle between the attempt of power to impose a uniform language and the attempt of those below to speak in their own dialects (heteroglossia).[49] The struggle between the multiplicity of internal voices and the monolithic voice of external authority breeds trauma.

Many theorists of postmodernism celebrate schizophrenia, or decentered fragmentation, as the cultural sign of postmodern political resistance to holistic models of self and society associated with the hegemony of the humanist paradigm.[50] My personal experience, knowledge of Romania, and scholarship all support different conclusions. For such theories fail as viable theoretical constructs when called upon to address the actual experiences of Romanians. Recently conclusions similar to my own have been argued eloquently by James M. Glass, who believes that the textual critique of postmodern resistance to *unicity* is not only "naive" but "dangerous." These theories collapse before the *actual* conditions that real people with multiple personalities suffer; and they cannot account for, or move toward, healing the terrible incapacitating fragmentation and the agonizing internal struggle for unity without which it is impossible to survive and function. Glass asks, "Is it not equally as important to understand and interpret the world from the point of view of the victims themselves?"[51] Scarry approaches this question from a slightly different position. She insists that trauma sometimes causes so much suffering that "the person in pain is . . . bereft of the resources of speech . . . [so] that the language for pain should sometimes be brought into being by those who are not themselves in pain but who speak on behalf of those who are."[52] Yet while trauma may be so severe that victims might require someone other than themselves to speak, recovery depends upon victims speaking for themselves.

Mute, but gesturing, Lia wrote the language of internal spaces on the surface of her body, words that — although reversed and unreadable — narrated her private suffering. Speechless and immobile, his body imprinted by another man with an inscription, Dan documented the interdependence of the psyche, identity, and ideology in history. The Perjovschis' art provides ocular witness to, and gestural voice for, the prolonged psychological, intellectual, and physical oppression that transformed Romania into a culture of trauma. Through their signifying bodies, they suggest means to express "the corporeal threat in social and political experience [and] the inexorable human link between subject and subject."[53] In such performances, the body and its languages may transform victimization into personal agency. "Write yourself," Cixous declared. "Your body must make itself heard."[54]

"The systematic study of psychological trauma depends on the support of a political movement," Herman has argued, a movement "powerful enough to legitimate an alliance between investigators and patients to counteract the ordinary social processes of silencing and denial."[55] Lia and Dan Perjovschi contribute to such an alliance by producing cultural signs that convert invisible pain into images able to be shared with, and scrutinized by, the public. Such actions impart the visual language of survivors and, however specific to Romania, remain paradigmatic of the kinds of representations found in cultures of trauma.

Analysis of the regularization of trauma is pressing and may advance understanding of its human consequences. Marked bodies and shaved heads visualize the aggregate forms of suffering. Should we learn to recognize them, we may reform. But I am not optimistic.

Afterword

Over the past two years since this paper was first published and immediately reprinted, I have had the privilege of lecturing widely on its subject in
the United States and abroad. Repeatedly, three identical questions have
emerged:

1. Why, if I choose to shave my own head or tattoo my own body, is this
   not an act of self-empowerment, a wresting of my own fate and identity
   from historical antecedents?

2. Can it be said that all historical examples of shaved heads and tattooed
   bodies conform to your paradigm and are "representations from cultures of trauma?"

3. Is there implicit in your argument a value judgment, moral or ethical,
   of people who elect to have their heads shaved or their bodies tattooed?

The frequency with which these questions have been posed by women (although not exclusively by women) necessitates a response, especially in the
context of this book. I am grateful to the editors for an opportunity to
expand and further explain my thoughts.

In answer to the first question, I would characterize my interlocutors'
cross-examination as urgent. Women have insisted that by choosing to shave
their own heads, they have refused both to surrender to classical representations of female beauty and have "taken control" of their own representation
and self-image. The shaved head, they insist, is a sign of personal agency, of
resistance, of independence from the paradigm of the erotic woman. They
have seized power from history, they persist. This argument has been made
by women of all age groups, sexual preferences, class, race, and education.
The aggressiveness with which this view is avowed is typified by a remark
made to me by three different women, on three different occasions, in three
different cities. Each one said she could "see me being shot" for my views.
Obviously, something profoundly critical to a woman's sense of self and
personal agency is at stake.

Especially since the mid-1970s in Western culture, alternative groups have
celebrated and practiced body modification; tattooing, multiple piercing,
scarification, and head shaving (even perceived as de rigueur and obligatory
by some marginalized or self-selected alternative groups) has been on the rise
and, as I noted above in a footnote, has become fashionable.[56] Writing on
behalf of such body modification, V. Vale and Andrea Juno, editors and
publishers of *RE/Search Magazine*, an infamous, internationally distributed
art journal, situated these practices "amidst an almost universal feeling of

powerlessness to 'change the world,'" and they insisted that body modification permits "individuals [to] change what they do have power over: their own bodies." They continue: "A tattoo is more than a painting on skin; its meaning and reverberations cannot be comprehended without a knowledge of the history and mythology of its bearer. . . . These body modifications perform a vital function identical with art: they 'genuinely stimulate passion and spring directly from the original sources of emotion, and are not something tapped from the cultural reservoir.' (Roger Cardinal) Here that neglected function of art, to *stimulate the mind*, is unmistakably *alive*. And all of these modifications bear witness to personal pain endured which cannot be simulated."[57]

These comments suggest that to mark the self is to make of oneself a work of art, to exact agency and self-representation from history, and to be "alive," not "simulated"—in other words, not a product of what Vale and Juno characterize as "civilization" with its "stifling and life-thwarting logic." But the equation of primitivism with agency is, as Marianna Torgovnick correctly observes in *Gone Primitive*, "a modern and post-modern . . . version of the idyllic, utopian . . . the wish for 'being physical' to be coextensive with 'being spiritual'; the wish for physical, psychological, and social integrity as a birthright, within familial and cultural traditions that both connect to the past and allow for a changing future. . . ."[58] Indeed, a woman (or individuated groups of self-selected women) cannot escape the history of cultural tradition by merely claiming to have done so.

My point has been that the semiotic universe of signs and representations that Western culture inhabits pervades all its practices. But moreover, because of the might of Western economies, technologies, weapons development, and communication systems, Western culture permeates the globe with its culture, leaving its own tattoo on social and cultural practices around the world.[59] Resorting to fantasies of resistance and agency or imitations of the "primitive" cannot change this condition any more than attempts to refuse negative representations by denial can reverse the overdetermined meaning and legacy of these signs.

The allegation that representations may be recuperated, seized from the histories in which they originate and with which they are in dialogue, is misguided and becomes little more than inflammatory rhetoric in the publications of such writers as Camille Paglia.[60] Paglia's idol, Madonna, equally falls prey to these illusions. Madonna's book *Sex* is nothing if not a compendium of the most audaciously gullible, simplistic, immature, self-destructive, and ultimately exploitative assertions on behalf of the notion that anything goes — including sexism, racism, self-abuse, masochism, and sadism — as long as the perpetrator claims its value as self-representation.[61] To say this is not to "loathe Madonna," as Paglia claims. I watch and listen to Madonna with the same fascination as anyone interested in the paradoxes and spectacles of entertainment culture; I even enjoy Madonna.

Paglia and Madonna are only the most flamboyant examples of those who claim to control all aspects of their representation. They are joined by numerous academics who theorize that both the construction and reception of conventional signs may be subverted by projections of self that emanate from a spectrum of individuated needs and desires ranging from the butch-femme aesthetic to the heterosexual straight, from black (Michael Jackson is often the example offered here) to browns and whites.[62] Without belaboring this argument, my point is this: in an effort to posit agency outside of history, to escape history, a spurious kind of independence folds back on itself, creating a double indemnity — one has been damned to damn oneself. The effort to deny the interconnectedness of historical representations is akin to sleepwalking through time. It may be done, but at what expense?

While this response may seem to suggest a futility in altering history and asserting agency, I believe the situation is not wholly unredeemable, even if I am pessimistic. What I do insist is that certain kinds of historically loaded representations cannot be reversed *without* a thorough understanding of their embeddedness in a complex, overlapping cultural network of experiences, contexts, and conditions. That Ishmael Reed's advocacy to shave the heads of black feminists who collaborate with white feminists might be related to the French punishment of women who slept with Germans during World War II, that Germans' punishment of German women who slept with Jews during the same period, or that skinheads who advocate white supremacy are part of this matrix, is a dense web of shared violence and ugliness that few imagine can be aggregate. The idea that a woman or a man who elects to shave her or his head also participates in this configuration is even more odious to her or him. And I suppose this is why the three women who could "see" me "getting shot" for saying these things imagined such a violent reaction to my supposition: for in fact I do believe that people share the space and continuity in time with this historical structure, despite their loftiest aims.[63]

The other two questions require only a brief response, and the answer to the second one is an emphatic, "No." All generalizations are dangerous, and I even cautioned, at the beginning of this paper, about the use of terms. The concept of trauma itself, I pointed out, must be used judiciously. I offer it only as a model for examining cultural configurations and representations *if* one remembers not only the wide range of traumatic experience possible but also the differences of intensity and duration of these experiences. I insist that each trauma must be examined in and for itself; and in theorizing "cultures of trauma," I struggled to clarify that my examples are limited to themselves. Moreover, they are also limited to the Western Judeo-Christian tradition. I cannot, and would not, attempt to speak about pre-Columbian, African, or Asian instances of shaved heads, as I have been asked to do. But I will say that on the subject of monks, nuns, and other members of religious orders who shave their heads, it is prudent to point out that this practice usually signifies submission to a higher authority. That trauma is involved is entirely a different question.

Finally, in no way do I pass moral or ethical judgment on anyone who chooses to shave her or his head or wear a tattoo. Both my scholarship and artistic practice have been devoted to trying to understand the social structures and cultural representations that invent and perpetuate destruction and violence, that destroy and harm identity, that strip agency from human will, and that leave a legacy of despair in the world. Those are the subjects of this essay. To attempt to decode (by describing) these structures is very different from passing judgment on individuals who, in their attempt to resist these negative histories, may appropriate aspects of them. Rather, if there is a qualifying feeling that comes from my work, a personal opinion about the people who shave their heads or tattoo their bodies as signs of difference and self-empowerment, it is that I have empathy for the struggle.

In trying to make a contribution to that struggle, I hope this essay underscores the dangers of unconsciously perpetrating negative traditions. I selected examples of shaved heads and marked bodies because of their contemporary popularity and the connections I perceived between our current historical moment and the histories and practices of Western culture. No argument is perfect. Mine is flawed. But these imperfections spring from an imagination that seeks to contribute to the construction of a more humane interaction and a responsible relationship to history, the present, and the future.

Notes

1. I gave the first version of this paper, "Shaved Heads: Towards a Theory of the Cultures of Trauma," at the International Conference on War and Gender, Bellagio, Italy, August 1993. I am grateful to the organizers, Duke professors Miriam Cooke, a feminist specializing in the literature of the Middle East, and Alex Roland, a military

historian, for the opportunity to present this work. This text was subsequently published in *Stratégie II: Peuples Méditerranéens* 64–65 (July–December 1993): 95–117, and republished in a shorter bilingual French-English version in *Lusitania* 6 (1994): 23–40. My students Rebecca Katz, David Little, and Kathryn Andrews provided sound editorial comments. I want to especially thank Edward Allen Shanken, whose critical insight into the nature of my work helped me to strengthen and clarify my own thought.

2. The phrase "cultures of trauma" is part of the title of my forthcoming book, *DIAS: The Destruction in Art Symposium, Representations from the Cultures of Trauma*, a book that represents an extensive revision of my doctoral dissertation, "The Destruction in Art Symposium (DIAS): The Radical Cultural Project of Event-Structured Art," University of California, Berkeley, 1987. Only while completing this essay did I learn of two terms, shame culture and guilt culture, that might relate eventually to my own work. In a review of Bernard Williams's book *Shame and Necessity* (1992), Bernard Knox noted that Williams adapted the term "shame culture" from his Oxford professor, E. R. Dodds, who used it to discuss what Knox summarized as the culture "Dodds believed existed in Homeric times [that] puts high emphasis on preserving honor and on not being publicly disgraced." The term "guilt culture" was coined, Knox continues, by Ruth Benedict in *The Chrysanthemum and the Sword* (1946). She referred to "the allegedly more evolved guilt culture" which "emphasizes personal responsibility and relies on 'an internalized conviction of sin.'" See Bernard Knox, "The Greek Way," review of *Shame and Necessity*, by Bernard Williams, *New York Review of Books*, November 18, 1993, 42.

3. Michael R. Trimble, "Post-traumatic Stress Disorder: History of a Concept," in *Trauma and Its Wake: The Study and Treatment of Post-traumatic Stress Disorder*, ed. Charles R. Figley (New York: Brunner/Mazel, 1985), 13.

4. Charles R. Figley, introduction to *Trauma and Its Wake*, ed. Figley, xviii–xix.

5. Trimble reports, for example, that Charles Dickens was unable to recover from having witnessed a horrifying railway accident in 1865, and Samuel Pepys became suicidal after a fire in his home. Trimble, "Post-traumatic Stress Disorder," 7. See also R. J. Daly, "Samuel Pepys and Post-Traumatic Stress Disorder," *British Journal of Psychiatry* 143 (1983): 64–68; and J. Forster, *The Life of Charles Dickens*, vol. 2 (London: J. M. Dent and Sons, 1969).

6. Some critical studies in post-traumatic stress disorder and its relationship to larger social and political frames include M. J. Horowitz, *Stress Response Syndromes* (New York: Jason Aronson, 1976); A. Egendorf et al., *Legacies of Vietnam*, vols. 1–5 (Washington D.C.: U.S. Government Printing Office, 1981); Robert J. Lifton, *Death in Life: Survivors of Hiroshima* (New York: Simon & Schuster, 1967); Lifton, *The Future of Immortality and Other Essays for a Nuclear Age* (New York: Basic, 1987); Richard Ulman and Doris Brothers, *The Shattered Self: A Psychoanalytic Study of Trauma* (Hove, England: Analytic Press, 1988); and Judith Lewis Herman, *Trauma*

and Recovery: The Aftermath of Violence — From Domestic Abuse to Political Terror (New York: Basic Books, 1992).

7. See Raymond M. Scurfield, "Post-trauma Reactions and Symptoms," in *Trauma and Its Wake*, ed. Figley, 233. See also Judith Lewis Herman, "Complex Post-Traumatic Stress Disorder," *Trauma and Recovery*, 121.

8. I am indebted to Judit Katona-Apte, United Nations World Food Programme, for this information and other comments put forward in her "Refugee Women: An International Existential Anomaly?" (paper presented at the International Conference on War and Gender, Bellagio, Italy, August 1993). See also Diane Weathers, "Impact of Refugee Camps," in *WFP and the Environment* (Rome: World Food Programme, 1993), 9–10.

9. On the subject of nuclear proliferation see, for example, Frank Barnaby, ed., *Plutonium and Security: The Military Aspects of the Plutonium Economy* (London: Macmillan, 1992).

10. A summary of that work appears in my essay "Survival Ethos and Destruction Art," *Discourse: Journal for Theoretical Studies in Media and Culture* 14, no. 2 (Spring 1992): 74–102.

11. Although the continental United States did not experience in World War II anything remotely similar to the destruction that occurred in Europe and Japan, it is clear that the increased militarization of U.S. economic and domestic life during the nuclear age had traumatizing effects. Robert J. Lifton and Eric Markusen refer to this result as the "genocidal mentality" in their book *The Genocidal Mentality: Nazi Holocaust and Nuclear Threat* (New York: Basic Books, 1990).

12. See Frank Capa and Robert Capa, *Photographs* (New York: Alfred A. Knopf, 1985), 162–65; Carl Mydans, *Carl Mydans, Photojournalist* (New York: Harry H. Abrams, 1985), 104. Ophuls's film includes extensive interviews with Pierre Mendes-France, Albert Speer, Sir Anthony Eden, Claude Levy, and others, but no comment at all from the women with shaved heads! Just prior to completion of this article, I found Alain Brossat's new book, *Les Tondues: Un Carnaval Moche* (Mesnil sur Estrée: Éditions Manya, 1993). Brossat's extensive research documents and analyzes the phenomenon of women with shaved heads from the perspective of medieval carnival and ritual.

13. Susan Sontag was one of the first to theorize about the sexual aggressivity (akin to rape) of the photograph in *On Photography* (New York: Farrar, Strauss & Giroux, 1973). See also Bill Jay, "The Photographer as Aggressor," in *Observations: Essays on Documentary Photography*, ed. David Featherstone (Carmel, Calif.: Friends of Photography, 1984), 7–23.

14. In the 5th century B.C., Herodotus accounted for the importance of women in the Persian Wars when he pointed out that "as for the carrying off of women, it is the deed, they say, of a rogue; but to make a stir about such as are carried off, argues a man a fool. . . . The Asiatics when the Greeks ran off with their women, never troubled

themselves about the matter; but the Greeks, for the sake of a single Lacedaemonian girl, collected a vast armament, invaded Asia, and destroyed the kingdom of Prima, hence they ever looked upon the Greeks as their open enemies." See Herodotus, *The Persian Wars*, trans. George Rawlinson (New York: Random House, 1942), 3, quoted in Barbara Harlow, introduction to *The Colonial Harem*, by Malek Alloula, trans. Myrna Godzich and Wlad Godzich (Minneapolis: University of Minnesota Press, 1966), xiv–xv. See also Sara Ruddick, "Maternal Thinking and Peace Politics," part 3 of *Maternal Thinking: Toward a Politics of Peace* (New York: Ballantine Books, 1989), 127–219.

15. For an extended discussion of the term "phallocratic," see Luce Irigaray, *This Sex Which Is Not One*, trans. G. Gill (Ithaca: Cornell University Press, 1982); and Jacques Lacan, "The Signification of the Phallus," in *Écrits: A Selection*, trans. Alan Sheridan (New York: W. W. Norton & Company, 1977), 281–291.

16. James M. Glass, *Shattered Selves: Multiple Personality in a Postmodern World* (Ithaca: Cornell University Press, 1993), 127.

17. On the subject of comfort women, I am indebted to Kazuko Watanabe's "Militarism, Colonialism, and the Trafficking in Women: Military *Comfort Women* Forced by the Japanese Imperial Army" (paper presented at the International Conference on War and Gender, Bellagio, Italy, August 1993). See also Iryumiyon Kim, *Emperor's Army and Korean Comfort Women* (Tokyo: Sanichi Shobo, 1976). On Bosnian pornography, see Catharine A. MacKinnon, "Turning Rape into Pornography: Postmodern Genocide," *Ms.* 4, no. 1 (July–August 1993): 24–30.

18. Hélène Cixous and Catherine Clement, *The Newly Born Woman*, trans. Betsy Wing (Minneapolis: University of Minnesota Press, 1986), 65.

19. Bertolt Brecht, "Ballade von der 'Judenhure' Marie Sanders," *Bertolt Brecht Gedichte: Ausgewahlt von Autoren mit einem Geleitwort von Ernst Bloch* (Frankfurt: Suhrkamp, 1977), 132–33.

20. Ishmael Reed, *Reckless Eyeballing* (New York: St. Martin's Press, 1986), 55.

21. Frantz Fanon, *A Dying Colonialism*, trans. Haakon Chevalier (New York: Grove Press, 1967), 39. I am grateful to Bruce Lawrence, Professor of Religion at Duke University, for the comments he made regarding Fanon during the Bellagio conference. Spivak is quoted in Barbara Harlow, introduction to *The Colonial Harem*, by Alloula, xviii. Harlow also points out that the French in Algeria and the British in India and Africa attempted "to collaborate with the women under the pretext of liberating them from oppression by their own men" and that this "would happen later in Iran during the Khomeini-led revolution against the Shah's dictatorship" (xviii–xix).

22. I am grateful to Judit Katona-Apte and Mahadev Apte for bringing this film to my attention.

23. James Ridgeway, *Blood in the Face: The Ku Klux Klan, Aryan Nations, Nazi*

Skinheads, and the Rise of a New White Culture (New York: Thunder's Mouth Press, 1990), 164.

24. Dick Hebdige, *Subculture: The Meaning of Style* (London: Meuthen, 1979), quoted in Ridgeway, *Blood in the Face*, 164.

25. The style, or fashion, of skinheads was rapidly assimilated by very different groups that do not identify with white supremacy, ranging from punks to neo-hippie ecological skins. Pop folk singer Sinead O'Connor's shaved head, for example, represents popular cultural icons of protest while the shaved and tattooed head of a current Parisian fashion model demonstrates how quickly style transforms ideology.

26. For a discussion of the abject, see Julia Kristeva, *Powers of Horror: An Essay on Abjection* (New York: Columbia University Press, 1982).

27. Toni Morrison, *Playing in the Dark: Whiteness and the Literary Imagination* (Cambridge: Harvard University Press, 1992), xiii.

28. Ibid., 51–52.

29. When performance artist John Duncan purchased a female corpse in Tijuana in the early 1980s for the purpose of necrophilious sex, his act was a desperate exhibition of this excruciating lack. Duncan's pain is palpable, however contemptible.

30. Cixous and Clement, *Newly Born Woman*, 64–65.

31. My research in Romania began in the fall of 1991. The following October 1992, I lectured on the subject of art and politics at the University of Bucharest and on performance art at the Nicolae Grigorescu Academia de Arta in Bucharest. At that time I began to discuss art and politics with many artists in the Romanian avant-garde and to do research that continues today in my work on cultures of trauma. All quotes from Lia and Dan Perjovschi date from my conversations with them in Bucharest in October 1992 and August 1993.

Katherine Verdery and Gail Kligman explain that many Romanians now believe that the December 1989 revolution was a coup that may have been plotted for up to two decades, a coup that may have been supported by the former Soviet Union, and a coup that was carried out by the National Salvation Front, reformed communists many of whom are still in control of the government and the Securitate. See Verdery and Kligman's "Romania after Ceausescu: Post-Communist Communism?," in *Eastern Europe in Revolution*, ed. Ivo Banac (Ithaca: Cornell University Press, 1992) 119.

32. The Romanian Securitate, unlike the German Stasi or the Russian KGB, has yet to be purged.

33. Primo Levi, an Auschwitz survivor, and philosopher Walter Benjamin both believed that the concentration camp was a microcosm of the external world. See Primo Levi, *Survival in Auschwitz and the Reawakening: Two Memoirs* (*Se questo e un uomo* [1958] and *La tregua* [1963]; New York: Summit Books, 1986); and Levi, *The Drowned and the Saved*, trans. Raymond Rosenthal (*Sommersi e i salvati* [1986]; New York: Vintage International, 1989). See also Pietro Fransisca, *Primo Levi as Witness:*

Proceedings of a Symposium Held at Princeton University (Florence: Casalini Libri, 1990); and Hans Sahl, *Walter Benjamin: Im Lager* (Frankfurt: Suhrkamp, 1972).

34. Katherine Verdery, *National Ideology under Socialism: Identity and Cultural Politics in Ceausescu's Romania* (Berkeley: University of California Press, 1991), 101. This is a complicated history involving claims made by Romanian intellectuals for the priority of Romanian cultural inventions and even historical events in the cultural and political history of Europe. Verdery carefully charts "protochronism" (temporal priority) in several chapters.

35. Ibid., 122.

36. Ibid., 107.

37. Ralph Earle, "On the Virtues of Distrust: An Interview with Andrei Codrescu," *The Sun*, no. 143 (October 1987): 8.

38. Katherine Verdery, "Nationalism and the 'Transition' in Romania" (presentation at Duke University, February 23, 1993).

39. Ion Bitzan, conversation with author, Bucharest, October 1992. Subsequent quotes by Bitzan come from this discussion.

40. Alexandra Cornilescu, "Transitional Patterns: Symptoms of the Erosion of Fear in Romanian Political Discourse" (paper presented at the annual meeting of the Modern Language Association, New York, 1992). Subsequent quotes by Cornilescu come from this paper.

41. Andrei Codrescu, *Monsieur Teste in America and Other Instances of Realism* (Minneapolis: Coffee House Press, 1987), 14.

42. Herman, *Trauma and Recovery*, 83.

43. See Henry Krystal, "Trauma and Affects," *Psychoanalytic Study of the Child* 33 (1978): 81–116, quoted in Herman, *Trauma and Recovery*, 84.

44. On the "conspiracy of silence," see also Haei Danieli, "The Treatment and Prevention of Long-Term Effects and Intergenerational Transmission of Victimization: A Lesson from Holocaust Survivors and Their Children," in *Trauma and Its Wake*, ed. Figley, 298–99, 307–8, 311; and Milton E. Jucovy, "Therapeutic Work with Survivors and Their Children: Recurrent Themes and Problems," *Healing Their Wounds: Psychotherapy with Holocaust Survivors and Their Families*, ed. Paul Marcus and Alan Rosenberg (New York: Praeger 1989), 51–66.

45. Herman, *Trauma and Recovery*, 9.

46. Verdery and Kligman, "Romania after Ceausescu," 143.

47. Elaine Scarry, *The Body in Pain: The Making and Unmaking of the World* (New York: Oxford University Press, 1985), 4.

48. Sanda Agalidi, "Notes on 'Vox,'" *Oversight* [Los Angeles] 2 (1990): 23.

49. See Mikhail Bakhtin, *The Dialogical Imagination* (Austin: University of Texas Press, 1981), quoted in Verdery, *National Ideaology under Socialism*, 122.

50. See Gilles Deleuze and Felix Guattari, *Anti-Oedipus: Capitalism and Schizo-*

phrenia (Minneapolis: University of Minnesota Press, 1975); and Jean Baudrillard, *The Ecstasy of Communication* (New York: Semiotext[e], 1987).

51. Glass, *Shattered Selves*, 158.

52. Scarry, *Body in Pain*, 6.

53. Kristine Stiles, "Synopsis of the Destruction in Art Symposium and Its Theoretical Significance," *The Act* 1, no. 2 (1987): 28–29.

54. Hélène Cixous, *Inside*, trans. C. Barko (New York: Schocken, 1986), 97.

55. Herman, *Trauma and Recovery*, 9.

56. The concept of alternative cultures is complex, and a full definition of this term is beyond my present aims. Provisionally, however, I am including people marginalized by any number of differences that separate them from what is conventionally agreed upon (even by the marginalized) as normative behavior and appearance. Alternative cultures then include individuals whose sexual preferences, social practices, age, class, education, and race, but also intelligence, creativity, and sensitivity, in some way or another, separate them from what they themselves might even consider normative.

57. V. Vale and Andrea Juno, introduction to *Modern Primitives*, special issue of *RE/Search* 12 (1989): 4. It is noteworthy that *RE/Search* began in the San Francisco punk scene as *Search and Destroy* (1977–1978). The original newspaper format was initially used when *Search and Destroy* became *RE/Search*, but the latter over time transformed into a glossy, trendy "scene" publication specializing in such heroes of camp culture as William Burroughs and J. G. Ballard and producing such special issues as *Incredibly Strange Films* (no. 10) and *Pranks!* (no. 11).

58. Marianna Torgovnick, *Gone Primitive: Savage Intellects, Modern Lives* (Chicago: University of Chicago Press, 1990), 245.

59. Recently my student Ducphong Nguyen told me a story her mother had recounted to her after hearing about my essay. There is a custom in some Vietnamese villages in which an adulterous woman is taken from her home, her is head shaved and her body covered with lime, and she is tied to a boat and then set adrift to die on the river. I have been unable to substantiate this story and have not been able to determine how old this custom may be or whether it reflects Western practices. But the parallel to the West is astonishing.

This is just one of many references individuals have given me regarding the pervasive evidence of trauma related to shaved heads and tattoos. I cannot list all of them here, but I should mention Ruth Mellinkoff's *Outcasts: Signs of Otherness in Northern European Art of the Late Middle Ages* (Berkeley: University of California Press, 1993). This book includes an entire chapter entitled "Hair and Heads: Close-Cropped, Balding, Hairless, and Shaved" (chap. 9). Thanks to Charlotte Houghton for this reference. My colleague Claudia Koonz also gave me several articles on the fraught conditions signified by tattoos and shaved heads in Ireland and Russia. A most compelling report states: "Since the collapse of communism and the decay of Russia's old social welfare system, statistics show that teen criminals are becoming even more violent and aggressive. . . . One of the most harrowing teenage crimes this year involved a group of boys who raped a 16-year-old girl and burned her to death in southern Russia. . . . Some [of these] teens also amuse themselves by getting tattoos, although getting caught often means serving in solitary." See Jennifer Gould, "Inside Russia's Gulag for Teenage Criminals," *Toronto Star*, May 30, 1993, F2.

60. Paglia's oratory, while silly and dismissable, is seductive because of the ways in which she summons myths of women and states of being (i.e., primitivism) that are familiar and comforting in a time of great change, when challenges to dominant patriarchal paradigms unseat all modes of behavior. For example, writing on Elizabeth Taylor's performance in *Suddenly Last Summer*, Paglia stated, "It is an astonishingly rich picture, full of the paradoxes of concealment and exhibitionism that make woman so elusive and so dominant" (17). On Madonna's video "Open Your Heart," she opined: "Responding to the spiritual tensions within Italian Catholicism, Madonna discovered the buried paganism within the church." This is the reason, she concluded, that "the old-guard establishment feminists who still loathe Madonna have a sexual ideology problem" (11). Paglia's summoning of a so-called mysticism of interiority, paradox, concealment, and exhibitionism historically associated with women is precisely the kind of thinking that reiterates and conforms to the phallocratic universe about which I have been writing. Furthermore, summoning the "pagan" in the church is calling forth the "primitive." See Paglia's *Sex, Art, and American Culture* (New York: Vintage Books, 1992).

61. See Madonna's *Sex*, ed. Glenn O'Brien (New York: Warner Books, 1992). The mere list of those who contributed to the construction of Madonna's "self-representation" — photographer Stephen Meisel, artist Fabien Baron, and producer Calloway — is telling.

62. See Susan McClary, "Living to Tell: Madonna's Resurrection of the Fleshly," *Feminine Endings: Music, Gender, and Sexuality* (Minneapolis: University of Minnesota Press, 1991), 148–66; and Lisa Lewis, *Gender Politics and MTV: Voicing the Difference* (Philadelphia: Temple University Press, 1990), esp. "Female Address Video (1980–1986)," 109–48. For these citations, I am grateful to Victoria C. Vandenberg, "Bodies, Gender, and Rock-n-Roll: Making Music Dance on MTV" (senior distinction thesis, Duke University, Women's Studies, 1990).

63. Angela Carter offers an excellent critique of the claims that women may appropriate signs of negativity as a representation or practice of self-construction and self-empowerment. See *The Sadeian Woman and the Ideology of Pornography* (New York: Pantheon Books, 1978).

Mandy Merck

MacKinnon's Dog

Antiporn's Canine

Conditioning

> *Is not the eternal sorrow of life the*
> *fact that in most cases human beings*
> *do not understand each other and cannot*
> *enter the inner state of the other?*
> — Ivan Pavlov
>
> *Treat your man like a dog!*
> *Reward him for good behaviour and*
> *he'll come when you whistle.*
> — Cosmopolitan

The following remarks deal with dogs, men, and the continuing debate on pornography. In declaring their relevance to women's lives, I am mindful of Tania Modleski's skepticism about the move in the late 1980s from women's studies to a "gender criticism" also engaged by considerations of masculinity: "What's in these new developments *for feminism* and for women?"[1] If (as would seem irrefutable) the central issue in the feminist debate on pornography is how that medium affects women, why bother about men?

My reply begins with the latest antipornography tract by the celebrated feminist legal theorist Catharine MacKinnon. In the ironically titled *Only*

Words, she argues that pornography is not speech but sex, not "an 'idea' worthy of First Amendment protection" but a stimulus to male masturbation employing representations of female subordination: "The women are in two dimensions, but the men have sex with them in their own three-dimensional bodies, not in their minds alone. Men come doing this." The pleasures of these autoerotic practices, MacKinnon argues, compel men to subsequent misogynist acts — whether rape, murder, harassment, or simple sexism. "Sooner or later, in one way or another, the consumers want to live out the pornography further in three dimensions. Sooner or later, in one way or another, they do. *It* makes them want to; when they believe they can, when they feel they can get away with it, *they* do."[2]

As I revised this article for publication, *Only Words* was greeted in Britain with the extensive publicity refused opposing feminist views. In part, this may be attributed to the British fascination with a "feminism" understood more than ever as the polemical excesses of eccentric colonials, whatever their actual politics (Greer, Hite, Dworkin, Wolf, Paglia, and now MacKinnon). In part, it may reflect the book's apparent compatibility with the Conservative government's increasing regulation of representation — as if to compensate for its deregulation of virtually everything else (wage minima, rail systems, banking practices, you name it).

This process recently reached its nadir when the murder of a Liverpool toddler by two ten-year-old boys, both children of impoverished and violent families, resulted in an amendment to the Criminal Justice Bill further restricting the distribution of films on videotape. This in a country where *The Exorcist* is still banned on video and where the photographic representation of sexual intercourse is also, and not incidentally, illegal. The attempts to win feminist support for such measures (attempts that have been successful in many quarters) make the analysis of MacKinnon's assertion that certain forms of representation are central to women's oppression all the more urgent.

If the clamor over *Only Words* yielded any benefits in Britain, it was to take such analyses beyond the meeting hall and the classroom and into the usually unreflective realms of the press. There, quite predictably, reviewers complained about the book's "breathtaking" and "lurid" rhetoric.[3] Typically, these observations were then set aside (rhetoric being seen as an unworthy, and certainly un-British, form of demogoguery) in favor of whatever was discerned to be MacKinnon's "central argument."[4] Here the reviewers may have been too hasty. Elsewhere other commentators (notably the American literary critic Stanley Fish and the political theorist Wendy Brown) have made MacKinnon's "supremely rhetorical" strategy the object of their inquiries, bearing down on "the logical and narrative structures of her prose" to analyze its potency as well as its political problems.[5] Encouraged by their example, I want to examine a recurring rhetorical figure in MacKinnon's writing on pornography, one that imbricates masculinity with bestiality in the discourses of behavioral psychology.

To begin, then, with a definition of pornography by Catharine MacKinnon. "Pornography," she has written, "works as a behavioral conditioner, reinforcer and stimulus, not as ideas or advocacy. It is more like saying 'kill' to a trained guard dog—and also like the training process itself."[6] The figure of the dog occurs frequently in MacKinnon's arguments, appearing whenever the subject turns to legal distinctions between words and deeds: "First Amendment logic, like nearly all legal reasoning, has difficulty grasping harm that is not linearly caused in the 'John hit Mary' sense. The idea is that words or pictures can be harmful only if they produce harm in a form that is considered an action. Words work in the province of attitudes, actions in the realm of behavior. . . . But which is saying 'kill' to a trained guard dog, a word or an act? Which is its training?"[7]

That passage is from a speech collected in MacKinnon's 1987 *Feminism Unmodified*. Two years later it was reprised virtually verbatim in *Toward a Feminist Theory of the State*.[8] And most recently, in *Only Words*, the published collection of MacKinnon's 1992 Gauss Lectures at Princeton, it is reworked under the heading of "a theory of protected speech": "Social life is full of words that are legally treated as the acts they constitute without so much as a whimper from the First Amendment. What becomes interesting is when the First Amendment frame is invoked and when it is not. *Saying* 'kill' to a trained attack dog is only words. Yet it is not seen as expressing the viewpoint 'I want you dead'—which it usually does, in fact, express. It is seen as performing an act tantamount to someone's destruction, like saying, 'ready, aim, fire' to a firing squad."[9]

MacKinnon's argument is part of a much-debated campaign to divest pornography of any legal protection as speech or expression. Her close collaborator, the writer Andrea Dworkin, has maintained that pornography not only *represents* sexual violence against women, it actually *is* that violence. The equation is not only one of words with deeds, but of resemblance with identity. As Dworkin argued in her 1979 polemic, *Pornography: Men Possessing Women*, "The valuation of women's sexuality in pornography is objective and real because women are so regarded and so valued. The force depicted in pornography is objective and real because force is so used against women."[10] Thus, if porn is real and so is the low status of women, and if the former depicts or narrates the latter, they therefore participate in the same, single reality, in which the relationship of image and act is not solely one of correspondence, or even causality. Instead, this "synedochal"[11] logic awards pornography a significant (often commanding) share in the ontology of gender itself. MacKinnon puts it more eloquently: "Gender is sexual. Pornography constitutes the meaning of that sexuality. Men treat women as who they see women as being. Pornography constructs who that is."[12]

In offering these definitions, Dworkin and MacKinnon refuse the distinction between representation and action that animates much of the juridical discussion of permissible and impermissible expression under the First Amendment: "Congress shall make no law . . . abridging the freedom of speech, or of the press." Until the 1960s, this amendment was interpreted to protect only the "expression of ideas" in the narrowest sense. But with the dissenting movements of the 1960s came the modern doctrine of speech and its enlarged protection for unpopular, offensive, or sexually explicit expression, unless such expression is deemed to incite immediate lawlessness (racist speech is only proscribed when it is judged to cause imminent and significant harm); offend community standards (the broader test for obscenity); or be harmful in ways recognized elsewhere in the law — blackmail, bribery, libel with "actual malice," conspiracy to commit crimes, discriminatory housing ads, yelling "fire" in the proverbial crowded theater. One of the most significant additions to this list of exemptions was formulated in the early 1980s, when workplace remarks to female employees such as "Did you get any over the weekend?" or epithets such as "cunt" or "tits" was ruled sexual harassment in a number of U.S. courts.[13]

It was the judicial success in this arena — the establishment of sexual harassment (including verbal harassment) in the workplace as discrimination in employment — which led MacKinnon and Dworkin to their next legal move, the 1983 attempt to classify pornography as sex discrimination under the civil rights ordinances of the City of Minneapolis, Minnesota. "Pornography," the new ordinance read, "is central in creating and maintaining the civil inequality of the sexes," and it went on to describe it as a "systematic practice of exploitation and subordination based on sex which differentially harms women," promoting "bigotry and contempt," fostering "aggression," and thereby reducing women's equality of rights to employment, education, public services, and the "full exercise of citizenship" itself.[14]

The upshot of this initiative was several years of judicial battles between the Minneapolis city council, which had passed it, and the city's mayor and civil rights officers, who opposed it; between the mayor of Indianapolis, Indiana, who passed a subsequent version, and the American Booksellers Association, which took the mayor to court; between antifeminist Christians who supported the initiative and antifeminist porn publishers who did not. Finally, the initiative divided feminists themselves, with a large group of writers, academics, and campaigners (ranging from Kate Millett and Adrienne Rich to Ann Snitow and Carol Vance) signing a Feminists Against Censorship Taskforce (FACT) brief opposing the ordinances' use of legally ambiguous terms like "degrading" and "objectification"; its neglect of other possible factors in women's subordination; and its apparent distinction between asexual women and sexually predatory men.

In reply to the argument of the City of Indianapolis that pornography conditions the male orgasm to female subordination, making such subordination a stimulus to a "natural physiological response" and thus leaving "no more room for further debate than does shouting 'kill' at an attack dog," the FACT brief declared: "Men are not attack dogs, but morally responsible human beings. The ordinance reinforces a destructive sexist stereotype of men as irresponsible beasts."[15]

There have been several juridical consequences of this canine controversy thus far: the U.S. Supreme Court upheld a Federal Court judgment against the Indianapolis ordinances by refusing to hear the city's appeal (1986); the Canadian Supreme Court found for MacKinnon's argument in the landmark decision *Regina vs. Butler* (1992); a British bill (which failed in 1989 and again in 1990) employed the ordinances' definition of pornography in order to restrict the sale of soft-core publications like *Playboy*; and Senate Bill 1521, better known as the "Bundy Bill" (which failed in 1992) would have made producers and distributors of "obscene material" liable for damages resulting from sexual offenses "foreseeably caused" by exposure to their wares. Although most of these initiatives have not been successful, their recurrence, as well as MacKinnon's newfound celebrity in the aftermath of Anita Hill's allegations against Clarence Thomas (allegations that notoriously included his workplace discussions of pornography), suggest that the "porn wars" are not over. To determine why, I suggest we turn from the regulation of pornography to a problematic that both antedates and animates it — the question of men and dogs.

My first observation is prompted by the FACT brief's ironic resort to the term "reinforces" in its critique of MacKinnon's use of conditioning theory. The discourses of behaviorism inform the terms of this debate, and feminist common sense in general, far more than we care to admit. And if FACT appropriated the very conditioning model it sought to challenge, this is not the only instance of the double talk, or ambivalence, or even disavowal, in which the pornography debate, and certainly its canine tropology, has been articulated. Indeed, behaviorism itself, as conceived by Ivan Pavlov and John Watson, is only one attempt to resolve the old dualities of human and animal, culture and nature, choice and compulsion, which find new expression in MacKinnon's dog. That dog descends from what Mark Seltzer has described as "the double discourse" that "insists at once on the artificial and on the natural character of the individual."[16] Following his influential reconfiguration of such apparent antitheses in his study of naturalist literature, *Bodies and Machines*, I'll begin with no less an authority on the canine condition than Seltzer's expert (and Pavlov's contemporary), Jack London.

London's Klondike tales are dog stories — stories whose central characters are not the prospectors of the Gold Rush or the MacKenzie River Indians, but Buck, White Fang, Brown Wolf, and Spot. The transpositions that turn sled dogs into psychologically elaborated protagonists and their drivers into mere "specks and motes"[17] in the Arctic wastes are part of a series of exchanges (between civilization and the wild, master and slave, California and Canada) in which men become bestialized, animals humanized, and everybody — as Seltzer points out — wears fur. In arguing that the violent pursuit of riches in the wilderness makes men no better (and quite possibly worse) than beasts, London could count on established connotations for the word "dog," which had long carried the meaning of a low or contemptible person. It also meant "male," both in canine terms (where "dog" is opposed to "bitch") and in human (where it is directed at men in sexual reproach or congratulation — "You dog, you").

And except for the odd mate or mother, London's dogs are a conspicuously male cast, matching the bachelor company of their frontier masters. If the latter should conventionally command the former, this opposition is also reorganized, with each species revealed as both compelling and compelled. The canine version of this double positioning is most simply rendered as "dog eat dog," a frequent occurrence in London's stories and a useful figure for his allegories of social Darwinism. Meanwhile, the masters are themselves mastered by greed, by their rivals for riches, and by "the great blind elements and forces."[18]

But if the lesson is that humans, like animals, dwell in a state of nature where only the strong survive, the nature of that nature remains uncertain (or, in Seltzer's description, "unnatural").[19] The very anthropomorphism that makes London's dogs into heroes undoes the bestial metaphor. What are men who are like dogs *like*, if dogs are like men?

In 1904, the year after London published *The Call of the Wild*, the Russian physiologist Ivan Pavlov was awarded the Nobel Prize for his work on digestion—specifically, the discovery that the secretion of digestive fluids is controlled by the nervous system. To observe such functions Pavlov used dogs—because they could be trained to lie still or stand in a harness for long periods of time, during which their gastric or salivary juices could be collected in surgically externalized pouches drained to the outside of the body. (Both the dog and digestion were merely convenient, if retrospectively striking, choices for neurological research: the longevity of the animals offered a way to do comparative studies of the same subject, while the secretions of digestion provided a medium for precise measurement—the volume of fluid produced in each procedure.)

In the course of these researches, Pavlov discovered that the nervous system initiates the flow of gastric juices in reaction to the taste of food, not its arrival in the stomach. The name he gave this phenomenon—"psychic secretion"—was itself a challenge to the prevailing division between physiological and psychological inquiry. Among the conventions still governing psychological investigation was the principle that research on animal behavior should be aimed at an understanding of the subject's conscious processes. Thus, to proceed with the question of psychic secretion, Pavlov's team was divided between observational physiologists and a colleague who undertook to analyze the "internal world" of the dog, assuming that the animal's "thought, feelings, and desires," as Pavlov later wrote, were "analogous to ours."[20] The eventual impossibility of reconciling this subjectivism with the experimental data of the laboratory led not only to the project's abandonment, but the breakup of the team itself. As Pavlov ruefully reflected, "Where is there even the slightest indisputable criterion that our conjectures are correct, that we can, for the sake of a better understanding of the matter, compare the inner state of even such a developed animal as the dog with our own? . . . And then, where is the knowledge, where is the power of knowledge that might enable us correctly to comprehend the state of another human being?"[21] In response, Pavlov discarded any pretensions to introspection for an objectivism that concentrated "on studying the correlation between the external phenomena and the reaction of the organism,"[22] effectively incorporating the psychical into his "physiology of the higher nervous activity."[23]

But of course Pavlov's research did not escape psychology (of which he is now deemed a founder) any more than it eluded anthropomorphism. (His dogs, mongrels raised outside the laboratory rather than bred for it, continued to be granted both names and "personalities," and variations in response among individual subjects were analyzed rather than aggregated. Moreover, Pavlov often diagnosed them with psychological disorders such as hysteria and catatonia.) One could say, however, that Pavlov "caninized" experimental psychology by directing its attention toward forms of behavior easily observed in dogs. Among these was the secretion of liquids.

After "psychic secretion" came the famous discovery that an autonomic or involuntary reflex (salivation at the taste of food) could be paired with a learned or "conditioned" one (salivation at the ringing of a bell). The result was a liquid measure of association, a quantifiable materialization of an ostensibly psychical process. "Here are facts," Pavlov declared, "which show that our psychical material may also be included in a definite scheme and that it is subject to certain laws."[24]

But if the dog's digestive system was the original medium for psychological positivism, it wasn't long before its other bodily functions were also investigated. Among Pavlov's researchers in the 1920s was an American, W. Horsley Gantt, who later became his translator and academic advocate. Gantt opens a 1949 paper with references to the giant woodcock of the Russian forests and the earthworm of the Baltimore suburbs. His interest is their sexual excitement and the way it inhibits other sensory functions, including those which would signal hunger or danger. The Russian woodcock is said to be tragically oblivious to the approach of hunters when it sings its "love song," while the worms disport themselves all over the Baltimore golf course each spring without regard to predators or passing foursomes. After a catalog of heroic male mating attempts (prefaced by an unapologetic citation of the masculine bias in the first Kinsey report), Gantt moves on to his central subject, the dog.

The *male* dog, I should say, since Gantt's subjects included Fritz the Alsatian, Peter the beagle, a male poodle known as "V3," and especially the mongrel Nick, subject of "the most meticulous and complete case history of a single animal to be found in the conditioned reflex literature."[25] These animals and others like them were subjected to a barrage of procedures to study conflicts of the drives between, for example, experimentally induced anxiety states and sexual excitement. As Gantt had observed on the golf course, sexual arousal can inhibit or block other sensations. Nick, in particular, exhibited symptomatic erections and ejaculations whenever he encountered stimuli associated with previous situations of anxiety. Years after one such experiment, in which anxious reactions were elicited by requiring dogs to make a difficult distinction between two tones of similar pitch (a distinction that determined whether the dog was fed), Nick would develop a "prominent erection . . . within a few seconds after the onset of the tone," Gantt enthused. "We could always count on Nick for a demonstration."[26]

As for the inhibiting effects of female arousal, Gantt notes in passing that bitches — like female cats — will accept food even during copulation. "A hint for Dr. Kinsey," he writes, "when he extends his study to the female."[27] Gantt himself had no inhibitions about extending his study to humans: he insists that "it is entirely within our right to believe that in man the sexual function may often assume the same dominant role, both excitatory and inhibitory, as we can show experimentally it does in the earthworm, the bird, the cat and the dog."[28]

The ascending scale on which Gantt concludes his report beckons us one step farther up the food chain, to the work of the British behaviorists H. J. Eysenck and D. K. Nias and their influential 1978 study *Sex, Violence, and the Media*. Here, with fulsome acknowledgement of the dog and the dinner bell, behavioral psychology moves to the human male, who proves remarkably like his canine predecessors. Not only does he sit still — on successive occasions — in an experimental apparatus described as a penis plethysmograph, but he exhibits an objectively measurable hydraulic reaction to certain stimuli, in this case films portraying "*fellatio, cunnilingus*, intercourse from behind, *soixante-neuf*, etc."[29] As for his female counterpart, despite admitted evidence of "considerable overlap" in reported rates of male and female arousal, Eysenck and Nias are at great pains to remind the adherents of "women's lib" that "high libido" and an enthusiasm for "pornography, permissiveness and impersonal sex" is correlated with masculinity — a proposition they support by questioning the "typicality" of women who volunteer for such studies, as well as adducing *every conceivable hypothesis* (anatomical, hormonal, evolutionary) for what they call the "biological basis of maleness and femaleness."[30] Another influential team of porn researchers, Donnerstein, Linz, and Penrod, are equally unrepentant about the male bias in their studies (whose typical subjects are college students), arguing that the highest incidence of rape, and indeed of all forms of violent crime, occurs in males between eighteen and twenty years of age.[31] But it took a contributor to the famed Meese Report on pornography to admit that the advantage of male subjects is the "independent and objective" evidence offered by "penile measures of arousal."[32]

The insistence of this penile positivism did not go unremarked by Andrea

Dworkin. In a 1985 essay wonderfully titled after Virginia Woolf's phrase in *A Room of One's Own*, "Against the Male Flood," she argues that obscenity law has historically treated the erection as a form of proof: "Empirically, *prurient* means *causes erection*." With the advent of a female judiciary and juries, however, both the test and the crime become obsolete: "In order for obscenity law to have retained social and legal coherence, it would have had to recognize as part of its standard women's sexual arousal, a more subjective standard than erection."[33]

But why should female arousal be deemed "a more subjective standard?" In a rare discussion of *women's* relation to pornography in *Toward a Feminist Theory of the State*, MacKinnon briefly reviews three such experiments. In all three, the female subjects reported less arousal than their physical reactions — notably vaginal lubrication — seemed to suggest. But where, in the case of men, the physical and psychical are read as indivisible, here they are detached. In a sudden rejection of the Pavlovian ontology she has so carelessly espoused, MacKinnon challenges the body's claim to truth: "It seems at least as likely," she writes, "that women disidentify with their bodies' conditioned responses." Where male tumescence and ejaculation proved the measure of an ideological effect, vaginal fluids are now described as "so-called objective indices of arousal." "Not to be overly behavioral," she continues, "but does anyone think Pavlov's dogs were really hungry every time they salivated at the sound of the bell?"[34]

Like MacKinnon, and despite her own protests to the contrary, Andrea Dworkin must also foreclose the question of women's sexual arousal to pursue her figure of a male flood. The legal strategy she proposes returns to the penis, whose erection and ejaculation become the index not simply of arousal (as in the obscenity test), but arousal by gender subordination. For, unlike obscenity, pornography is defined in this essay as "the conditioning of erection and orgasm in men to the powerlessness of women." It is also defined as "a woman being fucked by dogs, horses, snakes."[35] Here the canine saliva to which human sexual responses have been compared in the conditioning model is transformed into the fluids of orgasm — both human and animal — a lethal ejaculate that flows through this essay to become, in Dworkin's comments on Sade, an ocean. The pornographic writings and sexual crimes of the marquis are described as "waves on the same sea: that sea, becoming for its victims, however it reached them, a tidal wave of destruction."[36] (In her own comments on Dworkin's essay in *Only Words*, MacKinnon complains of "a society saturated with pornography, not to mention an academy saturated with deconstruction.")[37] As for bestiality, it is revealed to be pornography's primal scene ("a woman being fucked by dogs, horses, snakes") — the originary moment of a natural catastrophe ("a tidal wave") that liquidates both the proper relations of the sexes and the species. In what is paradoxically called the copycat effect, the dog in the pornographic scene (let's call him Dworkin's dog) transforms the spectator into another dog, MacKinnon's dog. Both the subject and the stimulus have been *caninized*.

Here the history of behaviorism offers us one final illustration. In an early attempt to extend Pavlov's principles to human behavior, the American psychologist John Watson also used a dog. This time, however, the animal was not the subject of the experiment but a potential stimulus. To demonstrate that phobias could be conditioned, Watson exposed a nine-month-old boy to a number of potentially frightening sights: rats, burning newspapers, and dogs. But the infant, "Albert B.," described as "just about the most famous child in the whole of psychology," exhibited no fear.[38] Watson then established that Albert *could* be scared, by the sound of a steel bar struck loudly with a hammer right behind his head. An experiment was devised in which a dog was brought to little Albert, and just as he began to reach for it, the steel bar was hit with the hammer. With three or four repetitions, Watson reported, "A new and important change is apparent. The animal now calls out the same response as the steel bar, namely a fear response." According to Watson, this result rendered the origins of animal phobias totally transparent, "without lugging in consciousness or any so-called mental process. A dog comes toward the child rapidly, jumps upon him, pushes him down and at the same time barks loudly. Oftentimes one such combined stimulation is all that is necessary to make the baby run away from the dog the moment it comes within his range of vision."[39]

In fact, this much-cited experiment in inducing phobia is one of the great fakes of scientific history. As the British psychologist Dennis Howitt relates, Watson never succeeded in conditioning the fear caused by the clang of metal to the sight of the dog. When he brought the two stimuli together, the loud banging made the dog bark, and the ensuing cacophony terrified the unfortunate infant (who was then sent home in a state, and as a likely model for the child tormented by his psychologist father in the 1960 film *Peeping Tom*).

What we find in the case of Albert B. is the other side of the canine coin that circulates in the behaviorist narrative — the dog who attacks. The docile subject of Pavlov's research becomes the phobic object of Watson's. And if pornography can accomplish this double metamorphosis, if it can turn men — if not into Circe's swine, then into MacKinnon's dogs — what does that make male sexuality? On the one hand, it becomes the experimental subject par excellence, a ready reflex that can be stimulated, trained, observed, and hydraulically measured. On the other hand, this creature of the laboratory may suddenly jump up, bark loudly, and wreck your experiment — unless your experiment was designed, like Watson's, to induce phobia in the first place. (This is not idle speculation in the case of Andrea Dworkin, who punctuates her study *Intercourse* — intercourse as male dominance — with the question "Are you afraid now?")[40]

But what should we fear most? The danger of a male sexuality trained in sexism or the danger of it wild? The unconditioned reflex or the conditioned one? Bred in the biomechanics of late-nineteenth-century thought, MacKinnon's dog collapses these oppositions to figure a bestial man most natural when most patriarchally cultured, most mechanically manipulable when most physically aroused. Despite both Dworkin and MacKinnon's reiterated description of male sexuality as a social, political (and thus potentially changeable) phenomenon, they simultaneously stress the unvarying domination on which it is said to be predicated. The effect is to represent male sexuality as dangerous by nurture *and* nature, because they've become the same thing.[41]

By 1916, Jack London's dog stories had made him a millionaire. In his reflections on the writer's relationship with his reader, the determinism that had crushed his characters "with the weight of unending vastness and unalterable decree" reemerged in his aesthetics.[42] In "Eight Great Factors of Literary Success," the best-selling author listed his ability "to select the symbols that would compel [the reader's] brain to realize my thoughts, or vision, or emotion."[43] Among the hazards of a certain anthropomorphism, we might list a strong theory of performativity. The allegorical dog seems to come with a master, someone or something that issues those unalterable decrees. In London's fiction this is not, as we first expect, man but "the marvelous power and influence of the environment."[44] In behavioral psychology, it is the efficacy of conditioning. In MacKinnon's writings, it is pornography.

In *Only Words* the author of the slogan "Porn is the image that acts" discovers speech act theory. Arguing that pornography is "constructing and performative rather than . . . merely referential or connotative," MacKinnon footnotes J. L. Austin's famous formula, "The issuing of the utterance is the performing of an action — it is not normally thought of as just saying something."[45] Such a theory requires at least an implicit utterance, and she reads one: "The message of these materials, and there is one, as there is to all conscious activity, is 'get her,' pointing at all women, to the perpetrators' benefit of ten billion dollars a year and counting."[46]

To get technical, as MacKinnon might say, such a command would not be, in Austin's terms, a *performative* but a *perlocution* — an utterance that *causes* an effect rather than one which *is* an effect.[47] The difference, to cite the philosopher's own examples, is between pronouncing the marriage vows (the performative "I do") and successfully persuading somebody to fire a gun (the perlocution "shoot her"). (The resemblance of the second example to Mac-Kinnon's firing-squad analogy in *Only Words* is probably not coincidental.) This difference matters because, whatever the consequences, a command is not identical to its effect in the same way that a vow is. Giving a pledge is not the same as giving an order. Not even the most persuasive utterance can be rendered as — to paraphrase Austin — "I convince you to get her."

To solve this problem, to establish that the pornographic message exercises the binding power attributed to the performative, MacKinnon might have moved beyond Austin to broader accounts of the "reiterative power of discourse to produce the phenomenon that it regulates and constrains"[48] — the definition of performativity favored by one of her most outspoken critics, Judith Butler, and, in *Toward a Feminist Theory of the State*, by MacKinnon herself. (There she propounds this Butleresque formulation: "Gender is what gender means. It has no basis in anything other than the social reality its hegemony constructs.")[49] But as MacKinnon admits in *Only Words*, such approaches "generalize the performative to all speech" (and thereby impugn the uniqueness that she now attributes to pornography in order to exempt it from constitutional protection).[50]

So *Only Words* takes the opposite tack, arguing that porn effects a particular performativity through its direction at an involuntary reflex. It isn't its content — "get her" — which distinguishes it from other sexist discourses, but its address: "directly to the penis, delivered through an erection."[51] MacKinnon concludes this description with the phrase "and taken out on women in the real world," but *Only Words* scarcely mentions the research on the social effects of pornography cited in her previous writings.[52] Instead (in a significant reversion to traditional definitions of obscenity), the erection is offered as the effect. (One can imagine Austin revising *How To Do Things with Words* to replace "I now pronounce you man and wife" with the bailiff's command in court, "All rise.")[53]

Such an argument deduces a performative from a performance, and not the performance of rape, or gender subordination more broadly, but the performance of sexual arousal. So potent is the erection's status as proof — of an imputed command at one end of the sequence and an imputed abuse at the other—that the alleged causal links between them are all but ignored in favor of the mere reiteration of the phenomenon itself. "In human society, where no one does not live, the physical response to pornography is nearly a universal conditioned male reaction, whether they like or agree with what the materials say or not. There is a lot wider variation in men's conscious attitudes toward pornography than there is in their sexual responses to it."[54]

But suppose we agree, if not to this particular estimate, then to the likelihood that pornography will stimulate sexual arousal. Let's say that this likelihood constitutes not only its use-value as a commodity but its presumptive definition—what the 1979 Williams Report on Obscenity to the British Home Office described as a "certain function or intention, to arouse its audience sexually."[55] We might take this argument a step farther and also agree that porn is "a real practice of sex using representations."[56] Or, as MacKinnon puts it, "Pornography is masturbation material. It is used as sex. It therefore is sex."[57]

But all sexual practices are not the same. Acknowledging porn's "excitatory" possibilities may raise moral questions about masturbation, but it says nothing about the abuse of women. If porn can "perform" erections (in the sense of stimulating them automatically or involuntarily), it does not follow that it performs harm to women "in the real world." The erection, most importantly, cannot "get her" without the cooperation of a man. Despite the "nearly universal" ascription of the conditioned condition to men, *Only Words* also posits man as master—in his "conscious attitudes"—whose dog is all too recognizable as that particularly animate entity, at once ungovernable and yet highly manipulable, the penis.

The familiar dualisms in which this opposition is articulated in the above-quoted passage from *Only Words* (the individual/society; conscious attitudes/conditioned reactions; reason/sensation) have most recently focused critical discussion of an even hotter topic than pornography—addiction. Following Eve Sedgwick's description of our culture's current addiction to addiction as its all-purpose alibi of compulsion and free will (in which our behavior is seen to be at once pathologically determined and voluntarily transformable),[58] Mark Seltzer has identified the principle's equally paradoxical prefiguration in the late-nineteenth-century plasma addict, the "living dead."[59]

Both the addict and the vampire also haunt the antiporn account, with MacKinnon seizing upon the first to characterize the porn-using rapist ("sexually habituated to its kick")[60] while Dworkin assimilates Bram Stoker's 1897 *Dracula* directly into the pornographic canon. Indeed, she describes the novel, with its climactic scene of Lucy Westenra's impalement by her fiancé in the sight of three male witnesses, as *the* founding spectacle of twentieth-century voyeurism: "an oncoming century filled with sexual horror; the throat as a female genital; sex and death as synonyms; killing as a sex act; slow dying as sensuality; men watching the slow dying, and the watching is sexual."[61]

The vampire Lucy is herself an example of this novel's "pathologies of agency," for she is both active and passive, Dracula's prey and an accomplished predator.[62] Seltzer pursues this ambiguity in the cybernetic figure of the dead steersman who, lashed to his wheel, pilots Dracula's ship ashore. But there is also the question of his passenger, the "immense dog" whose first act on landing (to tear out the throat of another large dog) reveals that it *is* its master.[63] If the bloodthirsty Count is the modern addict par excellence, as well as the chief prick of the new pornography, he is also a decidedly behaviorist character, with a canine condition to match: an obedient dog that moves to the (internalized) master's command and a wild dog that attacks.

Given the irrepressible binarism of the behaviorist problematic (mind/body, choice/compulsion, human/animal), the doubling that implicitly matches every dog with a master would seem inevitable. But even if it weren't, it would still be crucial to MacKinnon's project. Despite the bravado of her "nearly universal" model of male reactions to pornography, her moral appeal — the appeal that rallied men like the critical race theorist Charles Lawrence and the philosopher Richard Rorty to endorse her new book — requires that conscious attitude of male condemnation about which she professes such skepticism. For all her denunciations of psychoanalysis, MacKinnon is as reliant on a notion of a divided male subjectivity as any of her opponents.

And this, I suspect, is what makes the pornography debate, and its behaviorist rhetoric, so . . . undead. Not too much disagreement between the warring parties, but too little. Not only is feminism's popular theory of gender socialization a polite form of behaviorism, complete with "the patterning of reward, nonreward and punishment . . . and the principles of direct and vicarious conditioning,"[64] but even the supposed complexities of social constructionism are caught in the old tourniquet of agency and determination, as others have argued.[65] If our recent efforts to untie it have only twisted it tighter (in the agonistics of "ideology" or "the unconscious"), this may be, as Eve Sedgwick argues with a certain degree of exasperation, because they've originated in models, Marxist or Freudian, that depend on the very dualisms in question. MacKinnon's dog may have been bred in the "heroics of compulsion/voluntarity,"[66] but so have we all. And, most ironically perhaps, this model of the subject makes man — that exemplary human subject — bestial *in* his humanity rather than in spite of it.

And here I want to close with one final evocation of that canine figure. This is a scene that mingles the most desperate claims to humanity with sex, spectatorship, and slavery. In it, five men sit watching an act of intercourse in a stream of fluids. They are described "as dogs." They are also described as "erect." But this is not a passage from the porn wars. It is a story of slaves on a southern farm whose master calls them "men" but treats them mostly like animals. And so, of course, he will not let them marry. Nevertheless, for a year, all five of these men court a young slave woman. When a different man is finally chosen, he seeks some place apart for their first union: "And taking her in the corn rather than in her quarters, a yard away from the cabins of the others who had lost out, was a gesture of tenderness. Halle wanted privacy for her and got public display. Who could miss a ripple in a cornfield on a quiet, cloudless day? He, Sixo, and both of the Pauls, sat under Brother pouring water from a gourd over their heads, and through eyes streaming with well water, they watched the confusion of tassles in the field below. It had been hard, hard, hard sitting there erect as dogs, watching corn stalks dance at noon. The water running over their heads made it worse."[67] This extraordinary passage, from Toni Morrison's *Beloved*, also seems to be a gesture of tenderness to these men rather than any indictment of their terribly concentrated gaze. It *is* undoubtedly an indictment of a regime that compels both voyeurism and public sex, that treats people "like animals." But somehow the simile slips, and these men seem to be mastered not by their owner, or by the awful heat, or by an implacably cruel mode of production, but by their own sexual desires (desires that, we have already learned, have led them to intercourse with cattle). Instead of evoking an enslaved sexuality, these lines could be taken to suggest masculine sexuality *as* slavery. It says something about the obduracy of such ideas that even Morrison's men can become MacKinnon's dogs.

Notes

The epigraphs are from Ivan Pavlov, "Experimental Psychology and Psychopathology in Animals," *Selected Works* (Moscow: Foreign Languages Publishing House, 1955), 155; and *Cosmopolitan* (U.K. edition), April 1993, cover.

1. Tania Modleski, *Feminism without Women* (New York: Routledge, 1991), 5.

2. Catharine A. MacKinnon, *Only Words* (Cambridge: Harvard University Press, 1993), 17, 19.

3. Bernard Williams, "Drawing Lines," review of *Only Words*, by Catharine Mac-Kinnon, *London Review of Books*, May 12, 1994: 9; Marina Warner, "The Tongue Bites Deep," review of *Only Words*, by MacKinnon, *Independent on Sunday*, May 29, 1994, Review Section, 32.

4. Williams, "Drawing Lines," 10. The irony here is that the reviewers didn't agree on what that argument was, with Williams maintaining that it was really about the incompatibility of current U.S. law on equality with that on freedom of speech.

5. Stanley Fish, "Introduction: Going Down the Anti-Formalist Road," *Doing What Comes Naturally* (Durham: Duke University Press, 1989), 18; Wendy Brown, "The Mirror of Pornography: MacKinnon's Social Theory of Gender" in *States of Injury: Power and Freedom in Late Modernity* (Princeton: Princeton University Press, 1995).

6. Quoted in Wendy Kaminer, "Feminists against the First Amendment," *Atlantic Monthly*, November 1992, 114.

7. Catharine A. MacKinnon, *Feminism Unmodified* (Cambridge: Harvard University Press, 1987), 156.

8. Catharine A. MacKinnon, *Toward a Feminist Theory of the State* (Cambridge: Harvard University Press, 1989), 206.

9. MacKinnon, *Only Words*, 12.

10. Andrea Dworkin, *Pornography: Men Possessing Women* (New York: Perigee Books, 1979; London: Women's Press, 1981), 200–201.

11. A rhetorical strategy identified by Donald Alexander Downs, *The New Politics of Pornography* (Chicago: University of Chicago Press, 1989), 42.

12. MacKinnon, *Theory of the State*, 197.

13. See MacKinnon, *Feminism*, 155, for relevant cases. MacKinnon herself wrote, in *Sexual Harassment of Working Women* (New Haven: Yale University Press, 1979), 29: "Verbal sexual harassment can include anything from passing but persistent comments on a woman's body or body parts to the experience of an eighteen-year-old file clerk whose boss regularly called her in to his office 'to tell me the intimate details of his marriage and to ask what I thought about different sexual positions.' Pornography is sometimes used."

14. For the complete text of this ordinance, see Andrea Dworkin and Catharine A. MacKinnon, *Pornography and Civil Rights* (Minneapolis, Minn.: Organizing Against Pornography, 1988), 99–105.

15. Quoted in *Off Our Backs*, June 1985, 12.

16. Mark Seltzer, *Bodies and Machines* (New York: Routledge, 1982), 94–95.

17. Jack London, "White Fang," *The Call of the Wild, White Fang, and Other Stories*, ed. Earle Labor and Robert C. Leitz III (Oxford, England: Oxford University Press, 1990), 94.

18. Ibid.

19. Seltzer, *Bodies and Machines*, 155.

20. Ivan Pavlov, *Lectures on Conditioned Reflexes*, trans. and ed. W. H. Gantt (New York: International Publishers, 1928), 1:38–39.

21. Pavlov, "Experimental Psychology," *Works*, 155.

22. Ibid.

23. Pavlov, "Physiology of the Higher Nervous Activity," *Works*, 271.

24. Pavlov, "Experimental Psychology," *Works*, 155.

25. See P. L. Broadhurst, "Abnormal Animal Behaviour," in *A Pavlovian Approach to Psychopathology*, ed. W. H. Gantt, L. Pickenhain, and Ch. Zwingmann (Oxford, England: Pergamon Press, 1970), 177.

26. W. Horsley Gantt, "Psychosexuality in Animals," in *A Pavlovian Approach*, ed. Gantt, Pickenhain, and Zwingmann, 114.

27. Ibid., 112. (Kinsey and his team did speculate on a possible neurological explanation for female "diversion" during coition. See Alfred C. Kinsey, Wardell B. Pomeroy, Clyde E. Martin, and Paul H. Gebhard, *Sexual Behavior in the Human Female* [Philadelphia: W. B. Saunders, 1953], 668–69.)

28. Gantt, "Psychosexuality in Animals," 118.

29. H. J. Eysenck and P. K. B. Nias, *Sex, Violence, and the Media* (1978; reprint, London: Paladin, 1980), 244.

30. Ibid., 237.

31. Edward Donnerstein, Daniel Linz, and Steven Penrod, *The Question of Pornography* (New York: Free Press, 1987), 14–15.

32. Edna F. Einseidel, "The Experimental Research Evidence," *The Attorney General's Commission on Pornography: Final Report, 1986*, reprinted in *Pornography: Women, Violence, and Civil Liberties*, ed. Catherine Itzin (Oxford, England: Oxford University Press, 1992), 249.

33. Andrea Dworkin, "Against the Male Flood: Censorship, Pornography, and Equality," in *Pornography*, ed. Itzin, 520.

34. MacKinnon, *Theory of the State*, 148.

35. Dworkin, "Against the Male Flood," 522.

36. Ibid., 524.

37. MacKinnon, *Only Words*, 7.

38. Dennis Howitt, *Concerning Psychology* (London: Open University, 1991), 40.

39. John B. Watson, *Behaviorism* (1924; reprint, New York: W. W. Norton, 1970), 8.

40. Andrea Dworkin, *Intercourse* (London: Secker & Warburg, 1987), 129.

41. Judith Butler, "Disorderly Woman," *Transition* 53 (1991): 91, describes MacKinnon's account of male domination as "the second nature produced by a systematic misogynist practice."

42. London, "White Fang," 94.

43. Jack London, "Eight Great Factors of Literary Success," quoted in Labor and Leitz, eds., *Call of the Wild*, xii.

44. London, quoted in ibid., xv.

45. J. L. Austin, *How To Do Things with Words* (1962; reprint, Oxford, England: Oxford University Press, 1975), quoted in MacKinnon, *Only Words*, 121 (n. 32).

46. MacKinnon, *Only Words*, 21.

47. I am indebted to Judith Butler for this observation. See Austin, *How To Do Things*, esp. Lectures VIII, IX, and X.

48. Judith Butler, *Bodies That Matter* (New York: Routledge, 1993), 2.

49. MacKinnon, *Theory of the State*, 198.

50. MacKinnon, *Only Words*, 121.

51. Ibid., 21.

52. Perhaps because, as a 1990 report commissioned by the British government concluded, "Evidence of the adverse effects of pornography is far less clear cut than some earlier reviews imply. Inconsistencies emerge between very similar studies and many interpretations of these have reached almost opposite conclusions. . . . It is unlikely that pornography is the only determinant of sexual and other forms of violence and that pornography can be influential in the absence of other conducive factors." See Dennis Howitt and Guy Cumberbatch, *Pornography: Impacts and Influences* (London: Home Office Research and Planning Unit, 1990), 94–95.

53. Nevertheless, "All rise," like "Get her," would be a perlocution rather than a performative.

54. MacKinnon, *Only Words*, 37.

55. *Report of the Committee on Obscenity and Film Censorship* (London: Her Majesty's Stationery Office, 1979), 103.

56. Ian Hunter, David Saunders, and Dugald Williamson, *On Pornography: Literature, Sexuality, and Obscenity Law* (London: Macmillan, 1993), 184.

57. MacKinnon, *Only Words*, 17.

58. Eve Kosofsky Sedgwick, "Epidemics of the Will," *Tendencies* (London: Routledge, 1994), 130–42.

59. Mark Seltzer, "Serial Killers (1)," *Differences* 5, no. 1 (1993): 111.

60. MacKinnon, *Only Words*, 16.

61. Dworkin, *Intercourse*, 119.

62. Seltzer, "Serial Killers," 111.

63. Bram Stoker, *Dracula* (1897; reprint, New York: Bantam Books, 1981), 84.

64. W. Mischel, "A Social-Learning View of Sex Differences in Behavior," quoted in Stephen Frosh, *Psychoanalysis and Psychology: Minding the Gap* (New York: New York University Press, 1989), 173.

65. See Diana Fuss, *Essentially Speaking* (New York: Routledge, 1989), 2–6; and Judith Butler, *Bodies*, 4–12.

66. Sedgwick, "Epidemics of the Will," 138.

67. Toni Morrison, *Beloved* (New York: Signet, 1991), 33–34.

Kathy E. Ferguson

Writing "Kibbutz Journal"

Borders, Voices, and the Traffic

In Between

Life in Israel brings one into intimate contact with a variety of borders and an intense set of claims about identity. There are the obvious physical borders, the ones between disputed territories and hostile states, where people cross between contested places in search of work, or in the line of duty, or for renewal or revenge. Then there are the seemingly obvious cultural borders between contending identities, between Arab and Jew, women and men, immigrant and native-born, religious and secular, dove and hawk. These too turn out to be contested spaces, hosting their own, often clandestine, border crossings. And then there are the furtive borders, woven into language practices and written onto bodies, which demarcate that which can be spoken from that which lies in silence.

"Kibbutz Journal" is part of an effort to engage these borders, to map their inclusions and exclusions, to chart the migrations they sustain and to attend to the utterances they authorize or forbid.[1] The journal was written during a four-month stay on a kibbutz in south-central Israel with my husband's family. The journal started out as a private space of writing, sought for the kinds of conversations that permit confusion, that allow intense feelings to explore their limits, that make listening possible. "Kibbutz Journal" became a public writing practice when I realized that I needed to keep this forum alive and to explore its possibilities with others. The journal format allows me to feel my way through a very complex set of practices, events, and histories, to navigate crosscurrents and accept derailments, without arriving at firm final conclusions. It allows me to be present in the writing, to both discern and rewrite my own inhabitations. It encourages me to write *through* theory rather than *about* theory, a move that is essential at some point in order to make the theories one's own. Theoretical reflection contains an unavoidable alienated dimension: it is an effort to understand something in terms other than those already present in the thing.[2] Theory's most fertile move is in this repositioning, wherein fresh links are forged between the prevailing terms of understanding and a different, contrasting terrain of meaning. By writing through the theories that shape my thinking, I hope to be able to address multiple audiences: readers familiar with, say, Foucault or Irigaray or Bakhtin will identify their ideas, while readers unfamiliar with these theorists can still engage the ideas without knowing their source. Theories are tool kits, and while there are times when one needs to write about one's tools, in this journal I can best reflect upon them by putting them to work.

Conventional academic writing tends to crowd out both the personal and the tentative; it requires firm arguments and clear resolutions; it stands at an unambiguous distance from its material. I have no neat narrative to tie up the loose ends here, no clear whole within which to subsume the fragments. The available narratives are part of the problem: the stories of Jewish resistance to Arab attacks and world indifference, or Palestinian resistance to Israeli repression and world indifference, or careful academic evenhandedness in the face of the intransigence of others — each of these arrangements of the story takes its place in the fixed landscape of available "positions" on the "Arab-Israeli conflict." It is this fixity that needs disturbing. But the I/i/eye writing is not outside these narrative strategies or outside the persistent demand for some overarching account of things. I turn to this kind of writing in the hope of creating a space to think against, perhaps even outside of, the prevailing curtailments of understanding. There is always a gap between what and how one writes, between what is told and the telling of it. This form of writing offers avenues for reflection on these asymmetries, perhaps more space for articulations ordinarily excluded.

"Kibbutz Journal" is part of an effort to write myself and my sons into a livable relationship with the social geography of Israel. My own location seems straightforwardly one of outsider: a U.S. academic visiting a kibbutz, a *goya* (non-Jew) marrying into an Israeli Jewish family, a feminist in the place that may well have invented patriarchy. But I cannot stay comfortably outside Israeli Jewish life, because my children have one set of roots, cherished links with family, openings to language and memory, in this troubled and troubling place. The journal offers a space for negotiating a peaceful identity space for my sons, a kind of belonging that is living and livable for them and for myself. Constructing these terms for Oren and Ari required mapping the available practices by which identity is constructed in Israeli life. I find these practices to be complex, appealing, disturbing, in some ways unacceptable. I want to connect us to Israel, but not always on Israel's terms.

But how can this be done on paper? What is the relation of writing to life? What kind of writing appreciates the manyness of things, is respectful of difference, is bold and careful, makes contact without appropriation? How can a writer let many voices speak in her text, avoid closure, and still articulate political commitments requiring judgment and action?

Hélène Cixous finds/creates something like this kind of writing as *écriture féminine*, a "textual way of spending" that offers a writer or reader (male or female) "a *living relation* with language and experience."[3] Michael Bakhtin calls on the term "heteroglossia" to get at the friction between contending forces in a text or a system, between what is admitted and what is excluded.[4] Pam Hiyashi coined the term "democratic text" to feature the political impulse at work in a textual commitment to plurality and a struggle against mastery.[5] While these different explorations of writing are not identical, they gesture toward a common direction, one in which "Kibbutz Journal" seeks to move. It's a direction shared by a number of other feminist writers, including Minnie Bruce Pratt, Toni Morrison, Gail Griffin, Patricia Williams, Trinh Minh-ha, Nancy Mairs, and others.

These visions of writing share a set of politicized commitments.[6] They are, in their different ways, typically open, fluid, exploratory, challenging, inviting, reflective. Verena Conley characterizes *écriture féminine* as "a writing, based on an encounter with another — be it a body, a piece of writing, a social dilemma, a moment of passion — that leads to an undoing of the hierarchies and oppositions that determine the limits of most conscious life."[7] Nancy Mairs describes "the aim that has underlain [her] work" as her desire "to nullify the splitting — of body from spirit, of critic from creator, of intellect from desire, of self from other."[8] Since hierarchies and dualisms are often written into our accounts of things, writing that stays within familiar limits is likely to reproduce those hierarchies and oppositions despite its intentions to do otherwise. Encountering another within a posture of openness, attentive to what Bakhtin calls "the internal dialogism of the word," lightens the impulse toward control and allows contending interpretive possibilities to emerge.[9] When Gail Griffin explores contrasting meanings of the word "professor," for example, finding both "to affirm openly" and "to make a pretense of," she cracks open the space of internal dialogism of her own vocation while she continues to inhabit it.[10]

This kind of writing employs a certain caution toward the terrain it explores, wary of premature closure. Bakhtin reminds us that "no living word relates to its object in a singular way," so efforts to pin things down once and for all are necessarily doomed.[11] Clarice Lispector writes that "the word shatters between my teeth into frail pieces."[12] Rather than seizing their prey, these texts "take the words in their hands and lay them with infinite delicateness close by things," trying for a proximity that allows multiplicity to endure, even to flourish.[13] Writing in this way sabotages the pretensions of the "god's-eye point of view," the bloated equation of objectivity with writing from nowhere.[14] These writings are located, knit closely into a place, a time, a body, a set of relationships, an institutional history, not because they are not generalizable, but because they need to recognize their particular partial perspective in order to connect with others. Mairs comments that "my text is flawed not when it is ambiguous or even contradictory, but only when it leaves you no room for stories of your own."[15] The "effort not to see violently" disempowers the colonizing gaze, engages without consuming, allows for movement and change.[16]

The presence of the author within the text facilitates listening and responding; the reader may feel that she or he could talk back, argue, laugh, weep. The texts encourage us to improvise. The author's presence is not that of static authority but of emergent participant, not so much writing about herself as writing herself. Cixous, speaking about/with Lispector, says, "It is what I write you that continues and brings *I* into continuity. But the *I* is no longer an author who masters."[17] Trinh Minh-ha remarks that she wants to be a writing woman, not a written woman.[18] Gail Griffin calls on "a constant interplay between anecdote and analysis, living and reading, experience and theory" to explore the very concrete navigations of her own voices and silences in her world of feminist teaching.[19] Karla Holloway and Barbara Ogur, in their essays in this volume, share this authorial practice.

These texts are often funny, indignant, earnest, confused, resentful, loving, vulnerable, bereft. Because the voices in them are emergent and unfinished, they do not always show themselves in a flattering light. Lispector wonders, as she disorders the expected temporal flow of narrative, whether she has "abandoned a whole system of good taste."[20] Patricia Williams places herself within the discourse of the law and the institutional circumstances of law school not as a heroic savior but as a contending, sometimes uncertain, participant — crumbling self-confidence, frayed bathrobe, and all.[21] Minnie Bruce Pratt's emergent voice finds no resting place in her struggles against racism and anti-Semitism, only a fierce, sometimes weary determination to "do her own work."[22]

The work these texts accomplish is often multisensory and multidimensional: Lispector concentrates on exploring taste, smell, and touch as ways of knowing.[23] Trinh juxtaposes stills from her films with italicized texts and multicolumned pages. Both Lispector and Trinh return often to the image of the hands: hands that move or pause, labor or rest, hands that seek another hand to hold. Lispector's character eats a cockroach to find the animal in herself; Toni Morrison's lives with ghosts, charting the crossings between life and death.[24] Interruptions and continuities are braided together, put into circulation, overflow, resist enclosure. They do not lay down the law so much as they make an appeal, issue a call.

The commitment of these texts to what Morrison calls "the living word" does not necessarily lead to an evasion of other kinds of commitments.[25] One of the tensions in this kind of text surfaces in the pull between openness to otherness, with its appreciation of difference and reluctance to judge, and commitment to political change, to a vision of equality, justice, or peace. Michael Du Bois has suggested that the key to political commitments within a democratic text is in the moment after the judgment, when a pledge or engagement is accompanied by a continued openness, a refusal of fixity.[26] Griffin's response to sexual harassment on her campus exemplifies this complex double posture: her anger is informed and complicated, but not derailed, by her meditations on the erotic dimensions of learning and the dissonance of female authority.[27] Similarly, Morrison's anger about Africanism, the "disrupting darkness" of racial imagery in American literature, is put forward in the service of more complex encounters with that literature, not its dismissal.[28]

Another tension in this diffuse project of feminist writing is that between the desire to disrupt phallocentric convention and the desire to communicate effectively. The risk of reinscribing phallocentric order in our texts is matched by the risk of failing to link up with our audience. Feminist disruptions such as those by Cixous and Trinh feature experimental writing practices, pushing the limits of linear order so as to sabotage the constraints of more familiar narrative devices. First-person narratives such as those by Mairs and Pratt resist convention in different ways — not so much by the organization of their texts, which are often quite controlled and orderly, as by the ways that the authors (and the readers) inhabit them. This can be a fruitful tension if each set of risks and desires is deployed to put pressure on the other. There is, finally, more than one way to write against the grain.

"Kibbutz Journal" hopes to participate in this project, to contribute to the collective conversations and enactments through which feminist hetero-glossia, *écriture féminine*, and democratic texts emerge. Unfortunately, and predictably, there are considerable risks to this kind of writing: the risk of being dismissed in intellectual circles for sentimentality and lack of rigor, in political circles for the absence of a clear agenda of action. The risk of offending people one loves. The risk of self-indulgence: once one begins to crack the facade of impersonality in writing; where is the line between useful self-exploration and self-indulgent narcissism? The risk of self-scrutiny becoming confessional, so that a move against power (of the dominant narrative) becomes reincorporated into power (of the judging gaze).

The brunt of these reservations has fallen most heavily on "Kibbutz Journal" in the context of my writing as a mother. On the one hand, the most consistent anchor I have found in my negotiations with Israel is that of a mother of sons who in some ways belong in that restless place. While of course other identity positions come into play, mothering recurs as my most compelling point of departure because it is as a mother that my questions about borders and identities in Israel most desperately matter to me. Mapping the identity practices of others can be an arrogant and judgmental act, the casual critical glance of the cross-cultural tourist. The concrete concerns of mothering require a more nuanced involvement: I cannot either dismiss or embrace the cultural terrain this journal charts.

But the terrain of mothering is itself fraught with difficulties. It is thoroughly overcoded with sentimentality, usually thought to be the opposite of rational deliberation. It seems to invite a biological misinterpretation in which appeals to a physical essence (e.g., "maternal instinct") replace analyses of a cultural practice. It marks a kind of power that is as capable of abuse as any other. It is deeply sunk into a cultural nexus that readily becomes maudlin about mothers while denying any real power to women. Mothering itself requires continuous reinterpretation, re-creation, in order to be inhabitable. While mothering guarantees no foundation, it provides both a potent starting point and a besieged investment. Mothering, critically construed, offers both my strongest motives and my most ambivalent tools in the effort to plot the topographies of identity available in Israel.

But of course there is no one Israel. There is more than one discernible voice, more than one detectable construction of who lives here and what they are about. A state or a society is never a simple or static thing; it is always a process of becoming. Global politics tends to be understood in unitary terms — i.e., we say "Israel" acts in a certain way on the world stage — but that common, one-dimensional way of speaking conceals great turbulence. One of the tasks of the Israeli state has been to mask this turbulence by defending its borders — geographic, cultural, linguistic — in ways that coopt or delegitimize its subversions. The less common views are hard to hear when the hegemonic voices are turned up to full volume. The dominant view becomes deafening, but the less legitimized views continue to intersect the identity practices in complex ways. They do their work on the slant, so to speak, uncaptured by the prevailing orthodoxy, but not unaffected by it.

On one level, the landscape of Israeli political and cultural life is amazingly diverse. There are the differences among/between the many languages of the immigrants and the official Hebrew; between *sabra* (Israeli-born) Hebrew and the Yiddish of the *shtetl*; between Hebrew and the widespread use of English in commerce, tourism, and diaspora fundraising; between Hebrew and the subterranean Arabic of the nearly one million Israeli Arabs (not counting the population of the occupied territories). There are also the discrepancies and antagonisms within the Hebrew-speaking population: between Ashkenazi (European) and Sephardic (Mediterranean) Jews, secular and religious Jews, conservative and radical Jews, Jewish women and Jewish men. There are the subtle contests between the available linguistic registers within which self-understanding can be constituted: between the images of globalism and nationalism, victims and warriors, remembrance and forgetting, nostalgia and irony. The self-understandings that people can articulate within Israeli society always hum with the energies of these interacting interpretive moments; the words they can speak are always already half someone else's.

Set against this unruly cacophony are the agents of unification — the state, the rabbinate, the media, the schools — and the relentless unifying drone of the discourse of "national security." On this level, the centralizing forces work at corralling the diversity within Israeli life, and thus at reinforcing the reigning claims to meaning. Further harnessing the dominant self-understanding is a particularly strident masculinity, a gendered underwriting of the central order. The dominant cultural forces are threatened by the manyness of things, the differences that put constant pressure on prevailing truth claims and self-understandings. The agents of unification attempt to tame the fractious dialogues, to marshal the (selective) resources of history, geography, and culture around a single understanding of what it means to be Israeli.

Mapping the spaces upon which these forces interrupt and reinforce one another requires detecting the resonances and incompatibilities among various ways of representing the world, and between ways of representing the world and ways of being in the world. One looks for the symbolic markers by which people establish and assess their sense of themselves. This way of looking at global politics seeks the locations in language that constitute people's sense of pride or shame, their fears and expectations, their resistances and resignations. It looks at the practices of power involved in struggles to maintain and to reformulate identities.

Charting identity practices is a dangerous business in that the people whose self-representations one is scrutinizing are always more than those representations. Identity practices are not the same as personalities. Rather, they are the cultural network of symbols and codes within which their residents must navigate. There is always slippage and contestation among the recurrent images anchoring the available understandings people have of themselves and others. One can locate such slippage by following identities as they travel, contrasting their reception in different contexts in order more fully to chart their relations. Encounters among different languages offer a space for reflection on the requirements of each. Identities on the move highlight the construction of the cultural categories they encounter, and might even occasion their reconstruction.

To illuminate the above discussion I have selected the following entries from my journal. Each addresses some dimension of identities — their production, maintenance, or subversion. Taken together, they suggest some of the commerce among gender, race, and militarism through which identity practices in Israel are put into circulation.

April 20

Oren and I went with Gili's father, aunt, and uncle to the magnificent Soreq caves in the Absalom Reserve. Awesome stalagmites and stalactites haunt the caves, and the air is wet and full of mystery. At the concession stand I found, much to Oren's delight, M&Ms for sale; I also found some fascinating productions of Israeli identity on the tourist postcards. In among the wide-angle landscape shots of the Sea of Galilee and Masada were two cards also evidently deemed by the Israeli tourist industry to be fitting mementos for visitors and the folks back home. One shows a close-up of a sabra, a cactus with large flat leaves and round, orange fruit. The caption states "The renowned Israeli sabra cactus, symbol of the Israeli temperament: prickly on the outside, sweet on the inside." Behind the cactus stand two young, attractive women in military uniform; wearing red flowers on their shirts, they stride forward with confidence and exchange friendly smiles. The cloudless blue sky shines brightly behind them. The card radiates reassurance. The military trappings on the cheerful young women are quintessentially Israeli, the prickly "outside" hiding the sweet feminine "inside." The women, like the cactus, are "in bloom," sporting flowers, promising new life. The young women smile at each other, happy with life; their military presence is folded into that contentment; all is well with the Israeli army, where beautiful young women serve their country with a smile. There is no mention of women's second-class status in the military, their obligatory presence there in perpetual subordination to men. No sign of what these charming, attractive soldiers might actually be doing, which is probably staffing the clerical ranks of the Israeli war machine. Do they, perhaps, call up the reserve soldiers who police the territories? Do they keep the files on suspected "terrorists"? Do they consider their hands to be clean? They wear their jaunty red caps at a dashing angle; they are proud and strong. Their beauty and boldness resides robustly in their military uniforms; the military presence is unremarkable in itself, imbricated thoroughly into what it means to be an Israeli.

A second postcard reproduces a reassuring militarized identity from a different angle. It shows three men, each wearing green military fatigues and sporting a different-colored beret—purple, red, brown. They stand with arms clasped around one another, backs to the camera, their faces hidden against a wall. Not "a wall"—"The Wall." The caption reads "Meeting of fighters at the Western Wall." Their faces are pressed up against the white-gold Jerusalem stone, which gleams hot in the sun. Their weapons hang from their shoulders; they appear to be weeping. Their bodies are slim and strong, their arms well muscled; they are strong enough to cry, perhaps for a fallen comrade, perhaps even for a slain enemy. Again, Israeli strength and youth, this time marked masculine, is interwoven with fatigues and weapons; to be a real Israeli *is* to be a soldier. In Israeli postcard iconography, the women soldiers are strong enough to serve their country, to *be* Israeli, with a smile; the men soldiers are strong enough to grieve at the costs of their military service while continuing to provide it. Serve, serve, serve; little room here to recognize young people with a different dream, a different strength. Little room for some other kind of Israeli.

The second postcard represents a line of Israeli kitsch going back at least to the creation of Zionism. In "The Kitsch of Israel" Avishai Margalit tells about a "bizarre controversy" in 1988 over the question "Should soldiers be allowed to cry at the funerals of their comrades?" "The general who opposed crying — or, more exactly, being seen crying — was a *sabra* born on a kibbutz; the one in favor of showing soldiers crying was a Polish-born survivor of the Holocaust. . . . The argument about the soldiers' tears goes to the heart of a fundamental issue about sentimentality in the Zionist revolution, the revolution that took it upon itself to mold a 'New Jew.' The New Jew was not supposed to shed tears."[29] For the *sabra* general, tears recall the helpless Jews of the ghettos and pogroms, history's victims. His rejection of public vulnerability aligns Jewish victimization with a no-nonsense, "stop whining and do something about it" revision. The Polish-born general is more representative of immigrant and diaspora Jews, the archetype of a righteous sentimentality. Sometimes this emotional register takes a universal turn, as in the mensch ideal, a good guy who is sensitive to the suffering of others. But more often it is channeled by state-orchestrated ideological production lines into an insular tribalism, as in the "we-love-Israel, the-world-is-against-us" form of self-justification.[30]

No one in this debate suggests that the military does not need a policy about soldiers crying or not crying, that such matters are private and none of the state's business. The production and deployment of images of young people in uniform is so central to Israeli self-understanding and so critical to its marketing of itself abroad, not to mention to its ideological and commercial tourism, that the constitution of the phenomenon as a public issue was self-evident. The postcard Oren and I secured along with our M&Ms is the heir of countless photographs, poems, songs, books, legends. Margalit writes: "The quasi-official symbol [of soldiers and sentiment] became the photograph by the veteran *Time* photographer David Rubinger which shows a group of unshaven helmeted paratroopers at the wall, in the middle of which one sees — *ecce homo* — a young, blond, lean-featured fighter with his eyes lifted upward and holding his helmet next to his heart. This altogether non-Jewish gesture of taking off one's hat at a holy place became the symbol of the return of the New Jew to the site of his holy temple."[31]

Margalit also indicates some of the sources of resistance to the earnest images of self-satisfaction. A popular rock song by female performer Sy Hyman criticizes the saccharine, sanctimonious tone of the "Shooting and Crying" literature, as does poet Dennis Silk in "On the Way to the Territories." Hyman's song is banned from the army radio station in Israel.[32] I remember some of Gili's stories about his days in the military, his indifference to patriotic exhortations and his small gestures of defiance. Yoram Binur's descriptions of his lackadaisical performance in the military in *My Enemy, My Self* are a refreshing change from most such memoirs, which seem to combine gung-ho soldiering with just the right touch of moral reflection.[33] It is crucial to keep evidence of these resistances and interruptions in mind, both to help explain the continuous onslaught of the prevailing identity practices and to marshal some resources against them.

In Israeli military kitsch, as in most state-produced excuses for killing people in war, the actual soldiers, their particular lives and concrete characteristics, are only important to the extent that they can be recruited into legitimacy-sustaining discourses. Margalit notes that Israel boasts "a thriving industry of books dedicated to the memory of fallen soldiers. It was almost invariably pointed out that they secretly read the poetry of Rachel ('the Israeli Anna Akhmatova') or Alterman ('the Israeli Gumilov'). These soldiers never got much credit for their love of poetry while alive, only after their premature deaths."[34] I am reminded of the book my friend Phyllis showed me called *The Perfect War*, by James William Gibson, about the U.S. war in Vietnam. The author talks about the production of the image of the unknown soldier: "The Pentagon, which waived its informal rules that 80% of a body must be recovered for it to be designated an Unknown, has now *intentionally destroyed all identification records related to the Unknown* to prevent inadvertent disclosure of information that might provide clues to the identity of the man intended to be a universal symbol of Vietnam battle dead."[35] The Israeli government is certainly not alone in marshaling the resources of kitsch-in-uniform to deflect criticism, to forestall unpalatable questions from grieving families, to paste over the recurrent cracks in hegemonic, militarized, national identities. But they have raised kitsch craft to new depths. In *In the Land of Israel*, novelist Amos Oz finds both Israeli and Palestinian authorities working overtime to produce "that delightful weepy sensation" which cements identity in the bittersweet warmth of shared self-pity, self-congratulation, self-indulgence.[36] Milan Kundera gives a wonderful explanation of kitsch in *The Unbearable Lightness of Being*: "Kitsch causes two tears to flow in quick succession. The first tear says: How nice to see children running on the grass! The second tear says: How nice to be moved, together with all mankind, by children running on the grass! It is the second tear that makes kitsch kitsch."[37] Margalit calls the second tear a "meta tear" — the glue holding together a state-orchestrated collective identity.[38] The Israeli military/state apparatus cannot refrain from politicizing and administering the grief of soldiers because it wants to control that second tear, the watershed that can either lubricate or dissolve a national identity.

April 24

The whole family went to Jerusalem on Saturday to show Gili's visiting aunt and uncle around. When we got to the Wailing Wall (with characteristic insolence, Gili calls it the Whining Wall), we met the now familiar mix of tourists, believers, and soldiers. I was standing with the kids when a woman with a decided U.S. accent approached me and asked if I wanted to pray. The conversation switched quickly to English, and she asked if I am Jewish. "No," I reply, knowing my answer will be unacceptable to her, "but my sons are half Jewish." Predictably, she dismisses this. "That's not possible," she claims. "You can't be a chicken and a bird at the same time." "A chicken is a bird," I jibe. The woman gives up on me and approaches my mother-in-law, opening her Bible, gesturing toward a page, and asking Batsheva why I did not convert to Judaism. I did not understand most of the ensuing conversation, but found out later that the woman wanted Batsheva to read a passage that asked forgiveness for allowing her son to marry a *goya*. Batsheva, bless her heart, shrugged her refusal and walked away. I sure married into the right family.

This incident evoked a smoldering resentment in me that comes somewhat as a surprise. What is at stake for me, that I keep attending to this woman's words? Perhaps it is because she represents the worst of the U.S. presence in Israel. The extreme Gush Emunim, the Kahane thugs, and other ultranationalist groups boast large numbers of immigrants from the United States in their membership. (So, of course, does the Left, including feminism.) Or perhaps it is simply because her narrowminded religious intolerance continues to irritate me. She personifies the arrogant pretensions of those who take the Bible to be a land-granting institution and assume their faith is an infallible and total guide to life.

These explanations, while they ring true, don't quite address the lingering feeling of assault that stirs my resentments. I think the incident rankles because that woman, and the many like her, would deny my sons the link to this place that I claim for them. The secular laws of Israel recognize half Jews and allow them to be citizens; and coming from Hawaii, to be *hapa* (half one ethnicity, half another) is commonplace. (Although ironically my children are not viewed as *hapa* in Hawaii because the category "Jew" is nearly invisible there, incorporated completely into the category of *haole*, or white person.) I claim a legitimate place for Oren and Ari in this vital, troubled land; it is one-half of their heritage, one-half of their stock of family, kin, community. I'm struggling to learn Hebrew to make it easier for them to do so, to give them at least a limited grounding in the language of their father and his people. Every holiday I try to teach the kids a bit more, to give them the cultural markers and practices that will make their Jewish side recognizable to them.

Sometimes this quest takes on comic proportions. Gili is so thoroughly secular that he is no help at all in these endeavors. Last December I put together a Chanaukka celebration, using a borrowed menorah and scrambling through Oren's books to find appropriate songs and recipes. When asked about Chanaukka, Gili thought for a moment and said, "Well, you sing some songs, eat some food, that's about it." "Some songs?" I asked indignantly. "Could you be a bit more specific?" Under prodding, he called home and asked his sister. Unhelpfully, Narkis said, "Well, you sing some songs, eat some food, that's about it." So we knitted together our familial version of the holiday, managed to have some decent latkes and kugel for dinner, and lit our menorah in front of the Christmas tree.

Oren resides quite happily within his *hapa* status. He proclaims cheerfully to his friends that he is "half Christian and half Jewish." (I hesitate at the label "Christian," wondering if I can stretch it to be a broadly cultural rather than religious category. If Gili can be a secular Jew, can I be a secular Christian?) But *hapa*-ness plays differently in different contexts. When we lived in Indiana, I took Oren to a nearby Methodist church to enroll him in preschool, so he could meet some other kids and have a big indoor gym to play in on cold winter days. Like every other preschool we looked at, this one began each morning with a prayer and the Pledge of Allegiance. I did not want Oren forced into these rituals, which are quite foreign to him but heavily over-coded for me. So when the teacher asked us our religion, as part of the application process, I replied (a bit evasively) "His father is Jewish." The teacher immediately assured me that, while Oren needed to be quiet during the prayer and the pledge, he was not required to participate in either. (We left the relationship between being Jewish and objecting to the Pledge of Allegiance unexplored.) The warm and enthusiastic young woman in charge of the preschool was thrilled to have a Jewish child in her class and immediately invited me to do a Chanaukka presentation for the children. ("Uh-oh," I thought to myself, "I'd better go do some research on Chanaukka!") But in the end there was no need . . . the teacher called me the next morning, regretful and apologetic. The church fathers had ruled that no Jewish cultural or religious practices were allowed in the classroom. She reported quite frankly that, in the opinion of the men who run the church, exposure to religious differences at such an early age was unacceptably subversive. "We only have these kids a few hours a week," she explained, repeating what she had been told. "We don't want to dilute our message." I suggested that religious differences could be viewed with interest and appreciation rather than fear, but it was clear that she had been disciplined and saw no way out. Oren could attend the school, she explained carefully, but Jewishness could not.

The church fathers in Indiana are not so unlike the orthodox woman at the Wailing Wall. For the men, Oren was not acceptable because he was too Jewish; for the woman, he was not Jewish enough. Both had territory to protect. Neither could appreciate the rich opportunities that his *hapa*-ness provides, to cross cultural borders, to appreciate alterity, to cherish the ironies and potencies of contrasting cultural practices.

There are different ways to do one's Jewishness. I do mine from the outside, so to speak. In Israel, in some ways I am a Jew . . . because, in the conflict with the Palestinians, it's clear which side I live with. Oren and Ari will come to their own terms with their *hapa* background, terms that I hope will contain affection and respect, along with a critical eye, for all the traditions they inhabit. But the woman at the Wailing Wall would deny them, and me, this room to negotiate. For her, Jewishness is not something you do, it's something you either are or are not; a being, not a doing. Jewish identity is fragmenting all around her (the last time we were here, the heated debates about the status of some of the immigrants took place under the rubric "What is a Jew?"), and my interlocutor is scrambling to put it back together, to make it one thing, to force me to do it "right" or not at all.

In *Storm from Paradise* Jonathan Boyarin talks about "the link between the given and the chosen" in his Jewishness.[39] He finds a constitutive double consciousness in Jewish identity: first, because Jewishness has been defined for millennia by its rejection and, second, because there was an historical beginning, in the time of Abraham, for the Jewish people. Jewishness, then, has always been defined in relation to what it is not, and to what went before. Giving Jewishness a history, and naming its intimate relationship as Other to that which rejects it, can help to denaturalize it as a category. When an identity is given a context and a history, it is harder to endow it with a timeless and unchanging status. (Although the struggles to define that history and give meaning to that context can quickly become occupied by inflexible orthodoxies.) Boyarin finds in Jewishness "a model of an elaborately inscribed identity constructed in the awareness of difference."[40] Viewing Jewishness as a complex inscription calls attention to Jewish identity as an act, a way of writing meaning onto life. Boyarin takes heart in the openings to otherness that a historically and relationally situated Jewishness can provide.

And so do I. When Oren was only a few days old, I found myself fussing, much to the amusement of a Jewish colleague, about his future bar mitzvah. Looking back, the real focus of my concern was the larger question of negotiating his participation in Jewishness. A relationally, temporally defined Jewishness can make some room for Oren and Ari, offer some welcome on the borders of an identity terrain defined as permeable and shifting, not rigid and fixed. Of course, they will ultimately have to negotiate that terrain for themselves, but Gili and I can either provide the resources to do so or withhold them, open doors or close them, sustain relationships or allow them to wither. My antagonist at the wall would foreclose these negotiations before they begin, denying the contingent linkages and partial affirmations that my sons require.

May 6

Today is Yom Zikaren, Memorial Day, dedicated to the memory of the over 17,000 soldiers killed in Israel's wars since the founding. Memorial Day looks backwards, mourning the fallen. Last night there was a ceremony on the kibbutz, today one at the *ulpan* (Hebrew school for immigrants), both accompanied by the nationwide sirens signaling a minute of silence, remembering. I stood last night with my arms around Oren thinking, please, no more wars, not for my sons, not for these children, no more killing. Would Israel's self-understanding shift if it could redefine the remembering more toward the future, toward a determination to avoid more death rather than a commitment to avenge past deaths? Did anyone else perform a silent revision, warding off future loss instead of acknowledging that from the past?

What selective memories are honored in this country of heroes and martyrs, knit together with blood and history. Everywhere there are memorials, ceremonies, official and unofficial rituals that define the past, capture it within the cruel and tragic boundaries of Israeli kitsch. Israel's kitsch, their categorical agreement with being, underwrites a militarized self-understanding. Heroes, martyrs, victims; suffering, persecution, survival. It is a gendered kitsch, with heroes and warriors occupying the masculine pole while victims carry the feminine. The hegemonic Israeli self-understanding is thoroughly masculine, the proud and manly warrior prepared to die for his country.

In Avishai Margalit's discussion of the "should soldiers cry" debate, he misses the gendered dimension of its kitsch. Everything about tears that the *sabra* disdains is coded feminine: helplessness, vulnerability, passivity, openness to others, grief in the face of loss. The prized "take-charge" mentality of the *sabra* is both a gung-ho masculinity and a strong-man resignation. The archetypic *sabra* soldier is eager to do what's necessary, regretful of its costs, yet proud to pay the price exacted. Marcia Freedman comments that Israeli schoolchildren learn, as a maxim, the words of a famous Israeli warrior, "It is good to die for one's country."[41] In *A Purity of Arms*, Aaron Wolf's account of his time in the Israeli army stresses the hero status accorded to soldiers by schoolchildren; he and his friends all wanted to be pilots or paratroopers.[42] (The girls cannot become pilots or paratroopers; do they dream instead of marrying them?) Gili says that as children they referred to Jews who would not defend themselves, contemptuously, as "soap." It is not a discourse that fields many openings for critical reflections on patriarchy, war, or racism.

The military inscribes itself on physical, social, and bodily landscapes in myriad ways. The ubiquitous brown uniforms on young bodies, machine guns swinging from shoulders, seem to inhabit every street, bus stop, restaurant. Military training writes itself on bodies, on their carriage and musculature, in a particularly public way in a society in which nearly every Jew has been or will be a soldier. Aaron Wolf recalls the identifiable bodily markings left by paratrooper training: "Repeated jumps from the Eichmann [a training tower] leave a paratroop trainee with burn scars along his neck that give me a certain amount of prestige in Israel, where everyone knows what they mean. When I hitchhike to the kibbutz on weekends, people who pick me up, seeing the burn marks, say respectfully, 'Oh. Paratroop training, eh?!' I am supposed to think of the burn marks as a badge of honor."[43] The symbolic significance of the characteristic burn marks has completely replaced their functional meaning, since the Israeli military no longer uses parachute jumps in combat. (They have been replaced by the more precise operations of transport helicopters.[44]) But the bodily markings of military prowess continue to provoke the admiration of schoolchildren and the respect of adults, and to underwrite a militarized, implicitly masculinized notion of citizenship.

Both "Arabs" and "women" are folded neatly into the metaphoric apparatus privileging Jewish, military, masculinity. "Women" (that is, Jewish women) take up necessary supporting roles: the plucky female officer; the loving wife back home; the devoted mother raising her children to be soldiers. They are coded feminine, positive, lesser than men but crucial and highly valued in their place. Not so dissimilarly, the representational practices creating "Arabs" also work the feminine side of the street. "The Arabs" are weak and stupid, not a worthy enemy but a sneaky and therefore dangerous one. "The Arabs" are a mystery, ruled by dangerous primal forces, inscrutable, disloyal to civilization. The Arabs play the woman to Israel's man, a deadly affair. They are coded feminine, negative, lesser than Jews, stirring both fear and contempt, yet in their own way necessary to the maintenance of hegemonic Jewish self-understanding. Could the widespread contempt for "the Arabs" — manifested frequently and casually even among my Labor Party friends who support "land for peace" — be a kind of self-contempt, a disdain for those who allow themselves to lose?

In *Keepers of the History* Elise Young finds a consistent intertwining of "Arab" and "feminine." She recounts a terrible incident on May 20, 1990: a group of Palestinians from Gaza are waiting at Rishon Lezion, a place outside Tel Aviv from which day labor can be arranged (commonly known as a slave market). A young Israeli man in army fatigues, carrying an automatic weapon, asks to see their identity cards. As the men offer the required cards, the Israeli opens fire, killing seven and wounding ten more. The media reports: "One Israeli driving by stops his car, jumps out, and dances around their bodies." The media further reports that "the murderer is himself a victim — of unrequited love. He told his girlfriend that if she would not take him back, he would go out and kill. Palestinians and women became confused in his mind."[45]

Young goes on to analyze women as an occupied territory, conflating Palestinian and feminine from the opposite political direction, with the intent of valorizing them as parallel victims. It is hard to know precisely what to make of this semiotic intersection of race and sex (Jew is to masculine as Arab is to feminine) when it is put to work by the killers as well as the defenders of the weak. The metaphors become even more slippery when complicated by the history of anti-Semitism, where it is the Jew who is feminized, othered, construed as irrational, dirty, and sinful, while the Christian passes as the implicitly masculine universal norm, the fully human "man."

June 9

Several times during my interviews and conversations I have heard someone say, about some other group perceived as a bit farther to the left, they've "gone too far." Dov says that the organizers of the Givat Haviva conference have "gone too far." Galia Golan says that Women in Black have "gone too far." Tamar and Sarit say that *Challenge* magazine, an English-language publication of the Israeli Left, has "gone too far." What does this mean? Sarit and Tamar interpreted it to mean that the offenders have, from the speaker's point of view, become too sympathetic to the Palestinians, to the point of identifying completely with them and forgetting that there is a legitimate Jewish point of view. But what is it, exactly, that is endangered? Is this a sexual anxiety, a fear of intimacy with the Other? Perhaps the offender has gone too far the way teenagers in the back seat of a Plymouth might go too far, committing an irrevocable act, somehow destroying their innocence and purity. Is this why the epithet "whores of Arafat" is so frequently flung at Women in Black? Or is it more generally about acceptance, a fear of accepting the other so they're not so Other anymore, and you, then, are not so special, so unique, so separate? Maybe "whores of Arafat" is similar to the white epithet "nigger lover," designating not primarily a sexual connection but a general, and illegitimate, acceptance of the other. And since acceptance of the other might be the first step toward the forbidden intimacy, the two could be wound up together. I wonder what "going too far" means from the Palestinian point of view.

The phrase "going too far" connects identity with a spatial metaphor, suggesting a link with the territorial dimensions of identity practices in Israel and in all modern nation states. Each people has and demands its proper place, always defined as a state. Jonathan Boyarin points out that the creation of the state of Israel was a convenient solution to Europe's "Jewish problem"; it got rid of the Jews without having to examine the state policies in Europe and North America that helped create the crises of Jewry.[46] Presumably the state of Israel will someday figure out that the creation of a Palestinian state could perform a similar clearing operation. Meanwhile, the territorialization of identity gives it a sharp either/or component: either our land or their land. Palestinians and Israelis both struggle to delineate their collective identities by establishing and maintaining themselves as nation states. Identity collapses into (existing or sought for) state power.

Boyarin gives a particularly striking example of the conflation of identity and territory: he cites "the recent arrest of an Israeli Jewish educator named Arna Mer on charges of 'identifying with the enemy.' The specific act she was censured for was going to the Palestinian town of Jenin to provide educational materials to school children."[47] Collective identity based on control of territory sponsors a zero-sum calculation: either we belong here or they do. Not both. No sharing.

One can imagine collective identities that are deterritorialized, knit together in some other ways, perhaps from shared memories, daily practices, concrete needs, specific relationships to people, locations, and histories. Such productions would be more narrative than territorial; they might not be so exclusive because they are not so relentlessly spatial. Connection to a particular place could still be honored as one dimension of identity, but its intensities could be leavened by less competitive claims. Participation in such identities could be self-consciously partial, constructed, mobile; something one does and re-does everyday, not a docile space one simply occupies and controls. Empathy across collective identities constructed as fluid and open could enrich, rather than endanger, one's sense of who one is.

Deterritorializing identity is a cultural shift likely to sound a bit premature to Palestinian ears; after all, I have a state, with the securities (and liabilities) of citizenship, from which to dream about uncoupling identity. So do the Jews. The Palestinians do not. Certainly everyone needs a secure and autonomous place to live; but must identity be so intensely bound up with the exclusive governance of territory? All territorializations of identity have a strong "let's pretend" dimension — in denying that anyone was there before, in ignoring competing claims, in cultivating a myopic nostalgia for lost origins. It may be that a deterritorializing of identity is a more promising path toward securing a Palestinian homeland than is the current battle between mutually exclusive claims to belong.

In that sort of world, Arna Mer's act would not need to be one either of a traitor or a hero. It could simply be a life.

Afterthoughts

I come back to the relation between writing and life. Is it possible to write oneself into a place and time, to slip or stumble through an intricate foreign landscape, to change oneself without losing one's way? The intriguing heteroglossia and appalling orthodoxies in Israeli life both invite and rebuff writerly advances. Writing across such shifting boundaries is a bit like looking through a window that is also a mirror: I am looking at others, looking at myself, looking at myself looking at others, on and on. The metaphor of the window/mirror gestures toward the vigorous back-and-forth such writing entails, the endless multidirectionality (and potential narcissism) of the self-reflective gaze. But this metaphor is also limited: it suggests a fixed frame of reference and a visual process of knowing. The writing process sought here is an active engagement, not a passive comprehension: I don't just look out a window at an Israel that is already there, but rather I reach with my words to bring the Israel that I see into focus, to shape the contours and name the possibilities that become speakable through the relations they entail. And this way of writing is multisensory, calling on the taste, touch, sound, and smell of things, not only the sight. There is a kind of affirmation in such sensory immersion, a desire to connect and to know. While the content of the words is often critical, perhaps judgmental, the process itself is an act of love.

Notes

1. This essay draws selections from *Kibbutz Journal: Reflections on Gender, Race, and Militarism in Israel* (Pasadena, Calif.: Trilogy Books, 1995). This chapter was first presented as a lecture entitled "Borders and Identities: Race, Gender, and Militarism in Israel" in the Women's Studies Lecture Series at Duke University, February 1, 1994. I have revised that lecture in light of the discussion that followed, when the focus of questions was on the creation of the journal and the writing practices it entails.

2. This definition of theory was offered by Mary Louise Pratt in "Multi-Culturalism and De-Colonizing Cultural Theory" (paper presented at a conference entitled "Multiculturalism and Representation," University of Hawaii at Manoa, April 28, 1989.

3. Verena Andermatt Conley, introduction to *Reading with Clarice Lispector*, by Hélène Cixous (Minneapolis: University of Minnesota Press, 1990), vii–viii.

4. M. M. Bakhtin, "Discourse in the Novel," *The Dialogic Imagination*, ed. Michael Holquist, trans. Caryl Emerson and Michael Holquist (Austin: University of Texas Press, 1981), 257–422.

5. Pam Hiyashi made this remark in my feminist theory graduate seminar, Department of Political Science and Women's Studies Program, University of Hawaii at Manoa, Spring 1994. My thanks to her and to the other students in that class for their careful attention to questions of voice, representation, and politics in feminist writing.

6. In calling attention to the intersections among these kinds of writing, I don't want to collapse them completely into one another or ignore important debates about/among them. While they are often controversial and clearly not the same, nonetheless they share a kind of pulse, an inclination toward the politics of voice and representation that has promise for feminisms. For further discussion of *écriture féminine*, see Ann Rosalind Jones, "Writing the Body: Toward an Understanding of *l'écriture féminine*," in *Feminist Criticism and Social Change*, ed. Judith Newton and Deborah Rosinfelt (New York: Methuen, 1985), 86–101; and Pamela Bunting, "The Body as Pictogram: Rethinking Hélène Cixous's Écriture Féminine," *Textual Practice* 6, no. 2 (Summer 1992): 225–46. For a discussion of Bakhtin, see Tzvetan Todorov, *Mikhail Bakhtin: The Dialogical Principle*, trans. Wlad Godzich (Minneapolis: University of Minnesota Press, 1984).

7. Conley, introduction, vii.

8. Nancy Mairs, *Voice Lessons: On Becoming a (Woman) Writer* (Boston: Beacon Press, 1994), 36.

9. Bakhtin, "Discourse in the Novel," 279.

10. Gail Griffin, *Calling: Essays on Teaching in the Mother Tongue* (Pasadena, Calif.: Trilogy Books, 1992), 165.

11. Bakhtin, "Discourse in the Novel," 276.

12. Clarice Lispector, *Aqua Viva*, quoted in Cixous, *Reading with Clarice Lispector*, 45.

13. Hélène Cixous, *Vivre l'orange* (Paris: Des Femmes, 1979), quoted in Trinh T. Minh-ha, *When the Moon Waxes Red* (New York: Routledge, 1991), 141.

14. Donna Haraway, "Situated Knowledges: The Science Question in Feminism and the Privilege of Partial Perspective," *Feminist Studies* 14 (Fall 1988): 575–99.

15. Mairs, *Voice Lessons*, 74.

16. Cixous, *Reading with Clarice Lispector*, 54.

17. Ibid., 25.

18. Trinh T. Minh-ha, *Woman, Native, Other* (Bloomington: Indiana University Press, 1989), 28–30.

19. Griffin, *Calling*, ix.

20. Clarice Lispector, *The Passion according to G. H.*, trans. Ronald W. Sousa (Minneapolis: University of Minnesota Press, 1988), 12.

21. Patricia J. Williams, *The Alchemy of Race and Rights: Diary of a Law Professor* (Cambridge: Harvard University Press, 1991).

22. Minnie Bruce Pratt, "Identity: Skin, Blood, Heart," in *Yours in Struggle: Three Feminist Perspectives on Anti-Semitism and Racism*, ed. Elly Bulkin, Minnie Bruce Pratt, and Barbara Smith (Ithaca, N.Y.: Firebrand Books, 1984), 41.

23. My thanks to Jorge Ferrandez for pointing out the conjunction of taste and knowing in Portuguese in my feminist theory graduate seminar, Department of Political Science and Women's Studies Program, University of Hawaii at Manoa, Spring 1994.

24. Lispector, *Passion*, 158–62; Toni Morrison, *Beloved* (New York: Alfred A. Knopf, 1987).

25. Toni Morrison, *Lecture and Speech of Acceptance upon the Award of the Nobel Prize for Literature, Delivered in Stockholm on the Seventh of December, Nineteen Hundred and Ninety-three* (New York: Alfred A. Knopf, 1994); see also Toni Morrison, *Playing in the Dark: Whiteness and the Literary Imagination* (Cambridge: Harvard University Press, 1992), 4.

26. Michael Du Bois made this remark during a discussion of heteroglossia and politics in my feminist theory graduate seminar, Department of Political Science and Women's Studies Program, University of Hawaii at Manoa, Spring 1994.

27. Griffin, *Calling*, 125–44.

28. Morrison, *Playing*, 91.

29. Avishai Margalit, "The Kitsch of Israel," *New York Review of Books*, November 24, 1988, 20.

30. Ibid., 21.

31. Ibid., 20.

32. Ibid., 20, 22.

33. Yoram Binur, *My Enemy, My Self* (New York: Penguin, 1989).

34. Margalit, "Kitsch of Israel," 20.

35. *New York Times*, May 29, 1984, quoted in James William Gibson, *The Perfect War* (Boston: Atlantic Monthly Press, 1986), 8.

36. Amos Oz, *In the Land of Israel*, trans. Maurie Goldberg-Bartura (New York: Vintage Books, 1984), 165.

37. Milan Kundera, *The Unbearable Lightness of Being* (New York: Harper and Row, 1984), 251.

38. Margalit, "Kitsch of Israel," 20.

39. Jonathan Boyarin, *Storm from Paradise: The Politics of Jewish Memory* (Minneapolis: University of Minnesota Press, 1992), xi.

40. Ibid., 66.

41. Marcia Freedman, *Exile in the Promised Land* (Ithaca, N.Y.: Firebrand Books, 1990), 32.

42. Aaron Wolf, *A Purity of Arms* (New York: Doubleday, 1989), 15.

43. Ibid., 191.

44. Ibid., 201.

45. Elise Young, *Keepers of the History: Women and the Israeli-Palestinian Conflict* (New York: Teachers College Press, 1992), 1, 2.

46. Boyarin, *Storm*, 121.

47. Ibid., 123.

Deborah Gray White

Private Lives, Public Personae

A Look at Early Twentieth-Century

African American Clubwomen

Sometime during the late 1920s, Mary Roberts Rauchert, a free-lance editor, reviewed the first draft of Mary Church Terrell's autobiography and counseled Terrell to write about her life as a woman, and not about her public persona. The book reads like a list of accomplishments.[1] In it there is much about her founding of the Washington D.C. Woman's Club, her years as the first president of the National Association of Colored Women (NACW), her work in the suffrage and civil rights movements — but there is little about her private self, her feelings and emotions. Rauchert thought Terrell ought to put more of her own problems into the manuscript, that she needed, for instance, to address "the very problem of friends." In what was a rather harsh but, relatively speaking, delicate criticism, Rauchert told Terrell that no life was completely "a cause," that the manuscript needed more about her family life; it needed more "heart"; that as written the book was "a little cold."[2]

While Rauchert's criticism seems a bit cold, it is impossible to read Terrell's autobiography without concluding that there was more than a grain of truth in Rauchert's report. Terrell's approach, however, was not very different from that of other African American women. Most were cautious about putting their private lives and histories in the hands of media that had for centuries stereotyped and slandered black women. Rather than take such a risk, they hid their private selves from the public.

Historian Darlene Clark Hine calls this self-conscious black female resistance. In an illuminating article entitled "Rape and the Inner Lives of Black Women in the Middle West: Preliminary Thoughts on the Culture of Dissemblance," Hine argues that "because of the interplay of racial animosity, class tensions, gender role differentiation, and regional economic variations, Black women, as a rule, developed and adhered to a cult of secrecy, a culture of dissemblance, to protect the sanctity of inner aspects of their lives." She further explains: "The dynamics of dissemblance involved creating the appearance of disclosure, or openness about themselves and their feelings, while actually remaining an enigma. Only with secrecy, thus achieving a self-imposed invisibility, could ordinary Black women accrue the psychic space and harness the resources needed to hold their own in the often one-sided and mismatched resistance struggle."[3]

In a 1987 article that I wrote on black women's manuscripts, I found that the secrecy Hine writes about was manifested in the paucity of black women's personal papers in libraries and archives. Scarred by the negative images and the adversarial relationships they traditionally had with public institutions, black women have proven reluctant to let go of any material that might reveal their private selves.[4] Thus, we have mostly the public personae of black women to analyze. In the case of early twentieth-century clubwomen, we have personae of proper selfless women: they built institutions such as libraries, settlement houses, hospitals, schools, and old-age homes. They defended black womanhood and organized antilynching campaigns. Night and day they served their race and their community.

Certainly, their accomplishments were important, in fact essential, to the survival of black communities. But what about the private lives of these women? If we look behind the veil of asexual Victorianism and public service in order to discover some of their true feelings, do we, as they feared, provide grist for the vilifiers' mills? Do their private feelings make us think negatively of them? I think not. I think, as Hines suggests, that what we really do when we look beyond the public personae is provide the basis for a more sophisticated analysis of black women. We make them real people instead of icons. We give them a depth of personality that is seldom associated, in history or in stereotype, with black women. And, equally important, we tell some stories that are seldom told. What follows is a peek at some of those stories, a quick look at the contrast between the private lives and public personae of a few twentieth-century African American clubwomen.

The issue of domesticity provides an interesting study of contrasts. There were few club leaders who did not at one time in their lives give a speech, write an article, or organize a mothers' club for the purpose of instructing black women on the importance of making homes clean and nurturing places. Yet few approached domesticity and motherhood with the same confidence they exuded in public. Margaret Murray Washington, for example, was childless herself, but helped raise her husband's children. She also helped organize the Tuskegee mothers' club and the E. A. Russell Settlement. She did all this despite her confessions that she was a "dull pupil" when it came to housekeeping, knew little about the care of children, and in fact disliked them.[5]

Mary Church Terrell saw the contradiction between her public pronouncements on the important role women played in the home and the lecturing and organizational work that ironically took her away from it. It troubled her. She was sure her public service was needed, but though she looked comfortable before the public, she was very ambivalent about what she was doing. It was too "wearing on the nerves," she complained, to take 5 and 6 A.M. trains, travel all day to reach one's destination by 11 P.M. or midnight, and then not be paid the previously agreed-upon lecture fee.[6] Then there was always the unexpected. Long train delays sometimes wreaked havoc on her schedule, and even worse, she once got her period on a train while hectically trying to meet an engagement in the Midwest. This particular event so exasperated Terrell that she considered giving up lecturing. To her husband Robert she wrote that she was "more and more convinced that a woman's place is at her own fireside."[7]

She felt especially guilty over her separation from her daughter Phyllis. Torn between the financial contribution she felt she should make to her household, the service she thought was her duty to perform for black women, and the desire to be at home with her daughter who "depends upon me to protect her," Terrell reasoned that the best compromise was to find ways of making money at home.[8] But that was easier said than done. When she was at home, her time was consumed with housekeeping and child care. Terrell did not complain about the latter as much as the former, for she truly felt that if she did not spend time with Phyllis and her adopted niece, Mary, they would fall prey to the omnipresent forces of immorality.[9]

Housework, though, was something else. Despite the fact that she sometimes had housekeeping help, Terrell, who sewed, varnished woodwork, upholstered chairs, and generally managed her household, found domestic work to be "a regular sepulcher in which a woman who wants to accomplish something burns her talent and time." This same woman who publicly lectured blacks on the value of "homes, more homes, better homes, purer homes," who praised the NACW for their efforts in starting mothers' clubs that taught black women "the best way to sweep, to dust, to cook and to wash," this same woman hated housework so much that she likened herself to a "prisoner bound with heavy iron chains which no amount of effort or determination or yearning of the intense kind can break."[10]

Her ambivalence about domestic work, however, was just something that she, like other black women, had to live with, just as they also had to live with Jim Crow. Forced segregation was inescapable. No matter where the club leader lived, as long as she had to travel to meetings on the railways, seek food and lodging, ride an elevator, or enter a building to get to an elevator, she was bound to encounter Jim Crow. But not all leaders handled the indignity the same way. The variety of responses reflects the variety of ways in which club leaders managed race and class on a personal level, as well as the ways in which race and class came together to affect the lives of some African American women.

Some black women during the late nineteenth and early twentieth centuries were brave in their resistance to Jim Crow. Like Rosa Parks, the catalyst of the modern civil rights movement, in 1884 Ida B. Wells refused to move from her seat in a "whites only" railway car and was dragged away by three white men. She sued the railroad and won her case, only to have the Tennessee State Supreme Court overturn her victory.[11] Similarly, Charlotte Hawkins Brown sued the railroads after twelve white men forced her from her Pullman berth near Aniston, Alabama. She won a small settlement, but, according to her, it was not enough to erase the indignity of regularly being put out of Pullman cars at all hours of the night. Especially painful was her feeling that, despite the compensation, "inconveniencing a Negro woman or humiliating her, in the eyes of the court, was never considered as any great outrage on personality."[12]

Jim Crow was such an outrage, though, that club leaders who could avoid the insult did so. Instead of using public accommodations and convention halls, they stayed with friends and held local and national meetings in black churches. On trips they packed food to eat so they would not have to search for restaurants that served blacks or go hungry on trains that served food only to whites. For the few who could get away with it, there was the option of passing.

Many NACW leaders were so light that they were often either mistaken for white or else they deliberately passed for white in order to enjoy the creature comforts usually denied to the dark-skinned. Victoria Earle Mathews, the founder of the White Rose Mission in New York, Josephine St. Pierre Ruffin, founder of the New Era Club in Boston and editor of the *Woman's Era* newspaper, Terrell of Washington, Fannie Williams of Chicago, Adella Hunt Logan of Alabama,[13] Sylvania Williams of New Orleans, and Alice Dunbar Nelson of Maryland were just a few of the prominent association women who at one time or another were taken for, or deliberately passed for, white. In many ways, these women had the best of both worlds: they enjoyed elite status in black circles, while being able to avoid the inferior treatment meted out to blacks. Because they did not pass all of the time, they did not have to cut off relationships with their black families and friends, which among other things would have meant moving to a different part of the country or world. In effect, even while being public advocates for black women, light-skinned NACW leaders, unlike their darker counterparts, had some control over when race would become an issue in their lives.

However, some control was not total control, as Terrell's records — the most complete on this subject — reveal. Terrell did sometimes travel in dirty and unventilated Jim Crow cars; while on the lecture circuit she was sometimes forced to enter back doors and take service elevators; and once while lecturing in Athens, Georgia, she was forced to eat her dinner in the kitchen with a dog.[14] Additionally, Terrell was discriminated against during World War I when she landed a job in a government office. Her boss hired her thinking she was white; when he later discovered his mistake, he dismissed her on false charges of incompetency and misconduct.[15] Despite these experiences, though, Terrell did not have to bear the full burden of color. Her near-white father had had advantages that allowed him to provide an upper-class upbringing for his daughter, including preparatory school, a college education at Oberlin, and a European study tour. Her diary and autobiography provide evidence that in her young and middle-aged years she frequently ate at white restaurants, sat in white sections of theaters, and held memberships in white organizations. Very often she traveled on trains in comfort as a white person.[16] She was not above moving from the Jim Crow railway car to the "whites only" car if the former was too crowded or dirty. More than once she traveled as a white woman to a destination where she was to give a lecture on the virtues of black womanhood and was not at all disturbed by the puzzled look on the faces of her black hosts when she exited the train from the "whites only" section. In fact, she once made light of her passing when she described her "leaps from the black to the white woman's role" as nothing short of "acrobatic."[17]

Alice Dunbar Nelson also left evidence of her passive passing. Not as confident as Terrell, she agonized over possible discovery on the night that she, her niece, and her stepdaughter arrived to take their seats at an Atlantic City show. She had bought three tickets from an agent who thought she was white. When she arrived with her darker-skinned companions, she feared they would be turned away: "I was conscious of misgivings, and a pounding in my throat when we approached the ticket taker. Suppose he should not let us take our seats? Suppose the ticket seller had sold the seats to me thinking I was white, and seeing Elizabeth and Ethel should make a scene. I choked with apprehension, realized that I was invoking trouble and must not think destructive things, and went on in." There was no scene, but Dunbar Nelson could not help wondering what life would be like without racial barriers. "How splendid it must be," she mused, "never to have any apprehension about one's treatment any where."[18]

While this sentiment was no doubt echoed by blacks of all complexions, the club leader who could pass faced a peculiar dilemma, one which especially revealed the potential for conflict between her public and private personae. Should the near-white club leader go through her day telling her race to whites who did not know her so that she could be degraded by second-class treatment, or should she just not tell people she was black and agonize or feel guilty over her passive passing? As a race woman the club leader was pledged to fight racism. Passing might be seen as complicity with an obnoxious practice that others, like Wells and Brown, risked life and limb resisting. It might be viewed as a selfish indulgence that was inaccessible to the masses of black people. On the other hand, though, resistance — even just a verbal objection — required nerves and courage that only a few possessed. Furthermore, the lone club woman, without the refuge of her organization, in a world where the black woman went unprotected by men or law, was vulnerable. If she put her personal needs first, did she necessarily forsake her public duty?

While there is clearly something paradoxical in the private passing for white of women who publicly defended black womanhood, on different levels it was perfectly consistent with their publicly avowed purpose to represent black women and speak for the race. What better agent of equality was there than a black who could be taken as a white? What better proof of the equality of the races than black individuals functioning in a "whites only" capacity with no one the worse off for it? Rather than betraying the race, perhaps they were proving to themselves and to their confidantes (usually future generations) that race in America was socially constructed to give whites an undeserved advantage over blacks.

This is the attitude Terrell took. It would be foolish to ignore the comfort and safety she gained by passing for white, but it would be equally foolish to ignore the fact that she did not feel guilty for passing. In a personally revealing incident, she traveled in the "whites only" car from Miami to Key West, Florida, in 1909 and talked freely with white women who wanted to know who she was. Rather than give her first and middle name, she cagily replied that she was "a Terrell." They in turn wanted to know if she was related to Governor Terrell of Georgia, for they saw such a "resemblance in the eyes." The tone of the diary entry suggests that as these women searched for visible evidence that they were traveling with southern aristocracy, Terrell was laughing at them.[19] To her, the episode was proof of the arbitrary, capricious, and constructed nature of racism. After all, as a mulatto she was supposed to be a sensuous seductress, but here she was sharing a train car with southern ladies who took her as a member of Georgia's ruling elite. Here in her private world was naked proof of her public pronouncements on the equality of the races.

This incident makes special sense if seen within the idiom of mediation.[20] Because the very light-skinned could literally go in and out of the white world, their perspective was potentially broader and less illusionary than that of the darker-skinned. Norma Boyd, a founding member of Alpha Kappa Alpha, a black sorority organized during the association's heyday, thought that the light mulatto's role as mediator was something special. According to her, had it not been for the "people who could pass for white and come back and report just how the other half does," the "darker people in our race would have had an awful time."[21] Whether Boyd was right is not as important as her perception of her special mediator role. She saw herself as an occasional spy in the enemy's camp. Apparently so did Terrell. This made these near-white club leaders anything but "tragic" mulattoes — those literary figures hopelessly caught between the black and the white worlds, being raised as whites only to discover, to their downfall, that they were by blood connection black.[22] If Terrell is any example, near-white NACW leaders identified with black America and were sincere in their advocacy of black women. They did have more political connections with whites, and their education, exposure, and general experiences made them more confident around whites than were most blacks. Still, while they had one foot placed tenuously in the white world, their anchor was dropped securely in black America.

Dropped as securely, at least, as many of darker complexion who accepted white cultural forms at the expense of black traditions. Despite Brown's brazen stand against Jim Crow, one cannot help but suspect that she had deep insecurities about being black. More than most club leaders, she lectured blacks incessantly on the need for refinement and culture.[23] Moreover, this dark-brown-skinned woman expressed a strange pride in revealing that she had an enslaved fair-skinned, blue-eyed grandmother who was a blood descendant of John D. Hawkins, the English navigator; that some of the blood of great southern slaveholders and railroad builders flowed in her veins.[24] Jane Edna Hunter, the founder of Cleveland's Phillis Wheatley Association, also seemed very insecure in her racial identity. Born of a dark-skinned mother and near-white father, Hunter was determined to "escape the curse" of her dark heritage. According to her biographer, Adrienne Lasch Jones, throughout her childhood and young adult years, Hunter associated blackness with poverty, contempt, and subjection. She was humiliated when she had to push her cousin's baby carriage through the streets of Charleston, because she thought her light brown skin made her superior to her darker-skinned relative. Although she eventually decided to dedicate her life to race work, there was always a nagging insecurity. Jones claims Hunter was "plagued by feelings of inadequacy" and "constantly worked to position herself to seem more important than she felt she really was."[25]

Of course, neither Brown nor Hunter was enveloped and protected by the black upper classes, and this had to make some difference in the way they handled personal issues of race. Unlike many of the near-white clubwomen whose class combined with color to make their lives relatively comfortable, both Brown and Hunter came from relatively humble backgrounds and both had very short marriages to men who did not provide an entrée to elite circles. In contrast to someone like Terrell, whose education was planned by her parents and whose husband was a municipal court judge, both Hunter and Brown came by their education and life's work rather haphazardly. Brown went to Cambridge, Massachusetts, schools, but had it not been for the generosity of a white philanthropist, it is doubtful that she would have had the one year of normal training she received before starting her own school in Sedalia, North Carolina. Hunter, on the other hand, lived with different relatives and benefactors after her father died, and could not attend school on a regular basis. Lacking the buffer and the anchorage that economic security and upper-class affiliation provided, Brown and Hunter practiced their own kind of "passing." They embraced white culture, or "passed" culturally, as a means of boosting their own sense of worth and ironically as a way of legitimating their "race woman" status.[26]

Regardless of complexion, however, dealing with whites, especially white women, was never easy. All NACW leaders had to harness their emotions and put on an artificial face before whites. Only in their private correspondence and in their diaries do a few association leaders let go of "the cause" and express their real feelings. At the heart of these feelings was a profound distrust of white people, despite the fact that many of them had white benefactors and an occasional white friend. Terrell, for instance, had many white acquaintances, some of whom dated back to her Oberlin days. Yet she likened speaking before white audiences as akin to going into battle. "I shall buckle on the armor," she wrote her husband before a talk in front of an Ohio audience. "It is a very nerve-wracking performance, this thing of representing my race and trying to please narrow-minded white people, too."[27] Margaret Murray Washington also had extensive white connections.[28] Still, she kept white women at arm's length. She found those who visited Tuskegee to be especially untrustworthy and devious — so much so that she never let them roam around the campus without a carefully selected escort. In a 1911 letter she labeled "somewhat confidential," she instructed Booker T. Washington's secretary to make sure that building attendants at Tuskegee knew when white women were visiting so that the latter could be properly escorted. Revealing in private correspondence what she would not dare say in public, she wrote: "I always try to give Southern women special attention because they can be so nasty."[29]

Washington could have received the advice that Charlotte Hawkins Brown's mother gave to her: "Try to make friends of those southern white people, for they can make you or break you."[30] Brown, whose normal school training was financed by Alice Freeman Palmer, the first woman president of Wellesley College, found that it was not only southern whites that she had to be wary of, but northern whites, too. She thought that in their eagerness to appease their southern friends, northerners were just as racist and just as disrespectful of black women.[31]

Her experiences with a group of northern white women also taught her that they could just as easily hurt her feelings. During the first years of the century, Brown began a relationship with women who eventually founded the Sedalia Club, a Massachusetts-based club formed exclusively to help support Brown's school, the Palmer Institute, in Sedalia, North Carolina. The correspondence between Brown and the white club members reveals the latter to be presumptuous and arrogant. Certainly Mary Grinnell could be described this way.

Grinnell donated outstanding sums of money to the school and in the process became somewhat of a confidante for Brown, who asked Grinnell advice on just about everything from running the school to love and matrimony. In 1910, right before her short-lived marriage, Brown asked Grinnell whether she should marry, and after a year, when the marriage broke up, she again asked Grinnell for advice on what she should do. Grinnell's responses seemed sincere enough. Before the marriage she had counseled Brown to consider whether she could turn herself away from her school and give full-time attention to her husband, and wondered if Brown's fiancé loved her to the point of suffering when not with her. After the two separated, Grinnell wrote sympathetically about the trials of life, reminded Brown that she still had her work, and told her to ignore the malicious gossip about the separation.[32] What had to be troubling to Brown was the fact that Grinnell avoided face-to-face encounters. As long as the relationship remained on a letter-writing basis, Grinnell was a friend. But when Brown tried to arrange meetings, Grinnell gave her the cold shoulder. She not only rudely rejected invitations to visit Palmer Institute, but she discouraged Brown from visiting her.[33] One of these snubs occurred during the time when Grinnell was advising Brown on her impending marriage. When Brown suggested that she visit Grinnell in New Bedford, Grinnell hedged. First she wrote that it would be okay but added that she would explain to her friends that Brown's visit was strictly business. Revealing her duplicity even more, Grinnell asked Brown, "Where would you stay?" She explained that she could not let her stay in one of her guest rooms because, as she put it, "my colored cook won't know what to think of me." Grinnell also claimed that she did not want to insult Brown by putting her in with the maid. Since in any case she did not want "to create any back door gossip," Grinnell thought it best for Brown to stay overnight with a "respectable colored family" which Grinnell wrote she would be happy to find.[34]

Brown's records do not reveal whether she went to New Bedford, but they do reveal that her relationships with other women of the Sedalia Club were equally frustrating. From 1902 to the mid-1920s, the white women donors demanded almost obsequious obedience to their every request. They told her that they trusted her to make the major decisions affecting her school, but then dictated instructions of the minutest detail.[35] Typical of the instructions she received on curriculum were those sent by Mrs. Frances A. Guthrie. Along with her $150 donation and boxes of boys' clothes were instructions for Brown to teach personal cleanliness, modesty, and basic reading, writing, and arithmetic. Girls were to be taught sewing, table setting, and millinery so that they would be useful to their employers and to their husbands. The parents of Brown's pupils, Guthrie insisted, were "nearly all very ignorant people," and so while she knew Brown was inclined toward offering her pupils "Higher Education," she advised her to abandon her dreams because "neither their parents, their possible husbands, or they themselves are yet ready to receive" such an education.[36] Since an angry rebuttal would have been self-defeating in such situations, Brown did what many clubwomen who needed white support for their projects did. She dissembled. She begged and she begged humbly. She "Uncle Tommed," but she kept her eye on "the cause" and over the objections of her financiers she expanded the building plant, the acreage, and the curriculum of Palmer Institute.

Brown's true feelings were revealed only occasionally. A hint of dissatisfaction with Helen Kimball, the initial donor of the school's land, is revealed in a discussion over the future of Kimball's maid, Mary. It seems that Kimball sent fifteen-year-old Mary to Palmer after promising the girl's mother to provide Mary with some schooling. At the end of one year Kimball wanted Mary to return to her domestic job, and Brown, knowing that Mary wanted to be a nurse, objected. Apparently Brown, who was known among blacks for her feistiness, made her feelings known in a letter that Kimball found objectionable. "I did not like the tone of your letter regarding Mary," wrote Kimball, who then proceeded to tell Brown that Mary would be a more "useful woman" earning money as a maid than she ever would be as a nurse; that the "longer she is kept upon books the harder *work* will be for her."[37] Brown's immediate response to Mary's leaving is not known. If, indeed, she got up the nerve to write more than a bold letter, there is no record of it before 1921.

That year, though, she exploded. In an effort to gain more control over their contributions, the Sedalia Club decided to collect money from individual subscribers and send it in a lump sum. They refused to give Brown the names of the people who had contributed for fear that she might independently solicit their help; and when the club sent their money, they dictated how it was to be spent. Brown was livid. In a rare instance when she did not sacrifice self-respect for "the cause," when indeed the two were inseparable, Brown wrote, "If the folks up there who give are not satisfied with the management of things they can withdraw. . . . I don't need anybody to help me."[38]

Brown wrote revealingly of the personal stress behind trying to reconcile the different "causes" in her life. She reasoned that the education of black youth, especially black girls, was, if not the greater goal, at least a method of countering negative stereotypes. Yet her northern contributors were forever urging her to increase her southern support, which came slowly, and only when she prostrated herself before southern monied interests. Aware that her self-effacing behavior on behalf of her school often negated efforts made by clubwomen to counter such stereotypes, she wondered in writing just how much of the black woman's pride would have to be sold for the cause of black education. "I have already gained the interest of some people who will give me money for the school, but absolutely have no regard for the rights of negro women in terms of courtesy," she wrote. "The question in my heart and mind, and God only knows how it hurts, is just what are they going to ask me to submit to as a negro woman to get their interest, for there are some men who occupy high places who feel that no negro woman whether she be cook, criminal or principal of a school should ever be addressed as *Mrs.*"[39] Brown agonized privately, but in public she continued to "wear the mask," and her school survived. Despite its always unstable financial standing, the Palmer Institute remained a substantial black rural educational institution until the 1970s.[40]

If the attitude of progressive white women was very frustrating, so were relationships between black women. It would seem that, with such unsure ground all around them, the bonds between the women of the NACW would be strong, that they would establish friendships that could weather the challenges of the times. Some friendships did develop, such as that between Margaret Murray Washington and Josephine Yates. Clubwomen also served as role models for each other. While Ursula Wade and Charlotte Hawkins Brown looked to fellow southerner Margaret Washington, Mary McLeod Bethune inspired Alice Dunbar Nelson.[41] But usually national black club leaders were not friends. Allies, yes. Friends, seldom.

So insidious were the forces against amity and sorority that club leaders prayed for deliverance. "Keep us, O God, from pettiness" was the first line of the NACW's prayer. It went on to ask for freedom from faultfinding and self-seeking; for strength to make them calm, serene, and gentle. Knowing that they were more or less united on the large issues of race, class, and gender, they feared the repercussions of "mistrissism"—the damage of personality conflicts. Their prayer reflected their fears: "Grant that we may realize that it is the little things that create differences; in the big things of life we are one. May we strive to touch and know the great common woman heart of us all, and, O Lord God, let us not forget to be kind."[42] To be kind, gentle, calm, and serene were traits that were critical for women striving to be examples of perfect black womanhood; they were also traits that easily escaped them. Although they knew this to be true, few understood why. The most thoughtful explanation was given by Wells. She attributed the constant discord to the fact that every decision was taken as a referendum on personality. Rather than women taking private feelings and domestic experiences as a point of departure for self-conscious political awareness and action, as happened in the 1960s and 1970s when activist women made the "personal political," women of the NACW made the political personal, taking every philosophical and tactical difference as a personal slight. "Always the personal element," lamented Wells. "It seems disheartening to think that every move for progress and race advancement has to be blocked in this way."[43]

Wells's comment was precipitated by one of her many clashes with NACW leaders. In 1900 she had a "falling out" with Agnes Moody, president of the Ida B. Wells Club (a club named in Wells's honor), because Moody felt Wells had usurped her power. Ten years later, after Wells had earned a reputation as a no-nonsense, uncompromising race leader, Wells was hissed off the floor at the NACW convention because the delegates thought that she was making a power play for the editorship of *National Association Notes*. That episode contributed to her sound defeat in the organization's 1924 presidential election, which went to Mary McLeod Bethune.[44]

Like Wells, Terrell had a particularly stormy career in the NACW. She would write the most stinging five- and six-page letters to fellow clubwomen over seemingly minor disagreements or incidents. Daisy Lampkins, Nannie Burroughs, Mary McLeod Bethune, Addie Hunton, Margaret Murray Washington — each received letters at one time or another with words from Terrell that were as sharp as darts. She also did despicable things. When, for instance, Bethune journeyed to New York from Florida in 1932 with the intention of visiting Terrell, who at the time was working for the Republicans and staying at the Waldorf Astoria, Terrell refused to see her, sending word to the reception desk that she was too tired. A shocked Bethune left New York the very next day.[45]

Almost all conventions or large meetings, national or otherwise, brought out some of the worst in the NACW leaders. Biennial election meetings were especially contentious. From this distance they seem more akin to political conventions than conferences organized around self-help issues. How else can we describe the 1920 meeting where then-president Mary Talbert began campaigning against her successor, Hallie Q. Brown, fully a year before the election was held.[46] In 1933, Illinois club leader Mary Waring won out over Brown in a bitter struggle that saw Waring distributing handbill propaganda as far south as Alabama, and Brown traveling the country giving speeches trying to convince clubwomen to support her in opposition to Waring.[47]

What made these encounters particularly discouraging was the personal ego that leaders invested in their partisan battles, making the conflicts very emotional, and making regional and national conventions anything but places to nurture friendships. At the eleventh annual Washington State convention of 1928, the tension level was so high during a debate on who should be sent to the national biennial that a delegate rose from her seat, walked to the podium, and knocked the chairwoman's bell (apparently used to maintain order) right out of her hands.[48] This episode was just a prelude to the bitterness that marked the national convention itself. Alice Dunbar Nelson remembered the convention as one "too exhausting to think of." She called Brown a "dirty little rat" for using unscrupulous methods to gain office, and she described the contest for executive secretary (between Sallie Stewart and Rebeca Stiles Taylor) as a "bitter war." On top of everything else, during the three-and-a-half-hour Executive Board meeting there was so much "dirty linen washed" that some of the members were reduced to tears.[49] This was not unlike a meeting described by Terrell where some very "unkind and unpleasant" opinions were aired when a member submitted a personal finance voucher for the NACW to pay.[50]

There certainly is no denying that behind the public veneer of perfect black womanhood, NACW leaders were very often mean and callous toward each other, venting anger and frustration that seemed to have no other outlet. Why was there so much discord? Why so much dissension among women who were natural allies? There is no question that Wells was right about the fact that club leaders were taking political and philosophical differences personally. But Wells analyzed only a symptom of the problem, not the problem itself. More central was the fact that racism and sexism made the NACW one of only a few outlets for black women's leadership talent, but its goals were too limited to effectively use all of the abilities of all of its leaders. This turned it into a political arena where clubwomen became rivals for office and influence instead of companions and friends in the cause of self-help. When we realize that color and class differences made for as much distance between the leaders of the NACW as it did between all other African American women; that many club leaders were just too self-righteous and high-strung, too sure that they and only they knew what the race needed, what women wanted, and the course that black women should chart, we draw closer to the reasons for the endless friction.

If this friction made the association's leaders less than perfect, it certainly did not make them less worthy representatives of black women. In fact, because they shared some of the same everyday concerns and experiences as the women they spoke for, they were potentially more effective. If we extrapolate from the varied experiences reported here, we see that like black women everywhere in America, NACW leaders worked outside the home, chafed under double-duty, and were torn between their work, their public duty, and their maternal responsibilities. Jim Crow was as much of an insult to them as it was to all black women, and though they did not work as domestics in the homes of white women, relationships with white women were very often a trying part of their lives. To the extent that they managed the exigencies of life under the restraints imposed by racism and sexism, and still managed to coordinate nationwide self-help projects, they were their own best arguments for race advancement.

But no matter how successfully it was done, the way in which these NACW leaders personally handled the exigencies of life as black women was not the basis on which they sought to make themselves models of black womanhood. Club leaders wanted only the public persona examined: the woman who was outwardly virtuous, self-sacrificing in race and women's work, and articulate in defense of black women. No doubt, on some level they understood that if their private lives were examined along with the public, they would not measure up to their own very rigid notions of perfect black womanhood, for contrary to their public statements and personae, their private lives revealed ambivalence regarding Victorian notions of homemaking and motherhood, a willingness to forsake resistance to racism for personal comfort, a tendency toward self-righteousness, and a penchant for the kind of politics which the NACW officially denounced. This did not make them less suitable leaders, however. It made them more effective because they were more, rather than less, like all other black women, who also adhered to a cult of secrecy and a culture of dissemblance.

Notes

1. Mary Church Terrell, *A Colored Woman in a White World* (Washington, D.C.: Ransdell Inc., 1940).

2. Mary Roberts Rauchert to Mary Church Terrell, n.d., Box 102-2, no. 44, Mary

Church Terrell Papers, Moorland Spingarn Research Center, Howard University, Washington, D.C. Rauchert's comment was similar to those made by editors and publishers. See Mathilde Weil to Terrell, November 19, 1932, Box 102-2, no. 40; and Herbert Jenkins to Terrell, April 15, 1927, Box 102-2, no. 29.

3. Darlene Clark Hine, "Rape and the Inner Lives of Black Women in the Middle West: Preliminary Thoughts on the Culture of Dissemblance," *Signs* 14 (Summer 1989): 95.

4. Deborah Gray White, "Mining the Forgotten: Manuscript Sources for Black Women's History," *Journal of American History* 74 (1987): 237–42.

5. Margaret James Murray to Booker T. Washington, October 26, 1891, and July 17, 1892, *The Booker T. Washington Papers*, ed. Louis Harlan, Stuart B. Kaufman, and Raymond W. Smock (Urbana: University of Illinois Press, 1974), 3:174–75, 248–49. Washington was twenty-seven years old when she admitted that she disliked children.

6. Mary Church Terrell to Robert Terrell, January 16, 1905, Container 3, Mary Church Terrell Papers, Library of Congress, Washington, D.C. See also Mary Church Terrell to Robert Terrell, January 16, 1905, Container 4.

7. Mary Church Terrell to Robert Terrell, August 18, 1900, Container 3, Mary Church Terrell Papers.

8. Mary Church Terrell to Robert Terrell, August 12, 1900, Container 3, Mary Church Terrell Papers.

9. Mary Church Terrell to Robert Terrell, n.d., Container 3, Mary Church Terrell Papers.

10. Terrell Diary, entries for November 29, 1909, and November 20, 1909, Container 1, Mary Church Terrell Papers.

11. See Paula Giddings, *When and Where I Enter: The Impact of Black Women on Race and Sex in America* (New York: William Morrow, 1984), 22–23.

12. Charlotte Hawkins Brown, "Some Incidents in the Life and Career of Charlotte Hawkins Brown Growing Out of Racial Situations, at the Request of Dr. Ralph Bunch," Brown Papers, Series 1, no. 2, Arthur Schlesinger Library, Radcliffe College, Cambridge, Massachusetts.

13. Dorothy C. Salem, "To Better Our World: Black Women in Organized Reform, 1898–1920" (Ph.D. diss., Kent State University, 1986), 106.

14. Terrell Diary, entries for February 24, 1905, October 15, 19, and 28, 1905, and April 5, 1908, Container 1, Mary Church Terrell Papers.

15. Terrell, *Colored Woman*, 250–59.

16. Terrell Diary, entries for January 28, 1908, April 9, 1908, July 26, 1908, February 9, 1909, April 4, 1909, and June 10, 1909.

17. Terrell Diary, entry for January 30, 1908.

18. Gloria T. Hull, ed., *Give Us Each Day: The Diary of Alice Dunbar-Nelson* (New York: W. W. Norton, 1984), 69.

19. Terrell Diary, entry for April 8, 1909.

20. Hazel Carby's discussion of this concept in a literary framework has relevance for historians. See Hazel Carby, *Reconstructing Womanhood: The Emergence of the Afro-American Woman Novelist* (New York: Oxford University Press, 1987), 89–94.

21. Norma Boyd, transcribed interview, Black Women's Oral History Project, Arthur Schlesinger Library, Radcliffe College, Cambridge, Massachusetts, 26.

22. Carby, *Reconstructing Womanhood*, 73, 187 (n. 24).

23. See Deborah White, *Too Heavy a Load* (New York: W. W. Norton, forthcoming), chap. 1, for more information on Brown and the need for culture.

24. Brown, "Some Incidents." See also Charlotte Hawkins Brown, "A Biography," Brown Papers, Series 1, no. 1, 17.

25. Adrienne Lasch Jones, "Jane Edna Hunter: A Case Study of Black Leadership," in *Black Women in the United States*, ed. Darlene Clark Hine (Brooklyn: Carlson Publishing, 1993), 12:25–31, 94.

26. Ibid., 50, 256. See also Tera Hunter, "The Correct Thing: Charlotte Hawkins Brown and the Palmer Institute," *Southern Exposure* 11 (September–October 1983): 37–43.

27. Mary Church Terrell to Robert Terrell, October 27, 1912, Container 3, Mary Church Terrell Papers.

28. Washington herself says she lived with white Quakers, but there seems to be some question as to whom she lived with as a child. See Harlan et al., eds., *The Booker T. Washington Papers*, 2:514–15 (n. 1).

29. Margaret James Murray Washington to Emmett Jay Scott, January 31, 1911, ibid., 10:565–66.

30. Brown, "Some Incidents," 5.

31. Ibid.

32. Mary Grinnell to Charlotte Hawkins Brown, January 25, 1910, September 6, 1912, December 18, 1912, February 17, 1913, July 12, 1911, Brown Papers, Series 2.

33. Mary Grinnell to Charlotte Hawkins Brown, September 21, 1915, Brown Papers, Series 2.

34. Mary Grinnell to Charlotte Hawkins Brown, March 4, 1910, Brown Papers, Series 2.

35. Most of Brown's correspondence between 1911 and 1917 demonstrates this point. See, for example, the 1914 Easter Sunday letter from Annie Howe to Brown. See also Kimball's instructions to Brown in letters dated August 17, 1909, December 1, 1906, March 6, 1907, March 22, 1902, and August 30, 1909, Brown Papers, Series 2.

36. Frances A. Guthrie to Charlotte Hawkins Brown, n.d. [ca. 1907], Brown Papers, Series 2.

37. Helen Kimball to Charlotte Hawkins Brown, April 9, 1908, Brown Papers, Series 2.

38. Charlotte Hawkins Brown to Mrs. Macmahon, October 14, 1921, Brown Papers, Series 2.

39. Charlotte Hawkins Brown to Mr. Stone, 1921, Brown Papers, Series 2.

40. Kathleen Thompson, "Charlotte Hawkins Brown (1883–1961)," in *Black Women in America*, ed. Darlene Clark Hine (Brooklyn: Carlson Publishing Inc., 1993), 173.

41. Hull, ed., *Give Us Each Day*, 352–53; Charlotte Hawkins Brown to Margaret Murray Washington, September 27, 1916, Brown Papers, Series 2; Josephine Yates to Margaret Murray Washington, September 11, 1908, Box 132, Washington Papers, Tuskegee University Archives, Tuskegee, Alabama; Jones, "Jane Edna Hunter," 74.

42. Minutes, NACW Nineteenth Biennial Convention, July 1935, Subject Files, Container 23, Mary Church Terrell Papers.

43. Duster, *Crusade*, 329.

44. Ibid., 271–74; Salem, "To Better Our World," 106.

45. Mary McLeod Bethune to Mary Terrell, October 1932, Terrell Papers, Howard University.

46. Mary Talbert to Charlotte Hawkins Brown, January 10, 1920, Brown Papers, Series 2.

47. Laura Terrell Jones to Mary Terrell, October 15, 1933, Container 3, Mary Church Terrell Papers.

48. Washington State Federation of Colored Women's Organizations, Eleventh Annual Convention, 1928, Nettie Asberry Papers, 1081, Location B III A 16/1, University of Washington Libraries, Seattle, Washington.

49. Hull, ed., *Give Us Each Day*, 250.

50. Mary Terrell to Mary McLeod Bethune, February 16, 1926, Container 7, Mary Church Terrell Papers.

Karla F. C. Holloway

Classroom Fictions

My Tongue Is in My

Friend's Mouth

When Zora Neale Hurston died in 1959, her former friend and companion, Fannie Hurst, wrote a puzzled note to Carl Van Vechten — a literary patron known to both Hurst and Hurston during the Harlem Renaissance years. You may remember Fannie Hurst as the novelist whose 1933 book, *Imitation of Life*, was twice made into a Hollywood movie. Hurst was puzzled when she wrote to Van Vechten — unsure as to why Zora had chosen to disconnect herself from their circle of friends, why she had been so silent in the years that followed her 1940s move from New York to Florida.

Had Hurst been able to look back over her own correspondence during those years, she would have found another note to Van Vechten. This one

was scripted shortly after a devastating series of circumstances that culmi-
nated in Zora Hurston's appearance in a New York courtroom — arrested on
charges (later proved false and dismissed) of a morals offense. The newspapers described her as being prostrate and hysterical in the courtroom,
agonized and terrified at the charges being levied against her. Fannie Hurst,
whose friendship with Hurston had already taken on what seem to me to be
troubling and patronizing tones, characterized the event this way in her letter
to Van Vechten: "The Zora incident (certainly staged I understand) is in her
fine old tradition. Naughty but nice."[1] She followed this superficial comment
with the drawing of a happy, smiling face.

The note betrays a stunning lack of compassion. Where was her sentiment
for her friend? Where was her voice, coming to the defense of a woman she
had paraded in hotel tea rooms dressed exotically as an African princess so
that they could, in that age of Jim Crowism, be served in a public dining hall?
Where was her empathy and advocacy? Frankly, I think Fannie Hurst had
gotten just about all she could have out of this friendship with Hurston — she
did not speak *for* her, in all likelihood, because she had never spoken *with* her.

I give this critical exchange of prepositions — for and with — a fairly hefty
responsibility. I want them to help me share with you what I see as a disturbing erosion of voice in our academic communities. It's my sense that we have
come to allow our scripts to stand "for" rather than "with" voice. Our scripts
allegedly testify to our sentiments and sensibilities, and yet, at the same time,
sufficiently veil our spirits so that the politics that our identities reveal to be
various, culturally and ethnically distinct, are shrouded away behind a script
that makes us all seem the same, when each of us knows that that is but a
fiction.

When my sister died in an automobile accident in October 1989, I had
already been silent for four months. What began fairly innocuously as a
persistent case of springtime laryngitis grew worse until, instead of an annoy-
ing hoarseness, I had no voice at all. The summer's surgery corrected the
vocal cord problems, and my larynx was slowly healing; but my sister's death
in the fall plunged me into an unforgiving silence that made me vulnerable to
the incredibly noisy chatter of my spirit. It was during that time I grew to
understand Zora Neale Hurston's character Janie.

You may recall that at the end of *Their Eyes Were Watching God* Janie
ascends the stairs of her home, moving to the upper room with her memories — a "spark of sunstuff" against the wall.[2] But I want you to remember an
earlier moment, just before the novel's closing scene, where Janie experiences
the most intimate encounter in the novel. Many readers and teachers divide

this novel according to the appearance of men in Janie's life. She had had three husbands/lovers (some behaved as if they were both, some behaved as if they were neither). We often discuss the book in our classrooms in three days—as if these three men (Logan, Jody, and TeaCake) have some mystical numerological powers. But the real intimacy does not occur until these three have been abandoned, buried, or killed. Then we come to understand the relationship Janie returns to—the one with her friend Pheoby—who is destined to reflect Janie's sun-touched aura. Pheoby enters Janie's yard by "the intimate gate." Their intercourse that night is verbal—Janie shares with Pheoby the riveting story that makes up the text of the novel. Declaring "mah tongue is in mah friend's mouth," she designates Pheoby to share her story with her curious neighbors.[3] These days this phrase—"my tongue is in my friend's mouth"—resonates for me.

When my sister Karen died, the loss of speech that had been purely physical feathered out toward my spirit and, in consequence, I experienced the overwhelming power of inner speech. As I think back on that year I believe it was that enforced silence that encouraged me to consider how comfortable I had become in letting my writing and the writings of others take the place of the exchanges that voice demands. So I choose a text for this essay—in honor of my culture's traditional practice of positioning a written text to *serve* (and I underscore this word) as a medium for voice. My text? The visual, verbal, and scripted moments in the lives of three women.

The first event I have already recalled—Zora Hurston's traumatizing moments in a New York City courtroom in the 1940s. The second involves law professor Anita Hill when she testified before the panel of skeptics on the U.S. Senate Judiciary Committee—a moment that is etched into our national consciousness by the visual records of the last decades of the twentieth century, which we owe to C-SPAN. The third is an incident that preceded the Anita Hill episode by two centuries. In 1772 Phillis Wheatley, a seventeen-year-old child captured from West Africa and brought to New England before her eighth birthday, sat trial.

Although Phillis Wheatley was only a teenager when she sat in a New England courthouse before her Boston jury, visual parallels between that scene and Anita Hill's testimony encourage a comparison. The austere chambers of law and politics housed both events. Professor Hill was separated from her interlocutors by a strip of federal green cloth that symbolized the judiciary. Because this was an ordinary draping for courtroom tables of eighteenth-century New England, it is likely that a similar piece of fabric also separated Phillis Wheatley from her panel of judges. In addition to visual parallels, skepticism, outright disbelief, and implicit derision frame both episodes, and the powerful presence of the judiciary stalked both the margins and the centers.

The governor of the Massachusetts colony led the inquisition of the young Negro girl, Phillis Wheatley, who had audaciously claimed authorship of a thin edition of poems she sought to publish in America.[4] Her examination by "some of the best judges," as was claimed in the preface to the eventually published book, would lead to their attestation that she had indeed authored the words in her book.

Two centuries later, law professor Anita Hill would find herself nearly encircled by a panel of white males who would listen to her claim the legitimacy of her words. Legitimacy in Hill's case was more relevant to a concept of accuracy than to the situation of authorship that was questioned in the Phillis Wheatley hearings. Hill's testimony before a gathering of senators who would decide on the viability of Judge Clarence Thomas's candidacy for a position on the Supreme Court was to verify both the words she had submitted in a sworn affidavit and the experiences those words described.

Zora Hurston is related to this pair not only through the courtroom visuals, but because she too was held hostage by script. The pages of what would be her last novel, *Seraph on the Suwannee*, which described a "knowing and a doing kind of love," were read into the court's record as if they indicated (or could indict) the character of the woman who wrote them.[5]

It is not significant for my discussion here that the words each of these women had written were either used to indict or to affirm their spoken testimonies. Instead my focus is on the fact that voice did not dispel the visual power of three black and female bodies whose authenticity was in great measure dependent upon the visual stereotypes that race and gender negatively confer. Additionally, I want to encourage us to interrogate the lack of presence our voices have in forums like these when our stories do not match the circumscribed narratives that are imposed upon us by national identity politics. I believe that these contemporary and historic politics — essentially versions of the politics of silence — are versions as well of sexism and racism. Speaking out is a dangerously engaged and disrespected behavior, especially when our voices would controvert the "evidence" of our bodies.[6] Supporting the written text (a subversive means of veiling the visual impact of identity) over and instead of our voices is no less enslaving than the system that Phillis Wheatley escaped only through the tenuous geographical boundaries that separated her from the southern colonies.

Intimately related to these politics of voice are the place and manner of our articulations. Script has become so professionally vital to us that we have learned to value it in place of what we say. Anita Hill was constantly queried — "Did you write it down?" "Did you keep a log?" "A journal?" — as if there *ever* were truth or value attached to women's journals and diaries at any time in U.S. history. Zora Hurston was held hostage by the text of her novel — a work of fiction, an imaginative exercise — sort of like the imagination Hill was accused of using in her testimony. We can only guess at Wheatley's experience. One contemporary critic imagines her having to translate works of Greek and Latin, or having to read aloud and comment upon the work of the English Romantics whose verse was like her own.[7] Their texts supplanted her own verse as if her poetry were as insubstantial as her legal status in the eighteenth-century British colony.

Disrespect for the distinct and identifying qualities of the spoken voice enters our classroom as fact and fiction, behavior and text. What is the consequence of academic posturing that values everything but the stories of our lives as the substance of our discourses?

Consider, for example, the studied contrasts of two forms of stories and learning that Jamaica Kincaid sketches in *Annie John*. Here is a classroom scene: "The morning was uneventful: a girl spilled ink from her ink-well all over her uniform; a girl broke her pen nib and then made a big to-do about replacing it; girls twisted and turned in their seats and pinched each other's bottoms; and passed notes to each other. All this Miss Nelson must have seen and heard, but she didn't say anything — only kept reading. . . . Midway in the morning, we were told to go out and stretch our legs and breathe some fresh air."[8]

As if to insist upon the contrast in the classroom scene she remembers that was controlled by the silent and reading presence of the teacher, Kincaid sketches another event in *Annie John* that occurs shortly after a neighborhood girl has died in the arms of Annie's mother: "At school, I told all my friends about this death. I would take them aside, so I could repeat the details over and over again. They would listen to me with their mouths open. In turn, they would tell me of someone they had known or heard of who had died. I would listen with my mouth open. One person had known very well a neighbor who had gone swimming after eating a big lunch at a picnic and drowned. Someone had a cousin who in the middle of something one day just fell down dead. Someone knew a boy who had died after eating poisonous berries. 'Fancy that,' we said to each other."[9] When Annie's teacher (presumably after putting down the book she was reading and turning her attention to the class) asks the students to write an "autobiographical essay," she encourages no conversation—they are told to spend the morning quietly in contemplation and reflection and then to write. Annie's essay is about swimming with her mother, almost drowning, being unable to find her mother, and her recurrent and frightening dreams about this near loss. Which narrative spilled over into Annie's classroom text?

Nigerian novelist Buchi Emecheta's recall of her classroom has similar parallels. While her teacher, Miss Humble, read Coleridge's "Christabel" to the class, Buchi dreamily replaced the sonorous drone of her teacher's uninterrupted voice with "the voice of my big mother with her head covered in white woolly curls, with her face shining in its sweat, with me sitting by her feet with the Ukwa tree giving an illusory shade from the bright moon, and the children [who gathered in response to her] call-song. At that moment it seemed to me as if every compound had emptied its young ones onto the moonlit sand to celebrate [her stories]."[10] Their voices are a part of her telling.

"We want stories we want stories," they respond to her call; and her telling included them. The children had asked to be told the narrative of their own community, and Emecheta's autobiography continues:

And when she opened her mouth to speak, the voice that came out was distant and mesmerizing.

"Whose father walked seven lands and swam seven seas to fight and kill a bad man called Hitilah?"

"It's me," I whispered hoarsely, afraid of disturbing the quiet grip her voice was having on us.

"Who is our come-back mother Abgogo?"

"It's me." This time I could not restrain myself any longer. I stood up proudly and this movement of mine startled all my little relatives sitting there on the sand at Otinkpu into reality. "It's her, It's her," their voices chorused. . . .

[Y]ears later I [remembered] being singled out for this treat—the treat of being the heroine of our big mother's *inu* story.[11]

Years later, Buchi Emecheta wrote her own story—her autobiography *Head Above Water*—where she was again at the center of the narrative, as she had been on the moonlit beach in Otinkpu. Which classroom's fiction—and I am opening the doors and transforming the boundaries of how we visualize a classroom—becomes text?

In fiction, especially richly woven into fictions by women, I have found countless alternatives to silent scribbling classrooms. These engage the kinds of learning, sharing, and exchange that privilege voice and strategically position the visions and creativity these evocative intimacies enable into our narratives. They offer us a lesson for our daily lives. This lesson, enacted in our public cultures and scripted into our private narratives, indicates how bountiful the blessings of voice can be.

Toni Morrison's fictional sisters in *The Bluest Eye*, Frieda and Claudia, know the evocative power of conversation. Morrison describes their listening to their parents' words: "Their conversation is like a gently wicked dance: sound meets sound, curtsies, shimmies, and retires. Another sound enters but is upstaged by still another: the two circle each other and stop. Sometimes their words move in lofty spirals; other times they take strident leaps, and all of it is punctuated with warm-pulsed laughter — The edge, the curl, the thrust of their emotions is always clear to Frieda and me. We do not, cannot, know the meanings of all their words, for we are nine and ten years old. So we watch their faces, their hands, their feet, and listen for truth in timbre."[12] Morrison's sisters benefit from a lesson like Paule Marshall's Selina Boyce in *Brown Girl, Brownstones*, who, like Marshall herself, learns more about life listening for the voices of her community than she learns in its schools. This classroom is her mother's kitchen where, on Saturdays, with the "kitchen full of fragrances," Selina and her friends learned the politics of colonialism, and racism, and sexism, learned the cooking and cultures and spirituals of the Barbadian women who came to her mother's kitchen. "The children watched from their corner — Selina leaning forward excitedly . . . the words living things to her. She sensed them bestriding the air — charging the room with strong colors. She wondered at her mother's power with words. In school she could sense the veil dropping over the children's eyes."[13] In school, Selina felt her voice had no power; but in her mother's kitchen "her mind would be flooded with eloquence."

How has it happened that this eloquence and passion, this truth in timbre and colors, have been nudged aside, replaced by our more formal classrooms in the university? Why have they been nudged, pressed beneath the written records of these testimonies? When did we learn to lose the visions that our voices can enact and enable?

I want to suggest that our classrooms offer us unique access to spaces where the power of the spoken voice can once again earn the respect, the position, and the privilege that are traditional endowments within my cultural community. And I want to suggest that it happens best when we place our tongues — tell our stories — in as intimate an encounter as we can create.

When I was forced into silence, by my own illness and then by the tragedy of Karen's death, everybody around me became quite noisy. My son went to the library and got a book (you'd have to know him to understand how phenomenal an event that was) and taught himself and then me (a rudimentary) American Sign Language. My father came to my house, called himself my amanuensis, and became my voice on the telephone with colleagues who came to visit and with students I needed to contact. My daughter read to me, although I tried to explain in halting and imperfect A.S.L. that I had not lost the ability to read — just speak. But she retorted, "You can't *hear* the stories." Empowered by a childhood of stories told — in twilight hours on our front porch, in bed, while braiding hair or ironing — she reversed the role and read to me in an exchange of love I will never forget. The wonderful women in my book club called me on the phone and talked as if I were responding — "Girl, and then do you know what she said — or did — or wore?" They must have seen me shake my head over the wires of the phone because they'd go on in these elaborate conversations as if I had indeed responded, and I listened because they were speaking *with* me.

I remember the eloquence and quiet passion of Anita Hill's friend and colleague, Ellen Wells, who insisted upon the absolute integrity of her friend when nobody would believe her. Ellen Wells spoke in concert with Anita Hill, commanding a dignity that those senators — shrouded in the high drama of the judiciary's chambers — could neither touch nor emulate.

That event makes me look back with not a little sadness at Fannie Hurst's note to Van Vechten. Hurst's voice was silently condemnatory when her friend Zora Hurston desperately needed its presence. I imagine that within that courtroom, Hurst could have held a significant power and sway, that she could have given the distraught and lonely Hurston some measure of support and a certain comfort. Instead we have evidence of a pathetic little note, representing in its slim message the meager support Hurston received too late and intimating a curious voyeurism rather than an intimate understanding.

And, finally, who spoke with Phillis Wheatley? We have evidence her "master" was present in the New England courthouse. Indeed we have evidence that he had led her to and encouraged these hearings — interested in her welfare we surmise, or perhaps we interrogate this event a bit more closely and wonder at his presence, knowing that she, like Zora Neale Hurston, died impoverished and abandoned by her supporters. Wheatley died of malnutrition. There was no nurturing of her voice — no matter how we interpret the courthouse scene.

However, what remains with us from each of these historicized confrontations is that testimony — shared, collaborated upon, evoked for evidence or for defense—holds within it the powerful and empowering text of the word. This brings me back to my opening fiction—the moment when Janie gives her story to Pheoby, sharing it with her because "my tongue is in my friend's mouth." And that fiction brings me worriedly to our classrooms and colleagues and collaborators in the enterprise of our academic and public lives.

Have we become so yoked by a maxim that makes equitable our academic publishing and the viability (and success) of our professional livelihoods that we have lost the resonant and responsive power of the spoken text? Are we as eager in our classrooms to let speech suffice for some situations as we are to rush it toward its "real and valued" purpose—writing? Does composition only mean composing the written rather than the spoken? Do we honor in-class speaking as well as in-class writing? Does our speech evoke a silencing substitution for conversation rather than an enabling accompaniment with other voices? Do we value eloquence but really mean evenly flowing prose rather than fluid and provocative speech? What would happen if we encouraged our students and colleagues to *tell* their stories too? What if our business meetings took time for narratives and examples from our lives outside our offices? In other words, would we learn something different about collaboration if we listened and spoke rather than read and wrote?

I come from a culture where *voice* is a birthright. Where being "well spoken" is a quality important enough to make a grandparent approve or disapprove of your significant other. Where Martin Luther King Jr.'s maxim about the "content of our character" was appreciated as much for its resonance as for its rightness. Where Toni Morrison's novels are read aloud so that we can feel and hear the shivering eloquence of her language. Morrison has spoken of her effort to "make the story appear oral, meandering, effortless, spoken . . . to construct dialogue so that it is heard . . . to always have the choral note."[14] Surely she meant these final words from her novel *Jazz* to be heard: "It's nice when grown people whisper to each other. . . . Their ecstasy is more leaf-sigh than bray and the body is the vehicle not the point. They reach, grown people, for something beyond, way beyond and way, way down underneath tissue. They are remembering while they whisper . . . they are inward toward the other. . . . I envy them their public love. I have watched your face for a long time now, and missed your eyes when you went away from me. Talking to you and hearing you answer—that's the kick."[15]

So I am left with this perspective on voice, my concern that the communities that surround us—political and academic, cultured, gendered, and otherwise diverse—gather together to value and affirm the ways in which our voices "kick." This is, you may rightly guess, important to me especially because the voices of people of color and women are the first to get silenced, disrespected, challenged, and disbelieved. In *Beloved*, Baby Suggs preaches a sermon that testifies to the way our spirits, our flesh, and our voices are diminished by the abuse of selecting one race, and one sex, as the norm.[16] Morrison writes: "And no, they ain't in love with your mouth. Yonder, out there, they will see it broken and break it again. What you say out of it they will not heed. What you scream from it they do not hear. What you put into it to nourish your body they will snatch away and give you leavins instead. No, they don't love your mouth. *You* got to love it. This is flesh I'm talking about here. Flesh that needs to be loved."[17]

Ours are the very voices likely to carry within them the resonances of those very principles and practices that once made voice so critical to retaining cultural memories. Women's voices told and remembered the stories of generations of cultures outside of the western world. Women's verbal artistry preserved, in praisesongs and griotic traditions, the accomplishments and events of families and villages. Women's voices literally carried the legacies of generations whose political marginality threatened the records of their presence. When our artists insist that we attend once again to the evocative power of voice, I think we need to listen. Alice Walker did not casually make the first words of *The Color Purple* italicized, isolated on the page, and prior to the rest of her text. These words—"you better not never tell nobody but god"—are subverted by the rest of the story that tells us relentlessly and insistently the story of Celie's abuse and salvation.[18] Celie's story brought the reality of sexual abuse and violence out and into public discourse. Walker's recent novel likewise contributes to our speech. There is now talk-show talk about female circumcision, and *Possessing the Secret of Joy* played no small role in this liberating conversation.[19]

Our voices do our work for us: as women, within our communities, in the midst of our families, among our artists; they must do this work as well and as insistently in our professions. When we share our stories, fiction or fact, we not only name, specify, claim, and celebrate our diversity but we evoke its power as well. We learn that the thoughtful reflectiveness of inner speech and the courageous conversations of our outer voices allow us to speak *with* rather than merely *for* those who have been silenced or who would be; to add the clamor of our collaborative and noisy voices to those whose testimonies are disrespected; and to harness the spiritual power of choric evocation—a power not unlike that in *Beloved* where thirty women gather together to send Sethe's dead daughter Beloved back to her own: "The voices of women searched for the right combination, the key, the code, the sound that broke the back of words. Building voice upon voice until they found it . . . a wave of sound wide enough to sound deep water . . . it broke over Sethe and she trembled like the baptized in its wash. . . ."[20] These friends, these women speak for Sethe who has lost the power of her own voice, sucked as she has been into the relentless whirlpool of a devouring mother love. After what I believe now was a requisite period of silence, I regained my voice too; but it had grown significantly deeper—enriched by the substance of my children's and friends' and family's voices.

Serious, sustained, and passionate conversations will assure us the vigor of our spirits and nurse the assertive power of our intellects. Feminist scholar Catharine Stimpson has recently argued that conversations encourage us to examine truths, they weaken totalitarian perspectives, and they permit catharsis. Of these lingering legacies of conversation, it's the catharsis I want to encourage. Catharsis brings me back to passion—that energy of spirit that maintains our psyches despite the fracturing blows of racism and sexism, poverty, abuse, and the various damages that the commodified enterprises of our societies can encourage.

If we lose our boldness and our passion, if we retreat away from the public response to women's bodies—the historical stereotypes and the persistently racist and sexist discourses they endure—we turn over to others who have no right to our privacy the very identities we believe our silence protects. Cultural critic bell hooks consistently argues that passion can disrupt boundaries, enabling in this deconstruction a space where people can interact and touch one another's differences in a way that is redemptive.

Redemption is critical not only for the injured, fragilized psyches of African American women who have relinquished boldness and passion, but also for those whose bodies are different from ours. They are male, or white, or differently sexualized—and they allow that identity patriarchal, racialist, or sexualized subordination of others. They lose their own souls, however, in the processes of patriarchy, racism, and sexism. So bound up are they in maintaining positions of power and authority, and so common to them is controlling, silencing language (like Clarence Thomas's response to the judiciary committee: "This, gentlemen, is nothing but a high-tech lynching") that the withering away of their own spirits is barely noticeable—until it is too late. Redemption would reconstitute their souls as well, giving them such passion and respect for themselves that they could not abuse others without the painful loss of those gains.

So let me close with a plea for an evocative and noisy redemption. Along with those in our classrooms, who learn to model our methods and material, and those in our professional communities whom we mentor and instruct in the intricacies of our busyness, let us be certain to gift them with our voices and theirs, celebrating in the conversations that we will certainly encourage the wonderful cacophony that makes our fictions and our classrooms — both our public communities and our private — so nurturing and so sustaining a ground. Let us assert the right to place our tongues and tell our stories anywhere we choose.

Notes

1. See the critical discussion of their relationship as reviewed by Gay Wilentz in "White Patron and Black Artist: The Correspondence of Fannie Hurst and Zora Neale Hurston," *Library Chronicle of the University of Texas at Austin* 35 (1986): 20–43. Jane Caputi explores the relationship between Hurst's *Imitation of Life* and Hurston's 1937 novel in "'Specifying' Fannie Hurst: Langston Hughes's 'Limitations of Life,' Zora Neale Hurston's *Their Eyes Were Watching God*, and Toni Morrison's *The Bluest Eye* as 'Answers' to Hurst's *Imitation of Life*," *Black American Literary Forum* 24, no. 4 (Winter 1990): 697–716.

2. Zora Neale Hurston, *Their Eyes Were Watching God* (1937; reprint, Urbana: University of Illinois Press, 1978), 231.

3. Ibid., 17.

4. See Henry Louis Gates's discussion of this event in "Writing 'Race' and the Difference It Makes," in *"Race," Writing, and Difference*, ed. Henry Louis Gates (Chicago: University of Chicago Press, 1986), esp. 7–9.

5. Zora Neale Hurston, *Seraph on the Suwanee* (New York: Charles Scribner's Sons, 1948).

6. I discuss the implications of "The Body Politic" (especially as the media capitalize on the powerful agency of visual stereotype) in greater detail in the chapter by that title in *Codes of Conduct: Race, Ethics, and the Color of Our Character* (New Brunswick, N.J.: Rutgers University Press, 1995).

7. Gates, "Writing 'Race,'" 7–9.

8. Jamaica Kincaid, *Annie John* (New York: Penguin, 1983), 39.

9. Ibid., 6–7.

10. Buchi Emecheta, *Head Above Water* (London: Ogwugwu Afo, 1986), 7.

11. Ibid., 8.

12. Toni Morrison, *The Bluest Eye* (New York: Holt, Rinehart and Winston, 1970), 18.

13. Paule Marshall, *Brown Girl, Brownstones* (Old Westbury, N.Y.: Feminist Press, 1981), 11.

14. Toni Morrison, "On the Spoken Library," *English Journal* 67, no. 2 (February 1978): 29.

15. Toni Morrison, *Jazz* (New York: Alfred A. Knopf, 1993), 229.

16. Toni Morrison, *Beloved* (New York: Alfred A. Knopf, 1987).

17. Ibid., 89.

18. Alice Walker, *The Color Purple* (New York: Harcourt Brace Jovanovich, 1982), 3.

19. Alice Walker, *Possessing the Secret of Joy* (New York: Harcourt Brace Jovanovich, 1992).

20. Morrison, *Beloved*, 261.

Barbara Ogur

Smothering in Stereotypes

HIV-Positive Women

Gena Correa's book *The Invisible Epidemic* knowledgeably details important aspects of the history of HIV in women: the slowness of the medical community and society in general to acknowledge the reality of infected women, the HIV manifestations particular to women, the special life circumstances of many infected women as caretakers of children and infected male partners, the vulnerability of many women to infection as a result of cycles of disempowerment related to abuse, poverty, and sexual exploitation, and the devaluation of the observations of the female caretakers of HIV-infected women that has also contributed to the invisibility of women within the epidemic.[1]

Correa also describes the curious phenomenon in which women are depicted in both medical and lay literature as the bearers of infected children and the transmitters of infection to men but somehow do not exist as infected people. Women have been underrepresented in AIDS clinical trials. Carol Levine refers to the "quadruple jeopardy" experienced by women in AIDS research: excluded because they are women and either potentially or actually pregnant, because they are members of minority groups and lack access to health care in general, because they are or are assumed to be drug users and presumed to be noncompliant, or because they do not meet the criteria for a clinical diagnosis of AIDS, which until recently may have disproportionately reflected conditions more common in men.[2] And while a number of spokespeople have described the experience of HIV-infected gay and bisexual men in film, literature, and nonfiction,[3] the experience of infected women, with rare exception, remains unarticulated.[4]

Throughout this period of women's relative invisibility in the epidemic, there have been voices of protest.[5] It is because of these efforts and those of the many women who wrote and spoke and agitated that we now have Centers for Disease Control AIDS definitions that more fairly acknowledge the conditions which are disabling and killing women. Recent CDC statistics showed an increase in reported cases of 111 percent in 1993, with a 153 percent increase in cases among women, a significant proportion of that increase reflecting new cases according to the CDC's revised definitions. Similarly, those establishing experimental protocols (such as the recently terminated 076 trial of AZT in pregnancy) might never have considered the health of the women participants without these efforts.

But there are other aspects of women and HIV infection that cannot really be addressed through policy changes or through agitation for resources. One of the most persistent of these problems is the refusal of most women to see themselves as potential victims of the HIV virus. In 1994, over a decade into the epidemic, over 40,000 women have been diagnosed with AIDS. In Massachusetts, 49 percent of women with AIDS do not have a history of injecting drug use; and the fastest-growing category of people with AIDS is heterosexual women. Yet most women do not consider themselves at risk. We have seen the science, the epidemiology, and it's not *us*. It's the prostitute's disease, the drug user's disease, the poor, lower-class woman's disease, the woman of color's disease, with perhaps the implicit suggestion that it is because of her drug use and promiscuous behavior that she contracted HIV, the woman from some far-away impoverished country with, again implicitly, unusual sexual practices. Or perhaps, if we are more socially aware, it's the disease of women victims of physical and sexual abuse. But *we* are not those women.

Feminist scholarship has often focused on the deconstruction of stereotypes of women, and particularly those stereotypes that restrict women's possibilities or divest women of power over their own health. This scholarship has taken a variety of forms, from the demystification and critical analysis of medical information, as presented by such groups as the Boston Women's Health Book Collective, to Deirdre English and Barbara Ehrenreich's historical-political analysis of women's health and women as healers, to the validation of personal history as a complex and rich source of data about such varied health issues as violence or sexual abuse, menstruation, sexuality, and childbirth.[6] In this volume, Karla Holloway insists that we listen to women's voices, as listening forces us as women and as scholars to come to terms with the realities of women's lives.

These are stories of women and HIV infection. The women are patients in the HIV clinic at the Cambridge Hospital in Cambridge, Massachusetts. Presently the clinic follows about 125 infected women out of 350 patients. By CDC epidemiology, the women are 49 percent white, 6 percent Hispanic, 4 percent Portuguese or Brazilian, 24 percent African American, and 18 percent Haitian; 46 percent have a history of injecting drug use, 42 percent are assumed to have acquired the infection through heterosexual contact and 1 percent through transfusion, and among 11 percent the source of infection is unknown. But these statistics tell us very little about these women and may even suggest some false truths. They have a more complex reality and subjectivity than epidemiological categories can capture. It is important neither to minimize the major issues of race, class, and lifestyle in influencing these women's vulnerability to the virus nor to smother them or us in the stereotypes of race, class, and lifestyle that threaten to keep them invisible and unsupported and ourselves ignorant of our own vulnerability to the virus.

The methodology for uncovering the complexities of their condition is the videotaped oral history. The subjects discussed in this article are patients of the Cambridge Hospital Multidisciplinary AIDS Program who participated in an interview with their primary care provider of the past two to five years. Through a use of open-ended questions and nonjudgmental facilitation, they were encouraged to talk about their lives before and after they became HIV-infected, with some specific questions relating to decisions made during adolescence, history of sexual or physical abuse, substance use patterns, sexual relationships, and their personal beliefs about why they became infected with HIV. The author edited the transcripts with the goal of presenting a chronological story of each woman's life in her own words. To validate the editing of the transcriptions, each woman was asked to read her story, to comment on whether it accurately portrayed what she wanted to say about herself, and to make any additions or corrections she would like. Only one factual correction was made. All four women expressed comfort in the validity of their personal stories and, in fact, appreciation at being heard. The interviews are part of a larger work in progress, in which a group of women patients in collaboration with women providers are using personal storytelling to try to place the epidemic in a more human context.

Donna is a thirty-eight-year-old white woman and mother of three. She would show up on the epidemiology tables as an injecting drug user.

"I moved out on my own when I was fourteen. I was supposed to get an apartment with some other girls and they never moved in, so I was always bouncing back and forth between jobs and my own place and my mum's. I was the youngest of three girls, and it seemed like we all did the same thing — we went from being real nice and homey to rebelling at about age thirteen or fourteen. The turning point for me was the Christmas when I was thirteen. She decided not to have Christmas — she said we were all too rotten — she'd always found everything wrong with everything we did. My sister had just had a baby and she was going to turn her out on the street. I said, that's it, if she goes, I go. I did what the others did, but I took it one step worse. I was the real rotten egg of the family.

"It was 1971. Everything was free love. I hung out in the square in Chelsea. I experimented with drugs a little bit, mostly speed, but I was never much into drugs. Then I got into the rough edge, hung out with the bike crowd and talked tough and brawled.

"I started working for the neighborhood youth corps and got accepted into this program to get trained as a respiratory technician. We had to go through hours and hours of tests. I was the youngest chosen in the country. I worked in that field for a long time, starting from when I was about seventeen. At that point I had started to settle down pretty much.

"I got married when I was nineteen. I didn't love him, although he was and still is a great guy. It was a marriage of convenience. We broke up within a year, but unfortunately not before I got pregnant with Erica. After she was born, I made the mistake of picking up my first drink — from the first one I was a blackout drinker, maybe because my biological father, whom I never knew, and also my stepfather, who raised me, were both alcoholics. I was a blackout drinker until I got into recovery two years ago.

"I kind of made peace with my mum when Erica was a baby. Up to then, I never could do anything right. After she was born, my mom took care of her while I worked and she started to act like Erica was hers. So one day I just took the baby and moved to Florida. Ever since then, she's never told me what to do with any of my kids.

"My second husband, Victor, is kind of the love of my life. Even though we're not together anymore, I know that we love each other and he will stand by me until the end. During the time we were together, he was drinking a lot and he was a mean drunk. I don't know if the boys ever saw any of the abuse, but I know Erica saw him hit me.

"I was never into IV drugs. I had tried cocaine once or twice and not that I didn't like it, but I said, what am I, nuts? I had always gotten upset whenever people brought that stuff into the house because of the kids. But it was during the time my husband had been picked up on his third DUI charge and put into jail for six months. I was really pissed. My whole IV drug period lasted maybe four months. I met this guy who was a coke user. I thought it was going to be companionship. Before I knew it, I was using coke with him and having sex where safety wasn't even considered. I figured it couldn't happen to me. I was a mother with three little children. But I got HIV. It only took one night—one night of unsafe sex, one night of IV use. Four months was plenty.

"The thing that got me so angry—when I told this other guy, he said, oh, I thought I was infected. I wanted to kill him. It wasn't just my life, I had three young kids. And it didn't just end with me. He just kept on going around and picking up other women. I tried to prosecute him, but they said they couldn't force him to get tested and as long as he didn't know he was infected, they couldn't arrest him. One of my friends said one night she couldn't stand it anymore—she saw him with this new girl in a bar and she went up and said what are you doing with him, don't you know he has AIDS?

"I think about that period as a time when I was very destitute, depressed. I've always felt the need for male companionship, a friend—I thought I'd found it with this guy, but it turned out he was just into getting high. I did things I'd never thought I'd do. I was shocked at myself. Fortunately I was able to stop completely after four months. I never in a million years thought it could happen to me or to anyone I knew.

"Ninety percent of me, intellectually, says this is not a punishment from God, it's just a terrible disease, and it is a really terrible disease, but anybody can get it. But I remember seeing this woman in *Common Threads*, a documentary about AIDS, saying that the majority of women get AIDS because of their strange and unusual lifestyle and it's a punishment from God. And that really clings to me, and I say, yes, it's possible. It's a small part, but it really still bothers me. Although most of me doesn't believe it, it's still that little part that can really get things out of control.

"I know I'm a good person. I would give and I have given the shirt off my back when somebody else needed it. I may not have lived a majority lifestyle, but I know I'm a good person. But I get caught up in — is it good enough?"

Rosemary is a white, forty-nine-year-old mother of three. She would appear on the epidemiology table as an injecting drug user.

"I come from a two-parent, Irish Catholic, middle-class household, both parents college-educated, the oldest child of four, the only girl. I was a very good student — Catholic schools. I started being defiant at about twelve or thirteen. Catholic philosophy didn't make sense to me. My parents were very strict. I became defiant — smoking cigarettes, drinking alcohol, sneaking out with boys. I also got raped — first sexual experience — at the age of twelve. My cousin drove me home from school one day with two other friends; he drove the car and they did it. Which, in some ways, it was almost like punishment for the transgressions I had been committing — I'd been breaking all those rules. It was a small community, so once that happened, you were a whore. And once that happened, people only asked you out to get one thing, and you gave that one thing to get the affection.

"I stayed in high school, finished with top honors, went to Boston College, dropped out in the first semester. They were peasants to me, very judgmental. So I dropped out, went to Boston, got pregnant, then went home, after deciding that I couldn't go through with the illegal abortion. My parents were supportive, which was pretty good for staunch Irish Catholic parents in those days, which was 1964.

"I ended up having a fight with my parents over a dog and her puppies and left home at 1 A.M. with a little boy, a suitcase, and a dog and five puppies. I went to the only friend I could think to go to, a friend who was black and gay and lived in Roxbury. I met and moved in with his next-door neighbor and had a baby daughter. He was killed in a car accident when she was three months old.

"A friend suggested I move to Amherst and go back to school because it was a supportive community for a single mother with a multiracial child. It was a great environment. I took Heather to class with me, John was in school. I finished 100 credits in two years, got a scholarship to go to graduate school at Smith. I'm not sure they got exactly what they'd bargained for because I was politically active in the black power movement my whole time there. I was drinking, but not to the point of dysfunction. I was involved in another frustrating relationship with a married man. He was a professor of black studies. That ended because I put too much pressure on. But in the meantime it had been a very positive relationship. We could never decide whether to sit up all night talking about ideas or make love — it was just that intense. I'd been all around the world, work-related, as a result of the relationship. At that time I really only wanted totality of his time and attention, and that just really wasn't possible.

"We broke up and I met another man, who was kind of the antithesis — he didn't have an inquisitive mind, he was macho — life was hell because we didn't belong together. I ended up pregnant and we married. He couldn't accept my other children, so when Sara was two I left him. I took very bad legal advice and ended up losing custody of Sara because she was the black child of a black man. She was deteriorating emotionally with him, so I moved back in, but after about six months I took Heather and Sara and ran — lived as a fugitive under aliases — got caught four years later on a kidnapping warrant.

"Actually it worked out okay. Sara went back with him for ten weeks and then his own mother threatened to report him to child welfare and he gave her up to me.

"Early, early on, in 1965–1966, I tampered with heavy drugs, IV a few times but never to any real degree. It was for sensation. Alcohol was different — alcohol was an escape — at times I drank heavily. But drugs were for sensation, recreation. If a little feels good, then more will feel better. That and the fact that it just couldn't happen to me. I think I've always tempted fate.

"To me, the only reason I would hesitate in dealing with this is because I think it would be easy for people to categorize — see, involvement with black folks, or see, IV drugs. I just don't want to further the stereotypes and let people blame the victims.

"I have no idea how I got it. Five to six years ago, I committed two highly at-risk behaviors around the time I probably got infected years ago. I used IV drugs one time with a friend who was a cocaine user, the first and only time I'd used in eight to ten years. And one night I picked up a stranger in a bar in New York City and had sex with him. And he wasn't a healthy person — he was also a cocaine user. I was aware of the virus, mainly because I had a lot of gay friends, but I knew . . . I remember the one night I used drugs, sticking the needle in semi-boiling water. I was aware that unprotected sex was a risk. I also grew up in an era when condoms were frowned upon by everybody — a man would just as soon not go to bed with you as use a condom. In a way, I think there is a self-deception because I'd been so much less promiscuous over the past five-year block, but it was back to that old thing — no, it doesn't happen to me — but it does and you don't get it from seamy, homeless men. You get it from professors and business people.

"I don't really consider myself to be living with AIDS. I think you go through two distinct phases — first you're dying with it. The whole focus is taking care of responsibilities. For me, I have to get Sara independent. You have been handed a death sentence. I think this is what families don't understand. They think you're not dying, you have eight or ten years before you'll be dying, but for the person with HIV, we want people to take care of us and be sensitive to us because we are dying, and the families can't sustain that for eight or ten years. My whole agenda is geared toward surviving four or five years to get done what I need to do, which is to get my child independent. I don't even know what I'd do if I had more time at this point."

Evelyn is a forty-nine-year-old African American woman whose infection would be listed as the result of heterosexual contact.

"My mother died in childbirth, so my grandmother brought me up. My father was a merchant marine and he would come around, but I basically didn't have that much contact with him because he was a drinker and my grandmother and aunts were staunch Christian Scientists and they didn't want to have any of that stuff.

"My teenagehood — I was the only black in the whole town of Winthrop, so I didn't really have any teenagehood — I didn't really have any boyfriends. The first boyfriend I had, I married him — seventeen and a virgin — double wrong.

"He was in the service in France. I got over there and had my first child nine months later, my second one eleven months later and was pregnant with my third child twelve months after that. It was 1965, the birth control pill had just been introduced, and there was a lot of controversy about it, but I said, give it to me.

"We stayed married for sixteen years and then I couldn't take it anymore because it was an abusive marriage. He was a drinker. The kids and I were basically scared. People are so quick to make judgments — well, get up and leave — but it's not that easy, especially if you've never worked before. This man used to get up in the middle of the night and put a gun to my head and say, I should shoot you, and I took that for years, and then one night I said — you know what? just blow them out, I'm tired. I decided this is it. I packed up my things and took the kids and came home.

"My aunt couldn't understand why I didn't want to stay with her, but I was independent. So I scrounged around and the first job I got was in

Sears—cleaning toilets. It was 1972. I hated that job like nobody's business. I finally saved enough to get my own place and me and the kids were sleeping on blankets on the floor but we didn't mind because it was ours. My daughter said, you know what, Ma, I never slept the night through until we moved here because I was afraid that Daddy was going to hurt you.

"During that time I had a couple of boyfriends, but it really didn't work out. The kids were young and I couldn't really see putting out all that money to get a babysitter and them not even contributing. But I had a lot of friends. And it was good for my kids because of me not really having had any freedom—now I had it and it was like we went through our teenagehood together. I'd dance to their music and I didn't really mind the noise.

"I met my ex-husband in 1984 and he treated me really nice. The kids couldn't stand him, but that's because he kind of kept to himself. But by that time I'd learned that I didn't have to let any man put his hands on me because I could take care of myself and my kids. Because by that time we had got rid of Sears and Roebuck toilets and we was working in Polaroid. Then I got a job at City in the emergency ward and I loved it, it was so interesting. I worked there for fourteen years. I've always loved taking care of people, especially the babies. And I've enjoyed myself—every year I go on trips with my three girlfriends.

"And then I started losing weight. And I had kind of heard rumors that Edner was sick—that he had tuberculosis and that he'd gone back to Haiti. I have a lot of mixed feelings about him. One part of me just hates his guts and the other feels bad because he was all alone. His family kind of ostracized him once they knew he had AIDS. I think he knew all along, even before we were together.

"For me it was a major problem, because he came to work at the hospital too. Nobody came out and said, he's got AIDS, but they'd say, you're losing a lot of weight, are you sick? It happened over and over until I hated to go to work. I guess I had it in the back of my mind, but I couldn't stand to find out. When I did get tested, it was kind of messed up—they don't use names, they use numbers, so I got my result that I was HIV on my birthday and that Monday when I went back to work, everybody knew that I had tested positive.

"Then a good friend recommended that I come here and it's made a big difference because I don't feel anyone's judging me, is she a dope addict or is she too fast? Because that's what you get. People hear you're HIV and some of them don't want to be around you.

"When I think about why I got HIV, sometimes I think about the expression what goes around comes around. Sometimes I think I must have done something to someone and it's like a payback.

"Then I also believe maybe it's God's way—a lot of time when there's a tragedy, it's like opening up a way for you to think. Like there's things I used to think were so important, like bills and stuff—it's not so consuming as it was. The important thing for me now is making good memories for my kids so that my baby can look back and say, oh yeah, Ma wasn't that down. I want my kids to have memories of me being well and laughing at life."

Darlene is a thirty-four-year-old African American woman who would be categorized as an injecting drug user.

"I was raised and born in Cambridge, Massachusetts. I have a real close family, my mom and dad and six sisters. When I was in eighth grade, my mother passed away. She was a diabetic and went into the hospital, and three weeks later, just before my eighth-grade graduation, they just came to school to tell me she had passed away. I was real close to my mother. The other girls they all felt close to her too, but somehow I just think that I was her heart. I didn't think I could live without her.

"I started hanging out with the teens at the teen center and started drinking and smoking pot, and I did that for a long time, running from my feelings. I did manage to get my degree, and I was going to go to college, but I was too busy drinking and drugging and having the fun life, what we called the fun life. I wouldn't call it that today.

"My mom and dad were real good parents. My father was kind of strict, but after my mother died, he was real quiet, raising the six of us alone. But he always stood up for us. I stayed with my dad up until I was in my thirties. The only reason we split apart at that time was because I got us evicted from the projects by my drinking and drugging. He took care of us. He paid all our bills, I didn't really have to do none of that. I took the extra money I had and used it on drugs. So me and my father had to split up. He went to live with his mother, and I went to a shelter with the kids. By that time I had found my kids' father, and him and me was running with drinking and drugs, and I wasn't thinking about nobody but myself.

"I started mainlining because I was hanging out with a group of older women who were doing it. And then I met Victor by way of my drug travels, because he was a runner on the street, and I thought, hey, this is the guy for me, he's got plenty of drugs, let me stay with him, and then once I'd had our first kid, we were hooked up. I know I pretty much got the virus through needle exchanging, because Victor hustled for me, he wouldn't let me go out on the street prostituting. He always provided for me and had me take care of the kids. It was a struggle because I had to wait all day for him to come back. He was the only one I would mainline with unless I was real sick and had a little left over and then I'd go to someone else and borrow their works. Plus, being addicts, if Victor and me was real sick, we might let someone use our works if they would give us some. So I think that's where I really got it. I don't know if it was from Victor or someone else.

"About that time, I had my youngest son, Jonathan, and they asked me if I wanted to get tested, because of having used drugs. And that's when I found out. I was like in a state of shock. I came out with, it's not me cause me and my mate are the only ones who use our works. I don't go around to shooting galleries and things. I think at that moment I wanted to commit suicide, because what I got out of it was, I was going to die in two years. I was lying up in Brigham and Women's Hospital looking out the window thinking, well, I might as well jump because my life is over, and then I thought, no, I might as well just keep using. For the next three years I didn't want to have nothing to do with getting treatment or even thinking about the virus.

"Victor never got tested, but then he started to have headaches and then he got paralyzed in his right arm and I thought, oh my God, he's starting to lose part of his body, this is real. And I watched Victor go through all the motions of getting sick and finally dying. This was somebody I'd been with for fifteen years and now I had to be there with these four children and nobody to help me.

"So I just got out of hand with the drinking. I didn't care about nobody. One day I didn't even pick Jonathan up after school. The next morning I got a call from his teacher saying I'd have to go to DSS to pick him up. All the way on the bus I was crying, and something made me get off at the church, because I'd gotten a lot of support there. I guess this was my time to have my kids taken away so I could straighten up my act. And that's when they helped me get into Women, Inc. DSS told me I had to go for twelve months, and I said, what am I going to do for twelve months? I'm going to die. And she looked at me and said, no, you're not going to die, you're going to get better.

"It was a really structured program and that's what I needed. And I said, damn, what kind of place is this? because they was asking me all kind of stuff like, what's my feelings? They said there's something along the way that kept you drinking and drugging. I said, no, it's just what everyone was doing. And that's when they got me to talk about my feelings and what I'd lost—my daughter, Victor, my mother, the boys. We worked on all my issues. I cried and cried. And after I talked about all my losses, they made me talk about the virus and we all cried and they held my hand. I just eventually came out of it. And I realized it's not my virus that's killing me, it's my drug addiction.

"I've had the virus now for seven years, and I'm feeling great. I don't have to feel down that I have the virus and I'm going to die some day. I keep myself up and I don't have to feel isolated because there's so much support I can have.

"I'm only thirty-four, but I've been through an interesting life. I'm feeling a lot better. I guess I've got all those issues up — not that I've finished dealing with them, but I've learned from the program not to keep that stuff inside. People come up and say, look how good you look, you don't look like you got the virus. And I say, that's because I don't think dead, I think alive. It's nothing to be afraid of, you can work with it. It's not a sin that you get it, to me it's been like a blessing. I don't know. I'm learning so much about myself, not just about the virus, but about being a woman."

Ruth is a forty-six-year-old white woman. She would appear on the epidemiological table as the heterosexual partner of a bisexual man.

"I grew up in a small town in southern Illinois, one of the only Jews in a place that allowed Jews in the same schools as whites (blacks literally lived and went to school across the tracks), but where there was pretty overt anti-Semitism. My family was supportive and loving toward me, but quite dominated by a charismatic and frequently moody father who was invested with a great deal of power and authority, not only within the family, but also in the small group of close friends.

"My mother's position was devalued and even belittled, and he was openly flirtatious with other women in the community. I experienced my teenage years as very painful, both as witness to my mother's pain and as a social misfit, a curly-headed Jewish intellectual in a sea of blonde, Protestant cheerleaders.

"I got out to Radcliffe College and found a more diverse and cosmopolitan environment. We were a group of men and women friends who explored the new social movements of the late 1960s and early 1970s, spiritual growth, leftist politics, communal living, sexual openness, some drugs. My relationships with men tended toward powerful charismatic individuals who were dissatisfied with committed monogamy. I committed to them and hung on over the years as they became emotionally more distant and even abusive. I graduated from college and began to travel around the country from one enclave of college friends to another, fell in love with a man who was an artist and a fisherman and broke my heart by impregnating and marrying one of my best friends. In 1971, after a year of floundering in depression, marijuana, and a series of even more unsatisfying relationships, I decided that I would never be happy anyway so I might as well be useful. I applied to and was accepted into medical school in Chicago.

"There I became involved in a more political community of friends. In 1975 I became involved with a man from a working-class, Puerto Rican background who was a medical school classmate and a member of our political student group. I became pregnant and married, but in 1979, after the birth of our second child, I discovered that my husband had had an affair with a man at work.

"For three years we tried to work it out. He promised to stop seeing men but fell into a depression and began frequenting gay bookstores, though assuring me that he was not having sex with anyone. This precipitated the end of the marriage in 1982. He set forth to explore his questions about his own sexuality, I became involved with a man who charismatically dominated our circle of friends (now in a Florida university community). He was permitted a great deal of covert sexual freedom within the community. Moreover, it was a small community of colleagues and friends, and in the early 1980s there was a significant rate of turnover and reformulation of relationships.

"In 1982 the first reports of Gay Related Immunodeficiency Disease came out. Although I still spent time with my ex-husband — going out for drinks, going dancing at the gay bars, even socializing with him and a succession of his male and female lovers — and often thought about resuming our involvement, especially when things were going badly with my new relationship, I was afraid to sleep with him. In 1987 he tested positive for HIV at a stage that indicated that he had been infected for a number of years, probably since a prolonged bout of the flu which he had experienced in 1983. He died in 1992."

In actuality, I am Ruth. I am not infected. But my points in making this personal are several: it could have happened to me, and, by extension, I could have been the vector to bring the virus to a large intertwined heterosexual community. In 1983 the epidemiological pigeonholing that allowed me to say, "Don't sleep with this man who sleeps with other men, but go ahead with this man who is heterosexually active with a lot of women," was protective. In 1994 for white women, it is a stereotype that is endangering us and will soon be killing us. For women of color, it has not been a useful distinction for a number of years, simply because the virus entered those communities earlier.

HIV is an infectious agent transmitted sexually and through contact with infected blood. As it spreads in epidemic fashion, we need to track the epidemic as it makes its way into and through populations. But we must be very cautious about what conclusions we draw from the epidemiology. The most consistent data are from the CDC, categorized by ethnicity, age, and by simplified risk behaviors. These data still show the majority of cases of AIDS in men who have had sex with men or in people who have used injecting drugs; it shows that the majority of U.S. women with AIDS are African American and Hispanic. However, since it takes eight to ten years for AIDS to develop after infection with HIV, these data are simply a reflection of where the virus was eight to ten years ago, a fossilized footprint.

The AIDS epidemic and its effects on women present enormous tasks. For modern medicine, the tasks of fighting the virus and its effects, of searching for preventative vaccines, of carrying traditional medicine's advances to all infected people even in this country, and then beyond to other parts of the world, have barely begun. There are powerful economic circumstances that make millions of women more vulnerable to infection, such as sexual exploitation, the forced disruption of families because of capitalist forms of deployment of labor, such as the mining hostels of South Africa or the migrant labor camps of Florida,[7] or the need for many women to remain in situations of domestic abuse for lack of education, skills, and support to live independently.

But there are clear areas where a distinctively feminist approach to analyzing some of the unique features of the HIV epidemic in women is critical. First, in the area of prevention, traditional efforts have focused on the dissemination of information. But HIV is transmitted in private, personal moments that have varying degrees of consensuality. Data suggest that 70 percent of all prostitutes and 80 percent of all women drug users have histories of incest.[8] But this is only the most clearcut example of women's sexual disempowerment. For the majority of women, preventing infection may not revolve around having information; most women know how HIV is spread. Protecting ourselves depends on our perception of our own vulnerability to the virus and then on becoming empowered enough to act in our own interest. When we see infected women as Other by virtue of stereotyping, we are able to avoid seeing ourselves as at risk. We have allowed the sexual relationships and behaviors of HIV-positive women to be defined during the era of ascendancy of the radical right by a stereotypical checklist of behaviors that good women do not do, and that women who get AIDS do. Number of lifetime sexual partners has been posed as a risk factor for HIV infection. But in the largest cohort of HIV-positive women described to date, of the fifty women who were infected heterosexually, the median number of sexual partners in the preceding ten years was three.[9] In fact, it has been suggested that the most powerful risk factor for the heterosexual spread of HIV is having one *infected* partner, not having multiple partners.[10] We need to reanalyze this information with the insights gained from feminist consciousness-raising in which women were permitted to share and legitimize their sexuality. This not only allows for the free expression of the realities of women's sexual behaviors, but also empowers women to begin to take control of them.

Moreover, even a more traditionally liberal perspective on HIV-positive women as victims of abuse, circumstances, or poverty somehow does not acknowledge the complexity of their lives and responses. Each of these stories has features of individual rebellion and resistance, of personal struggle and empowerment, of influence by or awareness of the concurrent historical changes in the role of women. It is in this complicated context that providing care to them and empowering them to avoid further spread of infection must occur. In this area, this project has provided exciting information. In every instance, erroneous, stereotypical, usually judgmental beliefs held by the treatment team were shattered, frequently with important implications for our ongoing clinical relationship. We became more aware of the issues in each woman's life which triggered impulses to use drugs or alcohol or to engage in unprotected intercourse, and were thus able to provide support or positive outlets at these times. More important, we came to respect each woman's strengths and learned to collaborate with these strengths in her care.

In the area of empowerment, the women who participated in this project uniformly commented on how good it felt to tell their stories. They described a feeling of wholeness, of being seen not just for the illness but as a complete person, with fewer feelings of isolation. This coming-out-of-the-closet phenomenon clearly can impact strongly on uninfected women to raise awareness of their vulnerability and to provide role models for empowering themselves.

Notes

1. Gena Correa, *The Invisible Epidemic* (New York: Harper Collins, 1992).

2. Carol Levine, "Women and HIV/AIDS Research: The Barriers to Equity," *Evaluation Review* 14, no. 5 (October 1990): 447–63.

3. Randy Shilts, *And the Band Played On* (London: Penguin, 1987); *Philadelphia*; *Longtime Companion*; *Savage Nights*.

4. See Correa, *Invisible Epidemic*; Diane Richardson, *Women and AIDS* (New

York: Methuen, 1988); Ines Rieder and Patricia Ruppelt, eds., *AIDS: The Women* (Pittsburgh: Cleis Press, 1987); Andrea Rudd and Darien Taylor, eds., *Positive Women: Voices of Women Living with AIDS* (Toronto: Second Story Press, 1992).

5. AIDS Coalition To Unleash Power, *Women, AIDS, and Activism* (Boston: South End Press, 1990); Multicultural AIDS Coalition, *Searching for Women: A Literature Review on Women, HIV, and AIDS in the United States* (Boston: Law Center, University of Massachusetts, 1992).

6. Boston Women's Health Book Collective, *The New Our Bodies, Ourselves* (New York: Simon and Schuster, 1984); Barbara Ehrenreich and Deidre English, *For Her Own Good* (New York: Doubleday, 1978); Ellen Bass and Laura Davis, *The Courage to Heal* (New York: Harper Collins, 1990); Emily Martin, *The Woman in the Body* (Boston: Beacon Press, 1987).

7. Michael Grey, "Syphilis and AIDS in Belle Glade, Florida, 1942 and 1992," *Annals of Internal Medicine* 116, no. 4 (February 1992): 329–34.

8. Mark Matousek, "America's Darkest Secret," *Common Boundary* 9, no. 2 (March–April 1991): 16–23.

9. Charles J. C. Carpenter et al., "Human Immunodeficiency Virus Infection in North American Women: Experience with 200 Cases and a Review of the Literature," *Medicine* 70, no. 5 (1991): 307–25.

10. Norman Hearst and Stephen B. Hulley, "Preventing the Heterosexual Spread of AIDS: Are We Giving Our Patients the Best Advice?" *Journal of the American Medical Association* 259, no. 16 (April 22–29, 1988): 2428–32.

Michael S. Kimmel

Men and Women's Studies

Premises, Perils, and Promise

Many readers are wondering, I would imagine, what I'm doing in such a volume of essays — or at the lecture series from which it came. More to the point, what is *any* man doing in such a volume? Why would a celebration of the anniversary of Duke's Women's Studies Program include a focus on men? As a scholar who researches men and their relationship to feminism, I can tell you that among women's studies programs nationally, Duke's has been one of only a handful that have understood, from the beginning, that women's studies is also about men because the discipline clears an intellectual space for talking about gender. I am not suggesting that among all the other things women's studies has to do, it must now also drop everything and take care of men in some vaguely academic version of the second shift. (I have heard arguments from men suggesting that women's studies must provide us with "a room of our own" within the curriculum, to appropriate the words of Virginia Woolf—and make sure that room has a rather commanding view of the traditional campus!)

When I say women's studies is about men, I mean that *women's studies has made men visible*. Before women's studies, men were invisible—especially to themselves. By making women visible, women's studies also made men visible both to women and to men themselves. If men are now taking up the issue of gender, it is probably less accurate to say, "Thank goodness they've arrived," the way one might when the cavalry appears in a western film, than to say, "It's about time."

Of course, making men visible has not been the primary task of women's studies. But it has been one of its signal successes. The major achievement of women's studies, acting independently and as a force within traditional disciplines, has been making *women* visible through the rediscovery of long-neglected, undervalued, and understudied women who were accomplished leaders, artists, composers, and writers and placing them in the pantheons of significance where they rightly belong. In addition, women's studies has rediscovered the voices of ordinary women—the laundresses and the sales-girls, the union maids and the union organizers, the workers and the wives—who have struggled to scratch out lives of meaning and dignity. For this—whether they know it or not, whether they acknowledge it or not—women all over the world owe a debt.

But in making women visible, women's studies has been at the epicenter of a seismic shift in the university as we know it. Women's studies has made *gender* visible. Women's studies has demonstrated that gender is one of the axes around which social life is organized, one of the most crucial building blocks of our identities. Before women's studies, we didn't know that gender mattered. Twenty-five years ago, there were no women's studies courses in colleges or universities, no women's studies lists at university presses across the country. In my field of sociology, there were no gender courses, no specialty area called the Sociology of Gender. We had, instead, a field called Marriage and the Family—to my mind the Ladies' Auxiliary of Sociology. By making women visible, women's studies decentered men as the unexamined, disembodied authorial voice of the academic canon and showed that men, as well as women, are utterly embodied, their identities as socially constructed as those of women. When the voice of the canon speaks, we can no longer *assume* that voice is going to sound masculine or that the speaker is going to look like a man.

The problem is that many men do not yet know this. Though ubiquitous in positions of power, many men remain invisible to themselves as gendered beings. Courses on gender in the universities are populated largely by women, as if the term applied only to them. "Woman alone seems to have 'gender' since the category itself is defined as that aspect of social relations based on difference between the sexes in which the standard has always been man," writes historian Thomas Lacquer.[1] Or, as the Chinese proverb has it, the fish are the last to discover the ocean.

I know this from my own experience: women's studies made gender visible to me. In the early 1980s I participated in a graduate-level women's studies seminar in which I was the only man among about a dozen participants. During one meeting, a white woman and a black woman were discussing whether all women were, by definition, "sisters" because they all had essentially the same experiences and because all women faced a common oppression by all men. The white woman asserted that the fact that they were both women bonded them, in spite of racial differences. The black woman disagreed.

"When you wake up in the morning and look in the mirror, what do you see?" she asked.

"I see a woman," replied the white woman.

"That's precisely the problem," responded the black woman. "I see a *black* woman. To me, race is visible every day, because race is how I am *not* privileged in our culture. Race is invisible to you, because it's how you are privileged. It's why there will always be differences in our experience."

As I witnessed this exchange, I was startled, and groaned—more audibly, perhaps, than I had intended. Someone asked what my response meant. "Well," I said, "when I look in the mirror, I see a human being. I'm universally generalizable. As a middle-class white man, I have no class, no race, no gender. I'm the generic person!"

Sometimes, I like to think it was on that day that I *became* a middle-class white man. Sure, I had been all those before, but they had not meant much to me. Since then, I have begun to understand that race, class, and gender do not refer only to other people, who are marginalized by race, class, or gender privilege. Those terms also describe me. I enjoy the privilege of invisibility. The very processes that confer privilege to one group and not another group are often invisible to those upon whom that privilege is conferred. American men have come to think of ourselves as genderless, in part because gender privilege affords us the luxury of ignoring the centrality of gender. But women's studies offers the possibility of making gender visible to men as well and, in so doing, creating the possibilities of alliances between women and men to collaboratively investigate what gender means, how it works, and what its consequences are.

In *Fire with Fire*, Naomi Wolf returns often to her book's epigraph, that famous line of Audre Lorde, "the Master's tools cannot dismantle the Master's house." Wolf believes that her book is a refutation of that position, and when one considers the impact of women's studies on the university and the culture at large, it seems that on this score at least, Wolf is quite right — that passionate, disciplined scholarship, inspired and dedicated teaching, and committed, engaged inquiry can contribute to the reorientation of the university as an institution. All over the country, schools are integrating "gender awareness" into their first-year curricula, even orienting the entire curriculum around gender awareness. Within the professional organization of my discipline, sociology, the Sex and Gender section is now the largest section of the entire profession. Gender has moved from the margins — Marriage and the Family — to the center and is the largest single constituency within the field.

Most commentators laud the accomplishments of women's studies programs in transforming women's lives, but it is obvious that women's studies programs have also been transformative for men. The Duke case is a particularly successful one: the popular house course "Men and Gender Issues" has been offered under the umbrella of Women's Studies for five years. Men Acting for Change (MAC), the campus group for pro-feminist men that has become a model for similar groups on campuses around the country, found a supportive harbor in the Women's Studies Program. The first time I came to lecture at Duke three years ago, my lecture was jointly sponsored by the Women's Studies Program and the Inter-Fraternity Council — the first time, I'm told, that those two organizations had cooperated on anything. Women's studies can — and does — forge creative alliances!

Essentially, however, the program at Duke and women's studies in general has centered around the same two projects as any other discipline: teaching and research. And to speak personally, the perspectives of women's studies have transformed both my research and my teaching. Women's studies made it *possible* for me to do the work I do. And for that I am grateful. Inspired by the way women's studies made gender visible, I offered a course called "Sociology of the Male Experience" in 1983 at Rutgers University, where I was then a young assistant professor. This was the first such course on men and masculinity in the state of New Jersey, and I received enormous support both from my own department and from the Women's Studies Program at Rutgers, then chaired by Catharine Stimpson. Today, I teach that course as well as a course entitled "Sex and Society" at Stony Brook to over 350 students each semester. Now, as then, the course is cross-listed with women's studies. But I also teach our department's classical sociological theory course, the course on the historical development of social and political theory. In that course, students traditionally read works by Hobbes, Locke, Rousseau, Smith, Marx, Durkheim, Tocqueville, Weber, and Freud. This is probably the most intractably canonical "Dead White European Men" course we offer in the social sciences. But it has become impossible for me to teach the works of those "great men" without reference to gender — without noting, for example, the gendered creation myths that characterize the move from the state of nature to civil society in the thought of Locke or Hobbes, or the chronic anxiety and loss of control attendant upon modern society documented by Tocqueville, Marx, Weber, or Freud. Moreover, I find that I cannot teach about the rise of nineteenth-century liberal individualism without including Frederick Douglass or Mary Wollstonecraft; nor can I teach about the late-nineteenth-century critiques of individualism without reference to W. E. B. Du Bois or to Charlotte Perkins Gilman.

If women's studies has made gender, and hence *men*, visible, then it has also raised a question about men: where are they? where have they been in women's struggles for equality? Taking my cues from women's history, I began to research men's responses to feminism. *Against the Tide* tries to provide part of the answer, a missing chapter from women's history: the chapter about the men who supported women's equality.[2] When I began *Against the Tide*, I mentioned to Catharine Stimpson, then dean of the Graduate School at Rutgers, what I intended to do. "A book about men who supported feminism?" she asked. "Now that will surely be the world's shortest book!" she joked. Of course, she knew better, but I did not really know what I would find. It turns out that in every arena in which women have struggled for equal rights — education (the right to go to college or professional school, the right to go to college with men), economic life (the right to work, join unions, receive equal wages), social life (the right to own property, have access to birth control, get a divorce), or political life (the right to vote, to hold elective office, to serve on juries) — there have been American men, some prominent, many unheralded, who have supported them: men such as Thomas Paine, who sat before the Declaration of Independence in 1776 and recognized that women would not be included under its provisions, although women had, as he put it, an "equal right to virtue." Men such as famed abolitionists William Lloyd Garrison and Frederick

Douglass, who campaigned tirelessly for women's rights from Seneca Falls onward. Men such as Matthew Vassar, William Alan Neilson, and Henry Durant, founders of Vassar, Smith, and Wellesley colleges. It was Durant, founder of Wellesley, who in 1877 called the higher education of women a "revolt": "We revolt against the slavery in which women are held by the customs of society — the broken health, the aimless lives, the subordinate position, the helpless dependence, the dishonesties and shams of so-called education. The Higher Education of Women is one of the great world battle cries for freedom; for right against might. It is the cry of the oppressed slave. It is the assertion of absolute equality."[3]

Pro-feminist men have included educators such as John Dewey, who urged that women be admitted to the University of Chicago and was one of the founders of the Men's League for Woman Suffrage, the nation's first pro-feminist men's organization. The group of pro-feminist men included W. E. B. Du Bois, Ralph Waldo Emerson, and Eugene Debs among the most vigorous supporters of woman suffrage. And there have been academic men such as Lester Ward and George Herbert Mead, to name but two, who pointed toward the scholarly study of women and opposed gender inequality. In one of his major treatises, *Applied Sociology*, Ward provided an epigraph for the advent of women's studies, arguing that "the universal prevalence of the androcentric worldview acts as a wet blanket on all the genial fire of the female sex."[4] Pro-feminist men are also policymakers such as Robert Reich, secretary of labor in the Clinton administration, who wrote a furious letter (reprinted in *Ms.* magazine) to a college president when his wife was denied tenure, and Representative Don Edwards of California, who has introduced the ERA in every session of Congress since 1974, as well as former Supreme Court justice Harry Blackmun, that vigilant defender of women's right to control their own bodies.

Supporters of women's equality have also included the less-celebrated men who simply lived out their principles of equality without fanfare. Men such as James Mott (married to Lucretia), Theodore Weld (married to Angelina Grimké), and Wendell Phillips, ardent abolitionist and suffrage supporter. In 1856, Lucy Stone called her husband, Henry Brown Blackwell, "the best husband in the world. In the midst of all the extra care, hurry and perplexity of business, you stop and look after all my little affairs," she wrote, "doing everything you can to save me trouble."[5] More than half a century later, Margaret Sanger quotes her husband, William, as telling her to "go ahead and finish your writing, and I'll get dinner and wash the dishes."[6] (She also comments that she drew the curtains in the kitchen of their first-floor

Greenwich Village apartment, lest passersby see her husband wearing an apron.) It appears that long before Ted Kramer and Mr. Mom, real men did housework!

Men *have* been there supporting women's equality every step of the way. And if men have been there, it means that men *can* be there and that they *will* be there. This legacy of men who supported women's equality allows contemporary men to join what I like to think of as the Gentlemen's Auxiliary of the Women's Movement. Neither passive bystanders nor the front-line forces — and especially not the leaders of those troops — men still have a pivotal role to play. Men can join this epochal struggle and provide support both individually and collectively. This strikes me as an utterly honorable relationship to feminism, quite different from an impulse I've encountered among newly enlightened men that goes something like, "Thanks for bringing all this to my attention, ladies. We'll take it from here." It also serves as an important corrective to many men's fears, which often boil down to "How can I support feminism without feeling like — or being seen as — a wimp?" To be a member of the Auxiliary is to know that the central actors in the struggle for gender equality will be, as they always have been, women.

But women's studies has done more than make the study of gender possible; it has made it *necessary*. The issues raised by women in the university and outside it have not "gone away" or subsided now that women have been offered a few resources and an academic room of their own. Women's studies has not been content with one room while the rest of the university goes about its androcentric business, any more than the women's movement has been convinced of its political victory because 100 percent of the U.S. senators from California in 1993 are women. Think about the shockwaves that rippled outward from Clarence Thomas's confirmation hearings over two years ago. Remember how the media responded to that event; recall the shameful way Anita Hill was treated by the Senate Judiciary Committee. The phrase the media used, as if with one voice, was that Thomas's confirmation would have "a chilling effect" on American women — that women would be less likely to come forward to describe their experiences of sexual harassment in the workplace, that women would be less likely to speak of the inequities and humiliations that permeated their working lives. Have the media ever been more wrong? Not only was there no "chilling effect," there was a national thaw. Women have been coming forward in unprecedented numbers to talk about their working lives. And they have not gone away. On campuses and off all across the country, women's studies students and faculty have joined in this virtual national seminar about men, masculinity, and power.

Gender as a power relation is the "it" that men "just don't get" in the current discussion. Women's studies scholars have demonstrated that masculinity and femininity are identities that are socially constructed in a field of power. Gender, like race and class, is not simply a mode of classification by which biological creatures are sorted into their respective and appropriate niches. Gender is about power. Just because both masculinity and femininity are socially constructed does not mean that they are equivalent, that there are no dynamics of power and privilege in operation. The problem with bringing men into this discussion about gender and power is that these issues are invisible to men.

In October 1991, after watching the hearings on television, I wrote a short op-ed piece for my local newspaper called "Clarence and Us," which described the ways in which the issue of sexual harassment had now been set before us and how men needed to rethink the issue of sexual harassment in our working lives. In subsequent months, I revised that op-ed piece into an essay with a new title — "Clarence, William, Iron Mike, Magic, and Us" — to include a few new names that would allow me to raise other issues, such as date and acquaintance rape and AIDS, that had been added to the growing national seminar. This became a lecture I deliver on college campuses across the country. But I have had to continually revise the title, because the issues not only have not gone away, but keep expanding. Today, I think the title of the lecture is "Clarence, William, Iron Mike, Magic, Senator Packwood, Woody, Tailhook, the Entire U.S. Military, Spur Posse, John Wayne Bobbitt, the Citadel, O. J. — and Us." With one more name, I won't be able to get through it without inhaling! How have men responded to this growing list? Some have taken a familiar defensive posture. "I'm not a rapist!" they shout. "And my family didn't own slaves! Leave me alone!" In fact, many advocates of "men's rights" paint themselves as the new victims of reverse discrimination. Declaring an equivalence between "wallet power" and "cleavage power," writers such as Warren Farrell claim that male power is a myth.[7] Other men have responded in the way some American men have always responded to women's demands to be heard: by running away. From Rip van Winkle to Robert Bly, men have run off to the woods, to sea, to the army, to the frontier, to outer space, in order to get away from women and breathe a sigh of relief. But neither political resistance nor mythopoetic retreat has made the issues that beset American men today disappear. In a sense, the men's rights and mythopoetic responses indicate to me the work that is yet to be done, as well as some of the obstacles that we will continue to encounter along the way.

Men are often confused about the question of power because some feminist insights do not resonate for men as they do for women. In its simplest formulation, feminism offered women a symmetry between their analysis of the world and their individual experiences. First, feminists argued, at the social level women were not "in power." This was an empirical observation, easily apprehended by anyone who cared to look. Every board of trustees of every university, every board of directors of every law firm and corporation, every legislature at every level in every state in the country — all were illustrations that women, as a group, did not have the power. Second, this aggregate analysis provided a social analogue for women's individual experience: women were not *in power* and women did not *feel* powerful.

To apply this symmetry to men's lives, however, missed something crucial in men's experiences. Certainly, at the political and institutional levels men *are* in power. But when that syllogism is presented to men — that individually, then, men must *feel* powerful — most men respond as if you came from outer space. "What are you talking about?" they say. "I have no power at all! My wife bosses me around. My kids boss me around! My boss bosses me around! I'm completely powerless!" This is a critical blind spot. All the economic, social, and political power in the world has not left individual men feeling powerful. The argument that men are powerful does not address the felt experience of most American men. Antifeminists and men's rights advocates do address that felt experience: "You're right, men have no power," they say. "Women have the power, in custody battles, in alimony, in the draft. Men are the real victims of reverse discrimination." And mythopoetic male bonders respond to that experience as well. "You're right," they say. "We have no power. Let's go off to the woods and get some. Here's the power ritual, the power drumming, the power chant." But power is not a quality one can acquire by trooping off to mythic summer camp for a weekend with the boys. At the individual level, power is experienced as a person's ability to do the kinds of things in his or her life that he or she wants to do. At the social level, power is an expression of the distribution of rewards and resources in a society; as such it is the property of groups, not of individuals. A gendered analysis must bridge these two levels, addressing both men's aggregate power and men's individual feelings of powerlessness. Much of the thinking about men has focused on opposite sides of the issue: antifeminists have seen individual men as powerless; many feminists have defined socially constructed masculinity as the drive for power, domination, and control.

I began the historical research for my new book guided by this latter feminist perspective.[8] Surely masculinity was nothing if not the drive for domination. Men were possessed with a craving for power and control. But the historical record has revealed a different picture: American men do not experience manhood as a drive for domination. Manhood is actually more about the fear of others dominating us, having power or control over us. We have constructed a vision of masculinity that sees others, especially other men, as frightening potential aggressors. We are afraid that others will see us as less than manly, weak, timid, frightened. We are afraid of not measuring up to some vaguely defined notions of what it means to be a man; we are afraid of failure. Acting masculine becomes a way to ward off the fears that we will not be seen as manly by other men, or by ourselves. What we call masculinity is more a defensive hedge against revealing those fears than it is the offensive and intentional initiation of aggression.

John Steinbeck wrote in *Of Mice and Men*: " 'Funny thing,' [Curley's wife] said. 'If I catch any one man, and he's alone, I get along fine with him. But just let two of the guys get together an' you won't talk. Jus' nothin' but mad.' She dropped her fingers and put her hands on her hips. 'You're all scared of each other, that's what. Ever'one of you's scared the rest is goin' to get something on you.' "[9] My reading of American history documents this theme. American masculinity has been propelled not by a drive for domination, but by fears of failure and fears that other men will "get something on you." In this sense, *homophobia* is the animating condition of American manhood. I do not mean homophobia in its current limited sense as the irrational fear of homosexuals or the fear of homosexual impulses in ourselves. It is those fears as well, of course, but it is also something deeper: homophobia is the fear of other men. It is this fear that propels many men to engage in the drive to dominate and to control. Homophobia keeps us isolated from one another, and eager to use what few resources we do have — racism, sexism, heterosexism, nativism — to dominate others lest they dominate us first. Such domination serves only as a hedge, keeping fears only temporarily at bay. If those other "isms" — racism, sexism, and the like — are compensatory mechanisms by which men can shield themselves from their fears of other men, then those who advocate equality for women, for people of color, for gays and lesbians, must also address men's deeper-seated homophobic fears. Since admitting fear is itself emasculating, these fears lie deeply buried in the hearts of men. We cannot even admit their presence, let alone work collectively to challenge the mechanisms that have placed those fears there.

Homophobia is part of our earliest experiences; it is inscribed into our psyches and becomes as familiar as our skin. Imagine, for example, a playground where a dozen five-year-old boys are happily playing. By asking one question, I would wager that I could immediately start a fight among the boys. The question? "Who's a sissy around here?" One of two things will likely happen. Two of the boys may square off, each pointing his finger at the other and shouting, in turn, "He is!" "No! He is!" before they come to blows. Or all the boys may gang up on the smallest, youngest, weakest boy and point at him in unison, shouting, "He is! He is!" Faced with a challenge that will haunt him for the rest of his life, he can either fight it out against overwhelming odds or take the more rational route and run away. Since this will forever brand him a coward, the manly response would probably be the less rational one. Now recall the 1992 Academy Awards presentations. As veteran actor Jack Palance came to the podium to accept the award for Best Supporting Actor in *City Slickers*, he observed that many Hollywood producers believed that at the age of seventy-one he was washed up as an actor, that he was past his prime. Then he dropped to the stage and commenced a set of one-armed push-ups. When he stood up and returned to the microphone, he clutched his Oscar tightly and notified a couple of hundred million viewers that he could "still get it up." "When does it end?" I groaned, wincing a bit from the pathos of a man old enough to be my grandfather still with something to prove.

When *does* it end? And why does it start so young? Why does it seem that men always have to prove their manhood? Why is masculinity such a relentless test, never assured, always in doubt? How is it that a man can spend a lifetime collecting the props that signify successful manhood—wealth, power, status, women—and have it all unravel in a flash because of a trivial innuendo? Why do men spend their lifetimes in pursuit of visible signs of strength, power, resolve, and courage, when our inner sense of manhood is ultimately so fragile? These are the questions that my participation in women's studies has led me to ask in my own research. And these are questions that are, at once, both scholarly and political.

Like studies of race and class, women's studies has made gender visible as a power relation, as an expression of the unequal distribution of rewards and resources in society. Women's studies connected that analysis to the social movement—feminism—that was about reallocating those rewards and resources more equitably so that women might make choices, widen their sphere of action, and claim their voices, their agency, and their lives. In the process, women's studies came to understand that those voices, agencies, and lives are very different among different women. Women, differently situated in society by race, class, age, sexuality, or region of the country, experience their lives in different ways. We have come to acknowledge that a singular construction of women's experience is inadequate.

The same is true for men. Women's studies has made gender visible to men, but it is not a monolithic, singular construction. There are many *masculinities*, many different definitions of masculinity, many different voices. These constructions of masculinity have taken shape on a contradictory terrain — a terrain of privilege conferred by gender, yet equally a terrain of inequality and powerlessness organized by race, or class, or sexuality, or ethnicity, or religion. Masculinity is about power, but it is the power of men as a group over women as a group, and additionally it is about the power of some men over other men. It is about the construction of masculinities within that field of power — the ways in which racism or homophobia, for example, construct the identities of both white men and men of color, of both heterosexual and homosexual men. Thus we speak of masculinities to denote this variety of men's experiences, and also of a hegemonic masculinity, a normative standard against which every other masculinity may be measured.

Many men resist the insights of women's studies because they do not understand how it relates to their experiences of not feeling powerful. They are told they are in power and must be aware of holding that power; yet they do not feel powerful. One of the most crucial tasks facing women's studies and the men who support it is to bring men into the discussion, to develop pedagogical techniques that will analyze men's power as a social group and simultaneously acknowledge men's individualized feelings of powerlessness, for it is only by acknowledging these *feelings* that we will be able to bring more men into the discussion. The ensuing conversation will further strengthen women's studies. Any metallurgist can tell you that the way to strengthen a metal, to make it stronger, more resilient, and more reliable, is not to add more of the same metal to it but to add different metals to it — to make an alloy. I would argue that diversity in women's studies, like diversity in the university, is certainly such a source of strength.

Men can learn so much from women's studies. And whether men acknowledge it or not, we need women's studies — desperately. All across the country, men are saying that they want to live more emotionally responsive lives, that they want their interior lives to play an increasingly important role, that they want to be more responsive lovers and better friends both with women and with other men. Virtually all men say they want to be better fathers than their own fathers were.[10] In every arena — the university, the workplace, the home — it has been women who have advocated precisely those changes that will allow us to live the kinds of lives we say we want to live. At home, women demand that we share housework and child care, that we also share the second shift — the home-based work shift that happens after the workplace shift is over.[11] In the workplace women campaign for family-friendly workplace policies, such as flex time, parental leave, on-site child care. These are not *women's* issues — these are *parents'* issues. And to the extent that men seek to be better fathers and better partners, men, too, have to make them our issues. On campus and in the workplace women campaign for an end to sexual harassment and an end to date and acquaintance rape. Surely, as long as women fear us, they cannot claim the sexual and emotional and intellectual agency that makes us desire them in the first place. If we want the kinds of relationships we say we want — relationships with women who are passionate, strong, sexy, women who are in every way our equals in desire — then we will want to join with feminist women in their struggles against these abuses of power. When women's studies makes gender visible to women, it not only reveals the ways in which women's lives have been obscured by traditional scholarship, but also provides to women a model of how engaged research, passionate pedagogy, and critical thought can be brought to bear to enlarge the range of opportunities open to them. And when women's studies fulfills its promise of making gender visible to men — or, even more acutely, makes it possible for men to make gender visible to other men — it also opens up the possibilities for men to live healthier, more emotionally responsive, more nurturing and compassionate lives, lives animated by a passion for equality and justice.

In 1917 New York City writer Floyd Dell wrote an essay in the popular magazine *The Masses* entitled "Feminism for Men." In it, Dell outlined how gender inequality also impoverished men's lives: "When you have got a woman in a box, and you pay rent on the box, her relationship to you insensibly changes character. It loses the fine excitement of democracy. It ceases to be companionship, for companionship is only possible in a democracy. It is no longer a sharing of life together — it is a breaking of life apart. Half a life — cooking, clothes, and children; half a life — business, politics and baseball. It doesn't make much difference which is the poorer half. Any half, when it comes to life, is very near to none at all."[12] In the first line of this essay, Dell underscores the promise of feminism. "Feminism is going to make it possible for the first time for men to be free," he writes. Women's studies has provided the opportunity for men to glimpse that possibility. And for that, we men can always be deeply grateful.

Notes

1. Thomas Lacquer, *Making Sex: Body and Gender from the Greeks to Freud* (Cambridge: Harvard University Press, 1990), 22.

2. Michael S. Kimmel and Thomas Mosmiller, eds., *Against the Tide: Pro-Feminist Men in the United States, 1776–1990. A Documentary History* (Boston: Beacon Press, 1992).

3. Thomas Paine, "An Occasional Letter on the Female Sex," 1775, and Henry Fowle Durant, "The Spirit of the College," 1877, in *Against the Tide*, ed. Kimmel and Mosmiller, 63–66, 132.

4. Lester Frank Ward, *Applied Sociology: A Treatise on the Conscious Improvement of Society by Society* (Boston: Ginn and Company, 1906), 232.

5. Quoted in Leslie Wheeler, ed., *Loving Warriors: Selected Letters of Lucy Stone and Henry B. Blackwell, 1853–1893* (New York: Dial Press, 1981), 151.

6. Quoted in Margaret Forster, *Significant Sisters: The Grassroots of Active Feminism, 1839–1939* (New York: Alfred A. Knopf, 1985), 252.

7. Warren Farrell, *The Myth of Male Power* (New York: Simon and Schuster, 1993).

8. Michael S. Kimmel, *Manhood: A Cultural History* (New York: Free Press, 1995).

9. John Steinbeck, *Of Mice and Men* (New York: Covici-Friede, 1937), 65.

10. Much of the work of Robert Bly and other mythopoetic men's movement leaders has been to provide a space for men to experience caring, nurturing friendships with other men, an implicitly counterhomophobic project. This is, to my mind, the most valuable contribution that project has made.

11. Arlie Hochschild, *The Second Shift* (New York: Viking, 1991).

12. Floyd Dell, "Feminism for Men," *The Masses* 5, no. 10, issue 38 (July 1914): 20; reprinted in *Against the Tide*, ed. Kimmel and Mosmiller, 361–63.

Cynthia Enloe

Feminists Try On

the Post–Cold War

Sneaker

Four years after the fall of the Berlin Wall marked the end of the Cold War, Reebok, the fastest-growing company in U.S. history,[1] decided that the time had come to make its commercial mark in Russia. Reebok wasn't the first sneaker company to target the Russian consumer. Adidas had been the front-runner in the country's sneaker market for several years, but its corporate strategy was to dump old merchandise on Russian consumers. Thus it was with considerable fanfare that Reebok's executives opened their first store, displaying brand-new wares, in downtown Moscow in December 1993. National Public Radio's reporter described it as "something out of a U.S. mall."[2] A distinctly up-market mall, at that. Reebok was selling track suits for $115; shoes on display were priced in the $100 range. A week after its grand opening, the store's happy managers described their sales as well above expectation. Their strategy also called for opening a similar store in Ukraine.

The opening of the Reebok store a stone's throw from Red Square seemed the perfect post–Cold War scenario: commercial rivalry replacing military posturing; consumerist tastes homogenizing heretofore hostile peoples; capital and managerial talent flowing freely across newly porous state borders.

On second glance, the scene in Reebok's gleaming Moscow store appeared somewhat more surreal. At the end of 1993, the average Russian monthly wage was a mere $40. And as President Boris Yeltsin's Western-approved economic restructuring was causing price rises on ordinary staples at the same time as it multiplied worker layoffs, many of Reebok's potential customers were anxious about just holding on to that $40 monthly income. Pumping up in Reebok's much-touted sneakers seemed far from many Muscovites' daily concerns.

Women in the city appeared to have particular concerns that would keep them from paying the admission fee that Reebok was charging at its door, much less trying on a $100 pair of sneakers. According to the municipal employment agency, women were 70 percent of all of the city's recorded unemployed in mid-1993.[3] While 20 percent of Russian men over sixty years old were living below the poverty line, 35 percent of Russian women over fifty-five were. Almost 60 percent of single parents, most of whom were women, reportedly were living in poverty.[4] On the other hand, just as in Chicago and Durham, so too in Moscow and Kiev, the success in selling sneakers depended in large measure on company marketers persuading children to pressure their mothers — married or single — to spend money on stylish athletic footwear. Women were often accorded a much higher profile as consumerist mothers in the public cultures of both entrenched liberal democracies and rawly nascent capitalist democracies than as policy-influencing citizens.[5]

The fall of the Berlin Wall and subsequent economic restructuring in the name of post–Cold War reordering, in other words, was no more a gender-free process than had been the Cold War that preceded it. It marked a radical rupture of gendered representations of both women and men, the very blatantness of which prompted several groups of professional women to join together in 1993 to launch the country's first women's political party, Women of Russia, in order to run a slate of candidates nationwide in the December parliamentary election. While not backed by the most explicitly feminist Russian women activists, Women of Russia's organizers wrote an electoral platform that was critical of those government policies that welcomed Reebok while at the same time undermining most women's economic and social security.[6] To the surprise of many political observers, who had brushed off the party and its candidates as a novelty item, Women of Russia garnered a very respectable 8 percent of the total national vote in the proportional representation electoral process, giving the party twenty-one seats in the new legislature.[7] The results of a widely quoted electoral poll by the All-Russian Center for Public Opinion and Market Research revealed that the voting patterns may have been more deeply gendered than even the turnout for Women of Russia suggested. Yuri A. Levada, the center's director, told reporters that his center's voter survey showed that it was *men*—especially (1) middle-aged lower-middle-class men in medium-sized cities with below-average education, (2) previously apolitical men under twenty-five living in bigger cities with above-average education, and (3) men serving in the military—who disproportionately cast their ballots for the right-wing nationalist Liberal Democratic Party led by the outspoken Vladimir V. Zhirinovsky.[8]

The end of the Cold War is occurring in a lot of different countries through a mind-boggling array of social processes. Those processes are virtually always gendered. That is, the peculiar forms of ideologized, militarized conflict that characterized the Cold War are coming unraveled in ways that depend on distinctive ideas about masculinity and femininity.[9] Taking Russian women's and Russian men's respective relationships to Reebok's new Moscow sneaker emporium—their desires, their tastes, their economic and political strategies, their explanatory theories—is one feminist strategy for making visible and making sense of how and why the Cold War is ending in the ways it is.

But those Reebok sneakers selling to a very thin slice of the Russian population do not appear on the Moscow shelves out of the blue. Each shoe—like those sold by its competitors, including archrival Nike, currently the world's leading athletic shoe company—has to be designed, engineered, manufactured, and transported before it can feed the gendered foot fantasies of Moscow shoppers. The very potency of the sneaker companies' advertising imagery can tempt one to ignore this mundane fact: Shaquille O'Neal's Reeboks are stitched by someone; Michael Jordan's Nikes are stitched by someone; so are your roommate's; so are your grandmother's. Those someones are women, mostly Asian women. No Asian woman stitcher, no million-dollar slam dunk. No Asian woman stitcher, no shopping mall desires fulfilled.

This was as true in 1980, in the depths of the Cold War, as it is in 1994, as the post–Cold War era is being entrenched. What has changed? The financial stakes have: by the end of 1993, athletic shoe sales in the United States market alone had reached an impressive $3.9 billion, 80 percent of that in various forms of sneakers.[10] Yet when we lace up our post–Cold War sneakers today, we are donning shoes that carry different representational political meaning than those we wore when the Wall and its architects forced a Russian shopper to stare longingly at Adidas rejects. During the forty years of the Cold War we women sneaker wearers in the West were donning a shoe that sent out the message that we had achieved liberation: after all, we had choice ("No, not the black Converse high-tops; I'll take the purple Nike low-tops"), and we could sprint right alongside our men up the corporate hill. Simultaneously, our sneaker-wearing sent out the message that the Communist countries' women were sadly benighted. They had no consumer choice, they had no stylish footwear to give them either the self-confidence or the bounce to compete with their men. Moreover, this message was not one of mere comparison. It was a message about entire political systems' superiority and inferiority in a dangerous global standoff. Since 1989, the multilayered message emanating from Western women's foot attire has changed, at least in part. Many of us capitalist consumer sneaker wearers are still imagining we have genuine choices and can use those sorts of choices to sprint toward liberation in the form of equality with our men. But now we are offering ourselves — our definitions of liberation — as models to emulate and thus as bases for hopefulness rather than scorn for women in Eastern Europe and Russia.

What also has changed are the abilities of women working in some Asian sneaker factories to organize effectively enough — without government suppression — to compel factory owners to bargain over working conditions, wages, and the very right to organize. The "some" here is crucial. For not all women stitching sneakers for the markets in Chicago and Kiev possess those capacities. Company executives are acutely aware of these differentials and choose their manufacturing sites accordingly. One of the crucial factors determining whether women stitching your and Michael Jordan's shoes can muster the resources necessary to force managers to engage in meaningful bargaining is the degree of authoritarianism in the political system under which those women live. The Cold War enhanced the power of many authoritarian regimes. Cold War ideology rested on the claim that the world was a dangerous place, so fraught with frightening enemies that only state militarization, centralization, and secrecy could ensure a citizenry's safety — safety from external foes and from their alleged internal co-conspirators. Such an ideology bred public passivity and repressed citizen knowledge and participation among all but a narrow circle of security elites. But because of the deeply gendered mortar holding its ideological bricks in place—that is, notions about which kinds of people could "handle" abstract scenarios and weapons technology—this Cold War cosmology was more exclusionary of women of all classes, but especially of women in economically and racially marginalized groups.

It is perhaps not surprising that it was South Korean women sneaker workers who were among the first to make use of the end of the Cold War to challenge the international corporate strategies of Nike, Reebok, and their chief competitors. By the end of the Cold War, Pusan, South Korea, had become the "sneaker capital of the world." This coastal city attracted European and North American shoe companies for several reasons. It had a location optimal for international transport to global markets; it had local Korean entrepreneurial men able to engage in joint ventures and to set up subcontracting factories; it had thousands of Korean women skilled and apparently willing to work under high-pressure conditions for minimal wages with little collective autonomy; it had a military regime in Seoul whose senior male officials were intimately tied to their U.S. government male counterparts through military alliances and the hosting of U.S. bases; it had a military regime whose economic formula included not only presumptions about Korean women's patriotic docility, but also state-sponsored women's organizations designed to inculcate women with those values.[11] It was an appealing package for executives in an industry like sneakers, which in order to generate profits needed to maximize market access and minimize labor costs. Pusan became a Cold War boomtown.

Feminist analysts of the Soviet Union and the Communist regimes of Eastern Europe have made us particularly aware of how certain state elites have had a stake in the feminized double burden. They have revealed how the masculinized senior bureaucratic and party officialdom of these countries legitimized and enforced the idea that the ideal woman, the patriotic woman, was a woman who was willing to work outside the home in a full-time job for the sake of boosting her country's GNP while simultaneously shouldering the main responsibility for her family's housekeeping, shopping (often an arduous task), cooking, and child care.[12] Feminist analysts of Western Europe also exposed how their government officials depended on many working-class women's paid work and middle-class women's unpaid work to construct industrial foundations for their modern states.[13] Cheapening women's labor further fueled the state's industrial takeoff and then provided the foundation for the second phase of industrial growth, the phase that would generate well-paying manufacturing jobs for men of the country's working class. But most Western feminist scholarship traced the potency of the Victorian myth of women's true "domestic" nature right up through the late twentieth century. Thus we may slip into the belief that the Cold War was fought between groups of state elites wielding mutually gendered yet opposing ideologies about state security: on one side of the Wall was the waged but exhausted double-burdened communist woman; on the other side of the Wall was the suburbanized but frustrated housewife. In reality the Cold War rivalry was more politically complex. Fervently *anti*communist regimes such as those in South Korea, but also in Taiwan, Singapore, the Philippines, Puerto Rico, and Guatemala each found the feminized double burden a useful ideological weapon to wield in their Cold War two-pronged campaigns for industrialized economic growth and social order.

Most of the writings on women factory workers in Third World countries — including my own — have recognized this double-burden-dependent state strategy; still they have not problematized the Cold War itself. They — we — also have featured only those women working in plants directly owned by foreign capitalists.[14] But this emphasis has overlooked one of the most important corporate innovations introduced in the 1980s in the international political economy of sneakers. Nike, the sneaker giant, began to refine its manufacturing formula. No longer, its Oregon-based executives decided, should Nike own its factories. Such ownership just heightened its corporate risk: it would have to be accountable for relations with the workers stitching its shoes. Much better, they concluded, would be a system in which they subcontracted the actual manufacturing of their sneakers to wholly owned foreign companies. Let *their* managers deal with the workers and with any local government agencies responsible for worker (or environmental) regulation compliance. Nike, for its part, holds on to control of those parts of the sneaker pipeline that give its officials the greatest professional satisfaction and the ultimate word on the product: design and marketing.[15] It may not be coincidence that Nike launched this no-factories formula in the late 1980s, late in the Cold War, just when women workers in Pusan were developing the resources to challenge both their government's and their factory managers' notions about "cheap women's labor."[16]

Executives of the major multinational shoe companies in general, and of athletic shoe companies in particular, have developed more and more intricate strategies for siting their factories and maximizing their control and profits while minimizing their risks and costs. It is not simply that they have selected Asia as a region and Asian women as assembly workers to optimize their corporate objectives. Between 1960 and 1990, they have made dramatic shifts *within* Asia. For example, in 1989 only 2 percent of Nike's shoes were produced by subcontractors—in China. Just four years later, in 1993, that proportion had leaped to 25 percent.[17] By the early 1990s, investors' interest was turning to Vietnam. The Cold War is ending in such a way as to add even more countries to the multinational sneaker factory site menu.

Taking note of these shifts might tempt one to imagine that the sneaker executives are omnipotent. They sit in their corporate "war rooms" looking at maps of the world on the wall, making calculations, and then implementing them, all without a hitch. In this portrayal women workers are reduced to helpless (and thus uninteresting) pawns. A woman in Pusan loses her job whenever her Nike—or Reebok or Adidas or L.A. Gear—subcontracting boss decides that assembling shoes in China's Guangdong Province better serves the company's interests. She didn't control the conditions that gave her her stitching job initially, and she doesn't control the conditions that eliminate her job a decade or so later—and her Chinese or Vietnamese successor will be equally powerless.

Such a portrayal implies that not just women employees are powerless. So are the fathers and husbands of these women workers who may rely on their sneaker stitching wages. So are the local municipal officials whose cities have been built up around these exporting factories. So are national government officials whose economic plans have been deliberately designed to make foreign companies' executives feel comfortable. Consumers are implicitly potent players, a fickle lot whose changing tastes can make or break a company, can drive it to seek ever more cost-saving labor sites. But consumers, because of their apparent apolitical consciousness and idiosyncratic nature, rarely are featured as deliberate actors by writers of international political economy studies—just as those who write about consumerist culture and consumers as public actors rarely trace the products under investigation back to their sources to discover who is doing what and with whom all along that decision-filled pipeline.

This misguided narrative assumption leaves as the only visible actors—the only actors, that is, whose assumptions, needs, calculations, and conclusions are monitored as if they mattered—the senior executives of the multinational corporations. One consequence of this tendency is that analysts commonly portray corporate executives as a solid corporate phalanx who appear to be globally omnipotent. Part of that appearance of omnipotence comes from never mentioning any but the most glamorous entrepreneurs by their names, never being curious about their ethnic and class perspectives, never looking at their particular career paths within and between companies in order to question just how a certain route through the corporate maze might reinforce particular presumptions about Cold War advantages, about dealing with male generals and economists and subcontractors of other nationalities, about the risks posed by militant women workers.

For instance, recently Nike announced that Thomas E. Clarke would replace Richard K. Donahue as the company's president. Donahue was sixty-seven, Clarke is forty-two. Clarke came up through the company as a marketing man, attracting a certain trade fame as the creator of the "Just Do It" advertising campaign. Although the *New York Times* financial section report does not mention his ethnicity or race, it would appear that Clarke is white and Anglo-Saxon, having grown up in Binghamton, New York, in the 1950s.[18] He went to college and then to graduate school, first in Florida and then at Pennsylvania State University, choosing to specialize in biomechanics. Clarke joined Nike in 1980 just after receiving his doctorate. With his scientific research interests, Thomas Clarke was an ideal fit with Nike, since their sneakers were on their way to becoming high-tech engineering products combining rubber, cloth, and petrochemically synthesized materials. Thus it made sense that young Clarke should be assigned by his superiors as a researcher at the Nike Sports and Research Laboratory in Exeter, New Hampshire, where he was promoted to director only three years later. Then in 1984 he moved out to the company's Oregon headquarters to head its central research and development unit. At this point in his career, Clarke chose (or was urged) to make a professional switch. In 1985, he moved from research to marketing, first directing the marketing of Nike's running division. By 1987, he was selected by his superiors to become director of marketing for the footwear division, simultaneously being promoted to divisional vice president and poised for two more promotions that would put him in line for president. Although the *Times* reporter's curiosity seems rather narrow, one learns here that a very rapid rise almost to the pinnacle of executive power at Nike can be accomplished without being posted outside the United States and without ever having to run a manufacturing operation that would require at least some contact with the employees who actually make the company's sneakers.

Feminist researchers, on the other hand, have been documenting precisely the women who make the sneakers and other goods for export—Mexican women cleaning and packing strawberries for American consumers who have come to expect fresh strawberries on their cereal even in February; Guatemalan women sewing men's shirts so executives in Dallas and Detroit can look stylishly authoritative; Barbadian women entering data in an industrialized office setting so that North American airline travelers can fly conveniently; Moroccan women weaving rugs so that residents of Frankfurt and Lyons can imagine that their homes have a touch of the exotic; Malaysian women assembling semiconductors so that high school students in the Bronx and Osaka can get their homework done more quickly.[19] Unlike many of the nonfeminist political economy commentators, these researchers have allowed the factory women their own voices. Women who stitch, assemble, punch, and weave are portrayed by feminist commentators not as pawns but as agents.

It is important to note here that a rather odd assertion has been gaining attention in some public discussions now taking place within the United States. It is the contention that feminists in the United States have portrayed women merely as victims, a portrayal that not only overlooks women's agency, but that alienates many self-respecting women who otherwise might become active in a broad-based women's movement in this country.[20] Such an assertion derives, I think, from a profound inattention to what has been going on within women's studies research in the last decade or more. Since at least the early 1980s, women's studies researchers here in the United States as well as in Western Europe — and feminist researchers working in oral history projects, labor unions, and local community projects all active outside academia — have produced scores of studies deliberately intended to reveal women's agency. Studies of long-forgotten married women's property rights campaigns, of women's mobilization against racialized slavery and against militarily sanctioned prostitution, of women's autonomous organizing within Europe's utopian socialist movements, of women's activism in the early textile labor movements, of women's diverse strategizing for the vote, of women's self-conscious maneuvering and theorizing within anticolonial nationalist movements — all of these investigations contributed to the burgeoning literature in the early phases of the Second Wave of feminism. At times, in fact, feminist researchers had to beware of coming down too enthusiastically on the side of women's agency. *Overestimating* the degree to which nineteenth- and twentieth-century women in Britain or the United States, Italy, or Egypt were not only participants but architects of their own fates could mislead the contemporary reader into *underestimating* the potency of the cultural and political forces they were attempting to influence.

Today, as well, if we are to make realistic sense of how women working in the international sneaker industry shape that industry, it is crucial that we overestimate *neither* the power of the globally mobile Nike executive *nor* the agency of the Korean woman who until recently stitched most of their sneakers.

Thus, as we return to the women workers in Pusan's sneaker factories, it is with several caveats in mind. First, if the politics of the Cold War helped to shape the gendered international sneaker industry between 1945 and 1989, then taking account of the post–Cold War's distinctive dynamics will be important to making sense of the gendered sneaker industry in the 1990s. Second, we need to link the cultural politics of consumerism explicitly to the politics of products' manufacture; if we continue to discuss consumer culture and manufacturing in splendid isolation from each other, we are not going to be able to grapple realistically with the gendering of power. Third, we should not assume that all women who work for multinational corporations are employed directly for those companies; the gender strategies of contractors' and subcontractors' executives must be monitored as well. Fourth, company executives may do their best to maximize their control of all the elements in sneaker production, but in reality they are not the only agents whose assumptions and calculations determine the gendered landscape of sneaker production; the gendered presumptions of national and municipal officials, of international lending institutions' officials, of labor union activists, of workers without organized representation — all need to be made visible. Finally, earlier feminist analysts have not treated even poor women solely as powerless victims; but as we continue this feminist project of making women factory workers' agency visible, we must detail when and how women's individual or collective activism results in increasing their effective control over their own lives — and when and why it does not. One of the places to begin such an analysis is with the South Korean women workers who organized on their own behalf, while we simultaneously remain attentive to the shifts in the global marketplace.

"I am thirty-two years old, married with two children. Now I work full time with KWWA on a voluntary basis."[21] Lee Jae Eun was describing her work with the Korean Women Workers Association to Filipino working women activists in 1990: "In the late '80s, there was a big debate within the [South Korean] Women for Equality and Peace. A group of women thought that women's activists should become involved with political activities and then bring women's issues into the political agenda. Others thought that they should concentrate on women's issues. During the process of improving women's situation [the latter group argued], the society can be changed."[22]

The politics of sneakers — as well as garments, textiles, electronics, and all other export industries that had been built on feminized factory labor in order to promote South Korea's Cold War industrialized economic boom — were about to be drawn into the politics of demilitarization and democratization. But how and how far women factory workers would become organizationally and ideologically involved was not at all certain. Just as in the revolutionary politics of France, Mexico, and Russia, in the civil rights politics of the United Sates and Britain, and in the anticolonial nationalist politics of Vietnam and Algeria, so in the antimilitarist pro-democracy politics of Brazil, Chile, and South Korea women had to weigh how best to relate their women's advocacy to other potentially, but not automatically, antipatriarchal movements.[23] Leaders (mostly men and a few women) of these latter movements all too often portrayed their causes — the overthrow of autocracies, abolition of racist laws, national independence, institutionalization of civilian pluralist electoral constitutions — as the "larger" causes. In their cosmology, women's rights became a subsidiary campaign, to be accomplished perhaps inevitably, perhaps simply later. In this scenario, explicit attention to women's needs and autonomous organizing designed to mobilize women in their particular daily situations were seen to be at best superfluous, at worst divisive. Yet the leaders and members of those groups that had prioritized the dismantling of attitudes, structures, and laws that systematically marginalized women and so privileged men were not so sanguine. Thus Lee Jae Eun and her colleagues stood at a political juncture familiar to women's advocates around the globe and across time.[24] Those activists who believed that women's issues had the best chance of being put on the national agenda if they gave up some of their autonomy and diluted their focus chose to join forces with the mixed-sex but male-dominated labor movement and its allied pro-democracy movement. Other women, including Lee Jae Eun, decided instead to form two new independent groups: the Women Society for Democracy and the KWWA. The former would concentrate on mobilizing white-collar women workers and housewives, while the latter organized women factory workers and raised their consciousness about women's issues.

One of the reasons Lee Jae Eun and her fellow KWWA activists made this difficult political choice is that they concluded that past mobilizations of Korean women factory workers had failed to produce action on the issues that most concerned the women themselves. In mixed worker organizations male labor activists quickly took over leadership roles: "In the seventies, the labour movement was led by women workers. In the eighties, we found that women were no more in the leadership of the labour movement. Most of the former women worker leaders were married. They had to stay home and take care of their families. . . . Through this experience, we realised that it was necessary to organise women workers separately for their liberation. . . . Many people in the democratic movement changed their way of thinking, but male-chauvinism is still very strong in the labour movement. There is not enough support for women workers' issues such as the issue of job security."[25]

The work of South Korean feminist scholar Jeong-Lim Nam exposes a complicated, but mutually reinforcing, Cold War relationship between labor activist patriarchy and militarized state elite patriarchy.[26] She warns us that it is not always, or only, women's position inside the family combined with cultural constructions of femininity which are to blame for the marginalization of women as manufacturing workers. Jeong-Lim Nam describes in detail just how South Korean women workers' labor was cheapened as well by the workings of state repression for the sake of fueling the country's economic boom and the foreign sneaker companies' profits. That is, as powerful as the marginalizing — and thus cheapening — effects were of familial and cultural sexism, women workers' mobilizing could not have been successfully checked without the weapon of state repression. South Korea's military rulers during the 1970s and 1980s passed specific laws, such as the Special Law Concerning National Security and Defense of 1971, that allowed for police to be used against striking workers in foreign-owned exporting companies operating in export-processing zones — that is, against precisely those work forces that were overwhelmingly female. The gendering of the state's repression gradually grew even more pronounced. As women factory workers become more politicized and more organized during the 1970s and 1980s, government authorities resorted more and more to sexual assault by riot policemen called into the factories — a tactic they chose not to use against male workers. According to Jeong-Lim Nam, this form of state repression was deepened in its silencing impact because of the cultural double standard that held a South Korean woman responsible for her sexual purity: "Sexual assaults such as stripping, kissing, fondling, threat of rape, and rape itself were used to control women's behavior. Since being raped or sexually harassed is such a stigma to an unmarried Korean women, sexual assaults were employed as a control mechanism for suppressing women's engagement in the labor movement."[27]

But why was the South Korean state so militarized during this era of (partially sneaker-driven) economic boom? And why did so many American and European executives of sneaker, electronics, and garment companies find that militarism so acceptable and reassuring? The story isn't complete without the Cold War. "National security" was a doctrine devised by many anti-communist regimes during the 1945–1989 period to justify suppression of domestic protest and dissent. The ideology of the Cold War encouraged not only government officials, but many journalists, labor union leaders, company executives, and ordinary citizens to imagine that the international system was so fraught with dangers that societies could not afford any activism that upset the established order. That order was profoundly gendered, and usually patriarchal. Thus it was that both Republican and Democratic U.S. administrations supported the militarization of South Korean political life. Thus it was that protecting sneaker and electronic export manufacturers from the outspokenness of women workers through police repression came to seem "normal" in the eyes of many foreign investors and their local subcontractors. What sustained the Cold War? Nuclear weaponry and state secrecy, yes. But also women-produced sneakers and police rape.

Now in the early 1990s, the landscape of South Korean politics is changing in ways that are prompting Nike, Reebok, and other foreign executives, along with their South Korean male subcontractor allies, to close their Pusan factories and look elsewhere in Asia for new manufacturing sites. As the South Korean military gradually lost its legitimacy due to its increasing reliance on coercion, and as the collapse of the Soviet Union made even its American backers less willing to support it at any cost, pro-democracy activists, now including autonomously organized women with a gendered agenda, succeeded in compelling the regime to allow popular elections and authentic opposition. Even the perceived threat of North Korean military invasion began to lose its popular credibility.

The results of the multistranded pro-democracy movement diminished the capacity of the state to protect local and foreign manufacturers from disaffected women workers and resulted in more open union organizing in the most feminized factories and more genuine bargaining between employees and managers over rates of pay, health hazards, and sexual harassment on the job. This achievement may help to explain why South Korean women working in manufacturing jobs narrowed the wage gap between themselves and their male counterparts: in 1980 South Korean women manufacturing workers earned 45.1 percent of the wages of male manufacturing workers; by 1990s they earned 50.1 percent.[28] To stave off assumptions that the mere passage of time created such progress, modest though it was, it is worth noting that during the 1980s in Japan, Singapore, and Sri Lanka the gaps between women's and men's manufacturing workers' wages *widened*.[29]

On International Women's Day in 1992, Korean women workers' groups held rallies in Pusan and five other cities. They commemorated a twenty-one-year-old woman worker, Kong Mi Kyong, who committed suicide as a result, they said, of intense work pressure and verbal abuse by her factory managers. Rally attendees also called on the now nominally civilianized government to halt their efforts to keep a low ceiling on wages and to perpetuate arbitrary dismissals. Finally, these South Korean women demonstrated their evolving analysis of gendered work conditions by calling for company child care centers to ensure women's right to work.[30]

As the silencing of women's voices became more difficult and the cheapening of women's labor less possible, Pusan began to lose its appeal to sneaker producers. Simultaneously, in Seoul's official circles, the shoe industry—along with other feminized factory-based sectors such as toys, textiles, and electronics assembly—began to be referred to as "sunset" industries. Newly elected, overwhelmingly male South Korean politicians and their senior technocrats started in 1989 to plan for an economic restructuring of the country. "Restructuring" is as gendered in South Korea as it is in Russia or the United States because it is designed to encourage some industries while abandoning others, to prioritize some skills while shelving others, invest public monies into some services while sharply cutting back on others—each characterized by sexual divisions of labor. Korea's feminist analysts see the state's abandonment of sneakers and textiles, combined with its new emphasis on steel, shipbuilding, and automobiles, as amounting to the *remasculinization* of the South Korean economy.

But it will not happen easily. "Restructuring" is far more than a technocratic euphemism. It requires women to be dismissed from jobs in which they have more conscious stake than they did even a decade ago, jobs in which they are better organized than they were under former repressive regimes. The KWWA has reported that between 1989 and 1990, 8,224 women workers employed in thirty-two foreign-owned companies lost their jobs when companies moved overseas.[31] As part of the same processes, more foreign companies decided to adopt the Nike model of international organization; that is, American and European strategists chose to stop hiring women assembly workers directly and instead to go through local subcontractors, thereby putting themselves at arm's length from the employees they might want to lay off at a moment's notice.[32]

Some Korean women have speculated, too, that the officials in Seoul might imagine that women laid off from a sneaker factory would be eager to switch to a new "service sector" job. They might even be willing to work as a disco dancer or a prostitute in the growing sex tourism industry, an industry that was launched during the Cold War by businesses that serviced American male soldiers, thousands of whom still are stationed in South Korea. But the attempt to translate this official assumption into economic practice may founder. It fails to take into account the fact that thousands of women factory workers now under threat of job loss have developed an understanding of their place in Korean society that connects ideas about mothering, sexuality, wage rates, public visibility, and autonomy.[33]

By the early 1990s, the South Korean entrepreneurs who make sneakers for Nike and Reebok began setting up new factories in China and Indonesia—two countries, one communist, the other anticommunist, governed by authoritarian governments legitimated by Cold War worldviews and distinguished by popular ideologies that marginalize women. At the moment, employers face only nascent autonomous women's organizing, but this may change in the context of subcontracting.

Riyanti is an eighteen-year-old junior high school graduate from the village of Klaten in central Java, the largest of Indonesia's islands.[34] Nike's cofounder and CEO, Philip Knight, has said that he would like the world to think of his company as "a company with a soul that recognizes the value of human beings."[35] For Riyanti, Knight's corporate aspiration translates into wages of fifteen cents an hour.[36] Her wages are not paid directly by Nike. Her bosses are South Korean factory owners who moved their Nike-producing sneaker factories to Indonesia from South Korea in 1989 when they concluded that labor costs there were becoming too high.[37] John Woodman, Nike's general manager in Indonesia, rejects the idea that these wage rates amount to exploitation of the mainly female work force hired by his subcontractors: "Exploitation? I don't think so. . . . Yes, they are low wages. But we've come in here and given jobs to thousands of people who wouldn't be working otherwise."[38] On another occasion, however, Woodman told researchers that he didn't really know what went on inside the sneaker factories. They weren't his factories. Nike just bought the product: "It's not within our scope to investigate."[39]

It is within the scope, but not the interest, of the military generals and their civilian economic advisers who have dominated Indonesia's political system for the past thirty years and have energetically courted European, Asian, and American investors. They are concerned about having enough jobs to absorb the thousands of new workers coming each year into the labor force. But they also are anxious because of the inherent instability of a political system that excludes so many Indonesians from effective roles in policymaking and yet has produced a social stratification that is widening the gaps between rich and poor. At the time of the 1993 government-controlled election, per capita income was a mere $650 — annual subsistence for Indonesians who daily can contrast their lives "to the glittering wealth that is on display in Jakarta, the capital, and other large cities."[40]

Nike and other name-brand sneakers that today are being made in Indonesia are being created out of a complex six-cornered relationship between American male general managers, South Korean (and Taiwanese and Singaporean and Indonesian) male subcontracting factory owners, Indonesian male generals and civil servants, men leading Indonesia's emergent opposition groups, women developing autonomous women's organizations, and Riyanti and her women coworkers. The women workers still appear to fit the image held by the sneaker executives and their subcontractors when they left Pusan's unhappy capitalist investors behind. " 'Tired?' Riyanti rolled her eyes and feigned collapse. She smiled, demure and uncomprehending, when asked about her low wages and long hours. 'I'm happy working here. . . . I can make money and I can make friends.' "[41] But Riyanti may be more than the package of feminine compliance she displays to a visiting journalist. Twice in that same year, 1991, Riyanti had joined her Indonesian women coworkers on strike, first to force the Korean company executives to accept their new union and later to compel them to comply with the government officials' newly instituted — but unenforced — minimum wage: $1.06 per day. These moments of defiance may be multiplied by the way the global economy's decision makers brought sneaker factories to Indonesia.

The typical model of the male-strategized, women-powered global assembly line that manufactures labor-intensive, competitive, light-industry consumer products is one that portrays footloose company executives moving from one Third World country to the next, welcomed in each by government officials eager to undercut the labor costs of their neighbors. In this scenario, the women who are likely to be hired or laid off by the working of this masculinized alliance are competitors with each other. If Riyanti gets a job, Kong Mi Kyong will lose hers. But this conventional scenario leaves out the possibility that the male executives and officials aren't the only ones who can talk to each other, to share advice, lessons, innovations. Increasingly, in fact, women workers in Asia and elsewhere are building organizational networks that are allowing them to exchange experiences and strategies explicitly designed to address women's own needs: how to convince fathers and husbands that a woman's going out to meetings in the evening is not evidence of her sexual promiscuity; how to overcome feelings of gratitude mixed with anxiety on the assembly line; how to develop organizational agendas that take into account family and community needs; how to build alliances with male workers and unionists without allowing women's analysis and goals to be smothered; how to acquire skills such as speaking in public, taking minutes, planning a strike, talking to journalists.[42]

In mid-1991 a delegation of Japanese feminists visited Indonesia. They were interested in finding out more about how their own lives and political activism related to those of Indonesian women. One of the factories they visited was in the government-created export-processing zone north of Jakarta. It was a joint venture owned and run by Singaporean and Indonesian capitalists. The owners employed 1,148 workers, 94 percent of whom were women. They were producing sportswear—not just sneakers but sports clothes—for both Nike and Adidas to sell in Europe and the United States. "The factory was dimly lit and packed with sewing machines and worktables on which were piles of materials. Workers here earned Rs. 2,500 (approximately $1.30) daily, working from 7:30 A.M. to 3:00 P.M. Workers usually work overtime. The expressions on the workers' faces were gloomy."[43] The Japanese women were hosted by Perempuan (Women's Solidarity) and the Women's Department of the All Indonesia Workers' Union (SPSI). These Indonesian women were cooperating with each other to build inter-Asian alliances even though they, like their South Korean counterparts, had each adopted quite different analyses about when and how to work with Indonesia's male unionists.

A year later, in 1993, three Indonesian women workers' organizers traveled to both Hong Kong and South Korea as part of an exchange developed by the Hong Kong–based Committee for Asian Women. A principal objective of the CAW exchange was to "build up solidarity linkage as plants from (Hong Kong and South Korea) are being relocated to Indonesia."[44] Integral to creating that solidarity in the face of structural competition was the efforts of Hong Kong and South Korean women workers to share organizing lessons with their Indonesian counterparts, many of whom were now working not only in the same industries but for the same employers. In turn, the Indonesian organizers described to their Hong Kong and Korean hosts how their government's lax enforcement of labor laws kept women marginalized, how government officials were promoting family planning contests inside factories with managers' assistance, how forms of harassment (e.g., taping over the mouths of women workers found talking among themselves) were used by managers, and how male coworkers often push women's demands to the bottom of the lists presented to government ministers.[45]

It is not clear yet just what tactics and strategies the sneaker factory owners and their name-brand corporate clients will adopt when challenged by this innovative cross-national women's organizing. The very fact that they will have to respond is new. There are new political actors on the world scene, women who organize out of their particular local needs and values while simultaneously deriving strength from international alliances. The political economy of sneakers in the past has been constructed — and refined — over the past three decades largely by male multinational executives, male government officials, and male subcontractors within the context of the Cold War, a gendered international system that justified militarized rule in the name of economic development for the sake of national security and interstate alliance security. It depended as well on those Americans, Europeans, and Japanese with the money to spend on items above and beyond daily subsistence to imagine that consumer choice was part of political freedom and thus woven into the way of life that was being defended by national security states and their militarized alliances.

Since 1989, the post–Cold War system has looked at first glance as one that simply allowed this political economy to spread. Russian and Ukrainian women as mothers now would imagine freedom to be the chance to buy Western-brand sneakers for their sons and daughters, maybe even for themselves, encouraged by the new official stress on women's potential for achieving feminine beauty. Chinese — and most recently Vietnamese — women would imagine their government's "openings" to the West, Japan, and the booming Asian Newly Industrialized Countries ("NICS" or "Tigers") to allow them to apply for jobs in foreign-owned and joint-venture sneaker factories.

But the post–Cold War political thinking among women in these countries may hold out the prospect for something less than a well-greased expansion of the Cold War sneakered relationships. To the extent that women in Russia and Eastern Europe seize public space in order to challenge the Americanized assumption that post-1989 democratization can be reduced to feminized consumerism *and* to the extent that women in South Korea can develop autonomous women-centered analyses and strategies for nonmilitarized, nonpatriarchal workplaces and find ways to share their lessons with Indonesian, Chinese, and Vietnamese women — to *this* extent, the Cold War sneaker may offer a less comfortable fit in the 1990s. And if it pinches, we may have to alter not just our shoe size, but our entire package of images about "Western" women, about Asian women, about Eastern European women, and perhaps about liberation itself.

Notes

1. Richard Barff and James Austen, "'It's Gotta Be da Shoes': Domestic Manufacturing, International Subcontracting, and the Production of Athletic Foortwear," *Environment and Planning* 25 (1993): 1103. I am grateful to Phi Pham for sharing her ideas with me about international sneaker politics at the very early stages of this investigation. A quite different version of this paper was published as "The Globe-Trotting Sneaker," *Ms.* 5, no. 5 (March–April 1995):10–15.

2. National Public Radio, *Morning Edition*, WNYC, New York, December 29, 1993.

3. Fred Weir, "The Kitchen Counterrevolution," *In These Times*, March 22, 1993, 22.

4. "Poverty of Numbers," *The Economist*, July 10, 1993, 40.

5. Ukrainian feminist scholar Solomea Pavlychko describes the intense pressures that mothers now feel as their children's desires are being constructed in new ways: by the burgeoning consumer market and the influx not only of foreign products but of European and American marketing techniques. Whereas only several years ago Ukrainian children collected stamps and then music cassettes, now they want to show off to their friends their collections of foreign candy wrappers (a Mars Bar wrapper has a special cachet). Reebok, Pavlychko reports, already is a well-known brand name among Kiev youngsters. Ukrainian girls are also now urged to long for Barbie dolls, thanks in large part to the glistening new Barbie store recently opened in Kiev by its U.S. manufacturer, Mattel. After seeing their daughters so unhappy among their more affluant schoolmates, some mothers have felt so guilty at not being able to afford the prized toy that they have spent money on a Barbie that they ordinarily would have set aside for more essential household supplies. (Solomea Pavlychko, Ukrainian Institute, conversation with author, Cambridge, Massachusetts, February 7, 1994. Her analysis of contemporary Ukranian feminism was presented at the Conference on Women in Russia and the Former USSR, University of Bath, Bath, U.K., March 31–April 2, 1993, and will appear as "Feminism in Post-Communist Ukrainian Society" in the forthcoming conference proceedings published by Cambridge University Press.) While a recent documentary explored the dysfunctional impact of Nike's and the Chicago Bulls basketball team owners' mutually reinforcing marketing strategies on the career aspirations of many African American boys in Chicago, the filmmakers neglected to investigate the consequences for these boys' relationships with their mothers, although those women would be among the most likely sources

of the money necessary for teenagers to purchase the expensive footwear. ("Be Like Mike," *Power Plays*, part 1, WGBH/PBS, February 7, 1994.)

6. For reporting on the Women of Russia Party, its origins, its leaders, and its policy analyses, see "Women's Group, Shakhray on Election Programs," *Foreign Broadcast Information Service*, November 29, 1993: 42–43; "Women of Russia Candidate List," *Foreign Broadcast Information Service*, November 24, 1993: 22–23; Reuters News Agency, "Women's Alliance Formed in Russia," *Globe and Mail* (Toronto), October 23, 1993; "Competing Visions," *Maclean's* (Toronto), December 27, 1993: 44–45; Linda Racioppi and Katherine O'Sullivan See, "Organizing Women Before and After the Fall: Women's Politics in the Soviet Union and Post-Soviet Russia," *Signs* 20, no. 4 (Summer 1995): 818–50; Nadezhda A. Shedova, "The Women's Movement and Women's Political Participation in Russia: A Look at Russia's Parliament [before the December 1993 Elections]," USA-Canada Institute of the Russian Academy of Sciences, Moscow, 1993; Richard D. Anderson, "Women Legislators in Russia [before the December 1993 Elections]" (paper presented at the annual meeting of the American Political Science Association, Washington, D.C., September 1–5, 1993). I appreciate Richard Anderson's subsequent correspondence with me in February 1994 in which he shared his analysis of Women of Russia's electoral relationship to more explicitly feminist Russian groups.

7. "Russian Parliament Outcome Unclear," *Boston Globe*, December 26, 1993.

8. Steven Erlanger, "Who Voted for Rightist in Russia? Most Nervous Men, a Poll Shows," *New York Times*, December 30, 1993.

9. I have tried to spell out this theme in greater detail in *The Morning After: Sexual Politics at the End of the Cold War* (Berkeley: University of California Press, 1993).

10. Jerry Schwartz, "In Shoes, the Great Outdoors Beckons," *New York Times*, February 13, 1994. Based on figures supplied by the (U.S.) National Sporting Goods Association, "sneakers" are a special category of athletic shoe, which excludes several different sorts of athletic footwear that the general public commonly thinks of as sneakers. Thus, to arrive at the total sales figure here of $3.9 billion, I have added the U.S. sales figures for the association's following categories: sneakers, jogging/running, basketball, tennis, and aerobic. Other athletic footwear categories that together make up the remaining 20 percent of U.S. sales in 1993 include hiking, soccer, golf, football, racquetball, and baseball. The Schwartz article was reporting on the rising sales of hiking boots among American consumers, especially among the middle-aged. For instance, in the United States from 1992 to 1993, hiking boots sales revenues increased by 27.2 percent, whereas basketball sneakers sales revenues increased by a mere 3.6 percent and aerobic sneakers sales revenues actually fell by 3.4 percent. Responding to — and perhaps fueling — this trend, Reebok has bought Rockport, an American shoe manufacturer well known for its hiking boots. Nowhere in this report, however, was information supplied regarding which women in which countries were

making the different styles of athletic shoes. The report also did not detail the consumer sales trends in other countries, such as Russia or Italy or Malaysia.

11. For a detailed analysis of the masculinist state formula of the post–World War II South Korean elite and of the ways in which that masculinization shaped the economic policies of successive Seoul regimes toward women, see Seungsook Moon, "Women for the Nation: Economic Development and Gender Politics in South Korea—1963–1992" (Ph.D. diss., Brandeis University, 1994).

12. See, for instance, Gail Lapidus, *Women in Soviet Society* (Berkeley: University of California Press, 1978); Mary Buckley, ed., *Perestroika and Soviet Women* (Cambridge: Cambridge University Press, 1992); Barbara Einhorn, *Cinderella Goes to Market: Citizenship, Gender, and the Women's Movement in East Central Europe* (London: Verso/Routledge, 1993).

13. See, for instance, Judy Lown, *Women and Industrialization: Gender at Work in Nineteenth-Century England* (Minneapolis: University of Minnesota Press, 1990); Angela John, *By the Sweat of Their Brow: Women Workers at Victorian Coal Mines* (London: Routledge and Kegan Paul, 1984).

14. My first effort to think through the relationships between militarization and the feminization of multinational corporations' manufacturing in Third World countries was "Women Textile Workers in the Militarization of Southeast Asia," in *Perspectives on Power: Women in Africa, Asia and Latin America*, ed. Jean O'Barr, Occasional Papers Series, no. 13, Center for International Studies (Durham, N.C.: Duke University, 1982), 73–86. My most recent writings with this focus on women as industrial workers are "Blue Jeans and Bankers," *Bananas, Beaches, and Bases: Making Feminist Sense of International Politics* (Berkeley: University of California Press, 1990), 151–76, and "Bananas Militarized and Demilitarized," *The Morning After*, 102–41.

15. For a report on Nike's manufacturing strategy and its relationships to its mainly South Korean subcontractors, see Mark Clifford, "Spring in Their Step," *Far Eastern Economic Review*, November 5, 1992, 56–60.

16. Organizers of Asian working women plan to raise the issue at the 1995 World Conference of Women in Beijing of subcontracting and of other new forms of global production and capital mobilization that have made the violators of women's rights "more invisible and distant." "Onward to Beijing 1995," *Asian Women Workers Newsletter* 13, no. 1 (January 1994): 10.

17. Barff and Austen, "'It's Gotta Be da Shoes,'" 1103.

18. "Nike Names Executive as President," *New York Times*, February 15, 1994.

19. There have been scores of these studies, many of which I have detailed in the notes to chapter 7 of *Bananas, Beaches, and Bases*, but new and lesser-known studies of women factory workers are mentioned regularly in *Asian Women Workers Newsletter*, published by the Committee for Asian Women, 57 Peking Road, 4/F, Room 403, Kowloon, Hong Kong. These include *Hurry on the Machines: Women in Clothing Factories Speak Out* (Johannesburg, South Africa: English Literacy Project, 1993); Ho

Shuet Yin, *Taiwan — After a Long Silence* (Hong Kong: Asia Monitor Resource Center, 1990); Chhaya Datar, *Waging Change: Women Tobacco Workers in Nipani Organize* (New Delhi: Kali for Women Publishers, 1989); *Women Workers in the Free Trade Zone of Sri Lanka: A Survey* (Colombo: Voice of Women, 1983); Kurt Petersen, *The Maquiladora Revolution in Guatemala* (New Haven: Orville H. Schell Center for Human Rights, Yale Law School, 1992); Amaryllis Tiglao Torres, *The Urban Filipino Worker in an Industrializing Society* (Quezon City: University of the Philippines Press, 1988); Carla Risseuw, *The Wrong End of the Rope: Women Coir Workers in Sri Lanka* (Leiden, Netherlands: Research Project on Women and Development, 1980); Carla Freeman, "High Tech and High Heels in the Global Economy: Women, Work, and Off-Shore Informatics in Barbados" (Ph.D. diss., Temple University, 1993); Lynn Bolles, *We Paid Our Dues: Women Trade Union Leaders in the English-Speaking Caribbean* (Washington, D.C.: Howard University Press, forthcoming).

20. Naomi Wolf, *Fire with Fire* (New York: Random House, 1993).

21. "KWWA Member Speaks," *Asian Women Workers Newsletter* 9, no. 3 (September 1990): 5.

22. Ibid.

23. See, for example, Sonia Alvarez, *Engendering Democracy in Brazil* (Princeton: Princeton University Press, 1990); Anne-Marie Hilsdon, *Madonnas and Whores: Sexuality, Violence, and Gender in the Philippines* (London: Zed Press, 1994); Maragaret Randall, *Sandino's Daughters Revisited: Feminism in Nicaragua* (New Brunswick, N.J.: Rutgers University Press, 1994).

24. A collection of case studies of organizing among Malaysian, Filipina, British, Indian Mexican, and other working women is Sheila Rowbotham and Swasti Mitter, eds., *Dignity and Daily Bread* (New York: Routledge, 1994).

25. "KWWA Member Speaks," 5.

26. Jeong-Lim Nam, "Women's Role in Export Dependence and State Control of Labor Unions in South Korea," *Women's Studies International Forum* 17, no. 1 (1994): 57–67.

27. Ibid., 60.

28. "Social Indicators," *Far Eastern Economic Review*, August 6, 1992, 6. The source for these wage data is the U.N.'s Economic and Social Commission for Asia and the Pacific.

29. Ibid.

30. "March 8th," *Asian Women Workers Newsletter* 11, no. 2 (April 1992): 5.

31. "Job Losses — Women at the Losing Ends Again," *Asian Women Workers Newsletter* 10, no. 3 (September 1991): 3.

32. "South Korea — Mass Retrenchment vs. Labour Shortage," *Asian Women Workers Newsletter* 11, no. 2 (April 1992): 14–16.

33. For oral histories of Korean women working in prostitution designed to service U.S. male soldiers, see Saundra Sturdevant and Brenda Stoltzfus, *Let the Good*

Times Roll: Prostitution and the U.S. Military in Asia (New York: New Press, 1992), 166–239. I am grateful to Seungsook Moon, a sociologist Brandeis University, for sharing with me her ideas about the relationship between the patriarchal underpinnings of the economic restructuring and prostitution (conversation with the author, February 10, 1994, Waltham, Massachusetts). Filmmakers Grace Lee and Diane Lee are currently completing a documentary film, entitled *Camp Arirang*, on South Korean women's experiences of prostitution connected with U.S. military bases.

34. Vernon Loeb, "$75 Nikes, 15 Cents an Hour," *Boston Globe*, December 30, 1991.

35. Philip Knight, quoted in "Naming Names," *Ms.* 3, no. 5 (March–April 1993): 92.

36. Loeb, "$75 Nikes."

37. Ibid.

38. Ibid.

39. John Woodman, quoted in Richard J. Barnet and John Cavanagh, "Just Undo It: Nike's Exploited Workers," *New York Times*, February 13, 1994. This article was adapted from Barnet and Cavanagh, *Global Dreams: Imperial Corporations and the New World Order* (New York: Simon and Schuster, 1994).

40. Philip Shendon, "Suharto of Indonesia, Re-Elected, Picks a Deputy," *New York Times*, March 11, 1993.

41. Loeb, "$75 Nikes."

42. Among recent academic studies of Indonesian women's workplace lives and their political organizing are Saskia E. Wieringa, "Two Indonesian Women's Organizations: Gerwani and the PKK," *Bulletin of Concerned Asian Scholars* 25, no. 2 (April–June 1993): 17–30; Dinae Lauren Wolf, *Factory Daughters: Gender, Household Dynamics, and Rural Industrialization in Java* (Berkeley: University of California Press, 1993).

43. "Visit Indonesia: Changes Start from Knowing the Reality," *Asian Women Workers Newsletter* 10, no. 4 (January 1992): 19.

44. "From the CAW Secretariat," *Asian Women Workers Newsletter* 12, no. 4 (October 1993): 20.

45. "We Are on Strike: Indonesian Women Workers Organize for Their Rights," *Asian Women Workers Newsletter* 12, no. 4 (October 1993): 1–3.

Sara M. Evans

Afterword

Women's studies began as the academic arm of "second wave" feminism. *Words* — on the page, in the classroom, and in the small group — were pivotal to feminist action. Themes of finding a voice and a space in which to speak and be heard resonate through the early literature of the women's liberation movement. This anthology demonstrates that after a quarter century of scholarship, "voice" remains a central concern for women's studies. We see here nuances and variations that could not have been imagined in 1970, but we can also observe some of the dilemmas that must be tackled by the next generation of feminist scholars if their passion for changing the world is to remain undimmed.

In the late 1960s and early 1970s, women regained their voices through a process of storytelling and naming. With the slogan "the personal is political," they analyzed inequalities in power previously understood as natural. Gathered in small consciousness-raising groups, women sought to redefine themselves and, with the new lens of feminism, the world. Some literally renamed themselves—reclaiming their "maiden" names or inventing new, matrilineal ones (Marthachild, Loisdaughter). They challenged the generic use of masculine pronouns and titles (chairman, fireman) and offered "Ms." as an alternative to the marital designations of "Miss" and "Mrs." Mimeographed papers flew around the country, generating a common language, though specific terms (e.g., "sexism" and "patriarchy") remained hotly contested and fluid.

Consciousness-raising was understood both as a process of theory-building and as personally liberating. Women described their own experiences in order to discover patterns, to look for structures of power in order to overcome individual self-blaming. They held nothing sacred, preferring to challenge the "naturalness" of received definitions of "femininity" and "masculinity" and to trace their implication in social structures (from the family to the corporation).

Consciousness-raising, then, was itself both a form of action (naming) and a ground for innovation and experimentation. Virtually any issue that came up for discussion in the semiprivacy of a small group could result in more public forms of action: consciousness-raising groups founded dozens of journals, health clinics, child care centers, bookstores, publishing houses, rape crisis centers, and shelters for battered women. Building women's studies programs was only one of many forms of institution-building.

In the late 1960s and early 1970s college and university students demanded (and sometimes taught) courses, searching in vain for scholarship that could answer questions raised in their consciousness-raising groups: why are women oppressed? what is the relationship between biological sex and sex/gender roles? what have been the images of and ideologies about women in past times and in other cultures? Students in on-campus consciousness-raising groups took these questions into their classrooms, and when they found them restricted to the sidelines, they created their own courses and then a curriculum. The women's studies classroom quickly became an extension of the consciousness-raising group, retaining an emphasis on active and participatory processes while rigorously demanding an encounter with scholarly traditions and paradigms. Both students and teachers understood that they had to challenge the paradigms of their disciplines just in order to ask the questions.

Women's studies classrooms were thrilling places. A generation of both graduate and undergraduate students joined their professors on the frontiers of knowledge. In discipline after discipline they created room to think, discursive spaces, by exposing the ways in which women have been rendered invisible and by experimenting with gender as a category of analysis. In literature they challenged definitions of the canon, of what constitutes a text. In history they proposed that the very definition of what history is — where it happens, what actions and changes are deemed to be "historic" — was extremely partial and limited. In sociology they noticed that, while gender occurred frequently as a variable, the presumed norm in most studies was male and women appeared usually as outsiders, exceptions, the unusual case. Similarly, anthropologists challenged perspectives on culture drawn primarily from male observers and male informants. Partial truths could no longer stand for the whole, and an endless array of new and challenging questions opened the way for dramatically new and challenging research. In virtually every discipline of the humanities and social sciences (and increasingly now in the sciences), feminist scholarship has become a major source of innovation and transformative knowledge.

The growth of academic feminism — measurable in the proliferation of journals, the formation of women's caucuses or committees in virtually every professional association, the changed content of mainline disciplinary publications — has remained linked to the multifaceted activist offspring of the "second wave." Indeed, women's studies proved to be a haven for feminism, continuing to grow despite the backlash of the Reagan era. Yet its very proliferation and growing sophistication and specialization has created distance between "academics" and "activists." They spring from the same root but increasingly do not speak the same language. Highly theoretical treatments of "social construction" and intellectual debates over essentialism, for example, seem far from the day-to-day concerns of activists working on welfare reform or rape and domestic violence.

Where the link has remained strong has been in the hands-on arena of public policy. Studies of comparable worth, for example, laid the foundations for both legislative and judicial strategies in the 1980s. Similarly, documentation of domestic violence, the feminization of poverty, and the consequences of divorce have provided ammunition for organizing and lobbying efforts. Policy research, however, has migrated to policy institutes and research centers, usually separate from women's studies programs and even freestanding outside universities. Despite common roots in the women's movement and a shared academic location, policy research centers and women's studies programs frequently have markedly different agendas represented in different understandings of politics. Policy research takes the liberal state as a given. Its goals are to lay the groundwork for policy initiatives designed to improve women's lives and their access to basic rights. Applied researchers in areas such as child care, comparable worth, labor law, and sexual harassment generally have close and ongoing relationships with activists in these areas.

In contrast, women's studies programs and departments focus on conceptual analyses, challenging, criticizing, and exploring virtually all cultural and political categories. They tend to be skeptical of the liberal state, and indeed have produced lengthy and astute critiques of its patriarchal nature. Most programs maintain links with community service providers such as domestic violence programs via internship study opportunities for their students. But the town-gown gulf remains significant.

It is instructive to ponder the transformation in feminist approaches through the evolution of women's studies. The problem of voice has been central to women's rights for a very long time. As Richlin shows in this volume, public speech in the ancient world was by definition a manly activity. Across many centuries even the women whose class and educational privilege permitted them access to public speech remained isolated, fundamentally outsiders. The power of this tradition was exemplified in the early nineteenth-century United States when women's efforts to shift from private to public speech met with ridicule and even violence. While Fanny Wright and the Grimké sisters were vilified for their daring, masses of women struggled with their own internal barriers to speech even in all-female semipublic settings. The first step for many was public prayer. Later, when suffragists adopted the tactics of public agitation, all they had to do was show up in a town square and launch into soapbox oratory to create a spectacle that rapidly attracted a crowd.

Disconnected from their own history, many early members of the "second wave" of feminism understood themselves to be breaking a silence for the first time. Their voices, located necessarily in individuals telling unique stories, sought to speak for and about women as a collectivity and to challenge a similarly monolithic patriarchy. Individual stories, as exemplars of group reality, could be powerful in settings such as abortion and rape speak-outs. Similarly, feminist scholars analyzed the voices of women as the basis for brilliant challenges to their disciplines. Yet both academic and nonacademic efforts to describe female culture, language, and common structures of oppression led to overly uniform and monolithic theories both about women and about patriarchal power. Simply to make statements about "women" —

without specifying which women — tended to evoke an unspoken norm that was white and middle class. As Audre Lorde put it, "As white women ignore their built-in privilege of whiteness and define woman in terms of their own experience alone, then women of color become 'other,' the outsider whose experience and tradition is too 'alien' to comprehend."[1]

Challenged by angry critiques of women of color and Third World women who demonstrated in eloquent detail the tendency of many feminist analyses to make an implicit presumption that women were white, middle class, and American, for the last decade and a half we have focused on the multiplicity of women's voices. For a time that exploration foundered theoretically on the very different premises of analytical traditions focused on gender, race, and class. When feminist theorists sought to show the overwhelming analytical power of gender, they rendered other forms of difference invisible. And not just race and class, either. Religion, region, sexual preference, and a host of other distinctions became indistinct in such a context. Yet the traditions of class analysis (whether Marxist or sociological) as well as race relations and minority studies had, in turn, a similar erasing effect on the consequences of gender.

The theoretical shift from structural and materialist analyses to poststructural discourse analysis has offered at least a partial resolution to the dilemma of feminist scholarship with its renewed focus on voice. This collection demonstrates just how powerful and creative that impulse has become. The authors, in enormously varied ways, invite us to imagine voices with which we may be unfamiliar and to hear new things in those we think we know. Silence, they note, is a fundamental condition of oppression. Just as speech has speakers and hearers, silence can result from a denial of voice or a lack of audience or both. They analyze the mechanisms of silencing and modes of resistance, including the contradictory traps of discourses, both verbal and visual. They use the tools of their craft — such as textual analysis and oral interviews — to bring additional voices into feminist analyses. Writers like Holloway also call passionately for more speech.

Current scholarship focused on voice has a striking continuity with its roots in consciousness-raising. The voice comes from within an embodied person — whether spoken, written on a page, or marked on the body. It is this specificity of the individual that permits the fullest exploration of difference, multiplicity, and complexity. Yet the emphasis on multiplicity has tended in recent years more toward fragmentation than solidarity.

As we try to imagine women's studies into the twenty-first century, however, we cannot build on these achievements if we do not also notice their limits. The emphasis on multiplicity, complexity, and subjectivity (as well as some of the highly specialized academic languages in which they have been explored) has challenged the category that lies at the center of feminism: woman. Not only does this intellectual challenge create a conceptual dilemma for women's studies, it also undermines political agency: in whose name can we act? is there a "we"? The emphasis of feminist scholarship on the forces that keep women silent and on voice as resistance to silence raises these questions but does not confront them very directly.

The political problem of reconstituting a "we" without erasing difference is addressed in part by the expectation that speaking and listening can elicit empathy, a sense of commonality. For example, stories of HIV-infected women confront the stereotypes more powerfully than any statistical measures. Storytelling makes the teller visible, confronts the audience with its own tendency to make those perceived as different (and threatening) into Others — a challenge to empathic listening. The effectiveness of these stories, gathered by doctors with roots in the feminist women's health movement, is a testimony to the continuing efficacy of consciousness-raising. The vision behind consciousness-raising was one in which the multivocality of each individual bespeaks a yearning for empathic understanding and the mutual identification with stories of victimization welds together morality and politics.

The very success of consciousness-raising poses us with new questions in the 1990s. Important as it is, the model of consciousness-raising is an insufficient one without further exploration of the nature of public interaction, of public conversation as well as public speech, and of power relations imbedded in new forms of global communication. The consciousness-raising emphasis on empathy, for example, too easily links to a politics of good (victim) versus bad (powerful). Self-righteousness can substitute for politics, and where it does, it leads to a reputation for political correctness that is costing us dearly. Those of us schooled in the movements of the sixties no doubt remember fondly the clarity of the civil rights movement, where the political goal of ending segregation was unquestionably aligned with the moral right. "Beloved Community" versus the KKK, however, represents a political vision that cannot encompass the messiness and complexities of most of modern public life.

A series of linked questions and problems suggest the avenues that women's studies may pursue into the twenty-first century. Voice, as imbedded in human experience, needs to be linked to public, conversational voices. Empathy and identification are critical aspects of the safe spaces of consciousness-raising groups. Analyzing victimization exposes the operations of power and the mechanisms of silencing. Our next task, however, is to theorize the *interactions* of voices. Feminist political theorists have already offered devastating critiques of the enlightenment concept of public and the notion of political actors as universal (male). To bring into the discussion of a Habermasian public the complex understanding of positionality and voice that feminist scholarship has built is extraordinarily promising, but feminist scholars have until recently eschewed such explorations.

What we have done so far is to break silences, bringing out voices and advocating strenuously for them. This, however, has not taught us much about how to have conversations once those voices are there. Some of the most eloquent work within feminist scholarship has concerned discourses of resistance — as explored, for example, by Stiles and Ferguson in this volume. Similarly, as Holloway urges more and more speech in our classrooms, she calls up the images of powerfully eloquent women whose resistance was silenced: Zora Neale Hurston, Phillis Wheatley, Anita Hill. But Holloway's passion hints at the messiness of speech as well — a messiness we must now begin to explore.

Holloway pleads (originally in speech but now on the page) for the spoken voice in women's studies classrooms. Spoken words imply listeners and respondents in the moment in which they are spoken — an interaction. They demand response. But are we ready for "an evocative and noisy redemption" in which we have to confront genuine differences in perspective and interest? Does "speaking *with*, not *for*" imply that only one perspective will be validated? Or can we imagine even our classrooms as public settings in which the purpose of speech is to articulate what is at stake, to tell the stories that explain our self-interest? Such a vision implies that listeners will not necessarily identify with each other because their interests and stories are different, even conflicting. Yet their task is nevertheless to listen well and to learn to understand (which is not the same as agreeing with) interests and points of view unlike their own. Listening must be distinguished from empathy. Empathy requires in some sense that the hearer vacate her position and assume the perspective of the other. Only when points of view are similar is it possible to identify empathically with another speaker and simultaneously to claim one's own position (for the reason that one is, in a sense, listening to oneself). To listen for differences as well as commonality, to recognize points of disagreement and understand their roots without suppressing one's own self-interest and point of view, however, is a different skill.

Such listening — and responding with similar speech — would shift the politics of the classroom from that of a "safe space," like the consciousness-raising group, to a "free space" that allows the exercise of political skills beyond the initial breaking of silence, skills that involve an active engagement with and use of power and not just resistance. The voices that now speak in our classrooms are remarkably different when compared with those of even a decade ago. This means that our conversations may be contentious, a speaking with but also an arguing with. If we can learn to demand respect rather than empathy, to encourage the full play of disagreement rather than rushing to premature (and frequently moralized) resolution, the noisiness of our classrooms can be an opportunity to build on the legacy of consciousness-raising by moving from safety toward freedom.

Note

1. Audre Lorde, "Age, Race, Class, and Sex: Women Redefining Difference," *Sister Outsider: Essays and Speeches by Audre Lorde* (Trumansburg, N.Y.: Crossing Press, 1984), 119.

Notes on the Contributors

Cynthia Enloe is professor of government at Clark University, where she also teaches women's studies. A scholar of women's roles in international relations and the military, Enloe has published *Does Khaki Become You?: The Militarization of Women's Lives* (1988) and *Bananas, Beaches, and Bases: Making Feminist Sense of International Politics* (1990). In the latter she shows that international relations is dependent on "artificial notions of masculinity" that are therefore open to radical challenge. Her most recent book is *The Morning After: Sexual Politics at the End of the Cold War* (1993), which deals with the gendered significance of the many changes occurring in the aftermath of the Cold War.

Sara Evans is professor of history at the University of Minnesota. She has been active in the women's movement for three decades, beginning in 1967 as an undergraduate at Duke University. Her first book, *Personal Politics: The Roots of Women's Liberation in the Civil Rights Movement and the New Left*, remains the most often cited work on the emergence of women's liberation out of the political cauldron of the sixties. In *Born for Liberty: A History of Women in America* (1989), Evans chronicles the diversity of American women's experiences from the colonial era through the 1980s. Evans taught her first course in women's studies in 1974 and continues to hold active leadership roles in women's studies on her campus today.

Kathy Ferguson is professor of political science and women's studies at the University of Hawaii. Her published work includes *The Feminist Case against Bureaucracy* (1984), *The Man Question: Visions of Subjectivity in Feminist Theory* (1993), and *Kibbutz Journal: Reflections on Gender, Race, and Militarism in Israel* (1995). Through her work in political theory, Ferguson has explored the social institutions of our time and the way they treat female subjects. She questions the ideologies they embody and points out their hidden assumptions and inadequacies. By examining metatheoretical assumptions about reality and truth, she finds openings to investigate contrasting visions of politics and identity in feminist theory. Ferguson advocates a complex approach to subjectivity — posing the self as a set of practices and performances instead of a fixed identity.

Nancy Hewitt, professor of history at Duke University, teaches American and comparative women's history courses focused on work, politics, and movements for social change. She is the author of *Women's Activism and Social Change* (1984), editor of *Women, Families, and Communities* (1990), and coeditor of *Visible Women: New Essays on American Activism* (1993). At Duke, she directs a Mellon seminar that brings together community activists and scholars to explore their mutual connections. Her current work examines work and politics among Anglo, African American, and Latin women in Tampa, Florida, from 1885 to 1945.

Karla Holloway is professor of English and African American literature at Duke University. Her work focuses on the intersections between linguistics, literary theory, and cultural studies, as well as theoretical linguistics and contemporary Third World women writers. Holloway's most recent book, *Codes of Conduct: Race, Ethics, and the Color of Our Character* (1995), explores the way in which the relationship between ethical decisions and ethnic identity (and identification) is a thematic subtext in contemporary African American life and literature.

Michael Kimmel is associate professor of sociology at the State University of New York at Stony Brook. He has received international recognition for his work on men and masculinity. His books include *Changing Men* (1987), *Men Confront Pornography* (1990), *Men's Lives* (1989), and *Against the Tide: Pro-Feminist Men in the United States, 1776–1990* (1992), a documentary history of men who have supported the struggle for women's equality. He is the editor of the scholarly journal *masculinities* and edits the book series Men and Masculinity for the University of California Press as well as a research paper series for Sage Publications. He writes frequently for newspapers and magazines. His new book is *Manhood: A Cultural History* (1995).

Mandy Merck teaches media studies at the University of Sussex. She has edited the film studies journal *Screen* and was senior producer of the British TV series *Out on Tuesday*. A collection of her essays on the problems of representing sexuality in popular culture, art, and film have been published as *Perversions: Deviant Readings* (1993). In this book, Merck's essays are themselves "perversions" as they stress irony and "deviance" from norms and avoid easy theoretical or critical categorizations in their critique not only of traditional theory but of feminist and queer culture and theory as well.

Jean O'Barr is the director of women's studies at Duke University. She has had a long career combining policy making, feminist teaching and writing, and campus activism. After more than a decade as the director of continuing education at Duke, she moved to the new women's studies program and became the editor of *Signs: Journal of Women in Culture and Society* from 1985 to 1990. She has published a number of edited collections and, most recently, a book of her own essays on building community and institutions on campus, *Feminism in Action* (1994). Her concern with documenting the ongoing evolution of women's studies and feminist scholarship drives her research, teaching, and political efforts.

Barbara Ogur is medical director of the Cambridge Neighborhood Health Centers in Cambridge, Massachusetts. She is a primary care internist practicing in a community health center that serves a multiethnic, but predominantly Spanish-speaking, population. Her major areas of interest include prescription drug abuse among women and access to care for traditionally underserved populations. This work has involved developing a multicultural midwifery program and AIDS services for African American, Hispanic, Haitian, and Portuguese patients and training medical students to take care of people from diverse and often disadvantaged backgrounds. Ogur's professional publications address women, mental health, and drug dependency.

Amy Richlin is professor of classics and women's studies at the University of Southern California. Her books include *The Garden of Priapus: Sexuality and Aggression in Roman Humor* (1983) and *Feminist Theory and the Classics*, coedited with Nancy Rabinowitz (1993). In her research, Richlin employs the most recent approaches to gender and subjectivity to explore ancient texts, using these texts to inform modern debates on gender. This exchange has led her to analyze issues ranging from aggressive male humor in Rome to the Clarence Thomas–Anita Hill exchanges. She calls into question attempts to set up impermeable barriers between historical periods; instead, she looks at the way historical continuities traverse periods and considers the political implications. Her studies of sexuality in antiquity form an "ethical history" of gender and material oppression. She examines the circulation of power in these texts — in content as well as form — in light of their social and moral contexts. Richlin demonstrates how learning about the past can lead to increased awareness of present problems, such as enduring brutality against women and the violence of sexual politics, and can contribute to the impetus to fight back.

Nancy Rosebaugh, program coordinator for women's studies at Duke University, is a graduate of Oberlin College and Duke Divinity School. Her background includes work in urban ministry and nonprofit social service agencies, and her present position involves her in planning programs for Duke graduate students and alumnae/i. Rosebaugh coordinates an annual graduate student research conference as well as numerous residential alumnae/i programs to bring feminist scholarship to out-of-school audiences. She organized the lecture series and symposium on which this volume is based and reveled in meeting outstanding feminist scholars and learning more about their work.

Kristine Stiles teaches art and art history at Duke University. She is an artist and scholar of experimental art and visual culture in its many forms — performance, conceptual, technological, ecological, and political. She also focuses her work on feminism and cultural studies. Stiles's writing on the postmodern avant-garde has brought her to research in Israel, Romania, and Vietnam during the last three years. Stiles received a Fulbright Scholarship for a joint appointment to teach at Bucharest University and the Nicolae Grigorescu Academia de Arta. Her books include *Theories and Documents of Contemporary Art* (1996) and *It Only Happens Once: The Letters and Performances of Carolee Schneemann* (forthcoming). Stiles is the 1994 recipient of the Richard K. Lublin Distinguished Award for Teaching Excellence at Duke University. She has lectured, published, and exhibited internationally.

Deborah Gray White is associate professor of history, women's studies, and Afro-American studies at Rutgers University. White explores what has become a nexus of controversy within feminist theory — the interrelationships among race, class, and gender. By giving voice to women long underrepresented in scholarship and ignored by traditional paradigms, she forces a reappraisal of these paradigms and illuminates the territory they obscure. In her book *Ar'n't I a Woman?* (1985), she explores the history of female slaves in the antebellum South, using slave narratives, WPA interviews, birth and death records, and court proceedings to define the parameters of slave women's lives. Her recent work, *Too Heavy a Load* (1994), studies black women's associational activities of the late nineteenth and early twentieth centuries.

Index

Sexuality: and homophobia, 162–63; Roman, 24–29; and violence, 38, 40–43, 80, 178–80. *See also* Masculinity; State

Silence: and law, 29–31; as resistance, 8, 38, 46, 49–53, 127, 187, 196; and state, 6, 29, 51–53, 134, 178–80. *See also* Voice

Space: and borders, 84–85, 101–3; gendered, 16, 100–102; ideological, 47, 153, 192

State: and capitalist consumption, 171–76; and gender ideologies/women as property, 23–29, 40–44, 99, 100–102, 169–71, 178–81; and images of domination, 6, 40–44, 50–51, 178–81; and nationalist ideologies, 170–84; and phallocracy, 44

Subjectivity: in analysis, 53–54, 71–72, 139–51, 154, 164, 175; of author, 4, 87–89, 102–5, 127, 149; embodied, 36–38, 74, 195; and writing, 85–90

Testimonials, 7, 9, 131–32, 140–51, 181. *See also* Oral history

Thomas, Clarence, 29–31, 69, 127, 134, 159–60

Verdery, Katherine, 46–47

Violence against women, 40–43, 133, 151, 192; pornography and, 67–78; and sexual harassment, 68, 88, 159–60, 164

Voice: academic, 125, 130–34, 190–98; and activism, 9–11, 138; and consciousness-raising, 151, 181, 191, 194; developing shared language, 7–9, 39, 52–53, 89; heteroglossia, 52, 86, 89, 102; as oral histories, 10; public vs. private, 106–7; relation to pornography, 66–78; and Roman speechmaking and masculinity, 17–20, 24; as subjectivity, 88, 151; as truth, 49, 125–29. *See also* Oral history

Walker, Alice, 133

Wheatley, Phillis, 126–27, 131

Williams, Patricia J., 86, 88

Women's studies, 153, 165, 191–92; and activism, 154, 190; at Duke University, ix, 4, 12–13, 153, 156; institutionalization of, 3; men in, 154–60; methods in, 175, 190. *See also* Men's studies

Work: domestic, 108–9, 171; gender and economic restructuring of, 168–82; sexual division of labor, 164–65, 171, 178–82; women's work organizations, 170–73

Writing: as conversation, 87–88; *écriture féminine*, 29, 86–89, 102; hegemony of, 127–28; journals, 8, 85, 191, 195; and language, 86–91; male hegemony in, 41, 89, 97; new models of, 7–9, 85–90, 129; as resistance, 7–10, 52, 188; theory in, 85